Anne Martinetti - Guillaume Lebeau - Alexandre Franc

AGATHA

THE REAL LIFE
OF AGATHA CHRISTIE

For Jean, Augustin and Gaspard: the essential trio...

A.M. and G.L.

First published 2016
by SelfMadeHero
139-141 Pancras Road
London NW1 1UN
www.selfmadehero.com

© Hachette Livre (Marabout), Paris, 2014

Written by Anne Martinetti and Guillaume Lebeau
Illustrated by Alexandre Franc
Translated from French to English by Edward Gauvin

Publishing Director: Emma Hayley
Sales & Marketing Manager: Sam Humphrey
Publishing Assistant: Guillaume Rater
UK Publicist: Paul Smith
US Publicist: Maya Bradford
Designer: Txabi Jones
With thanks to: Dan Lockwood

Anne Martinetti and Guillaume Lebeau would like to thank the dream team
at Éditions Marabout for their generous, unflagging support: Hélène, Laure,
Anne, Aline...

Alexandre Franc would like to thank Jean-Bernard Lauze, Frédéric Rébéna,
and Laure for the cover.

A CIP record for this book is available from the British Library

ISBN: 978-1-910593-11-0

10 9 8 7 6 5 4 3 2 1

Printed and bound in China

Anne Martinetti - Guillaume Lebeau - Alexandre Franc

AGATHA

THE REAL LIFE
OF AGATHA CHRISTIE

SELF
MADE
HERO

LONDON, 7 DECEMBER 1926

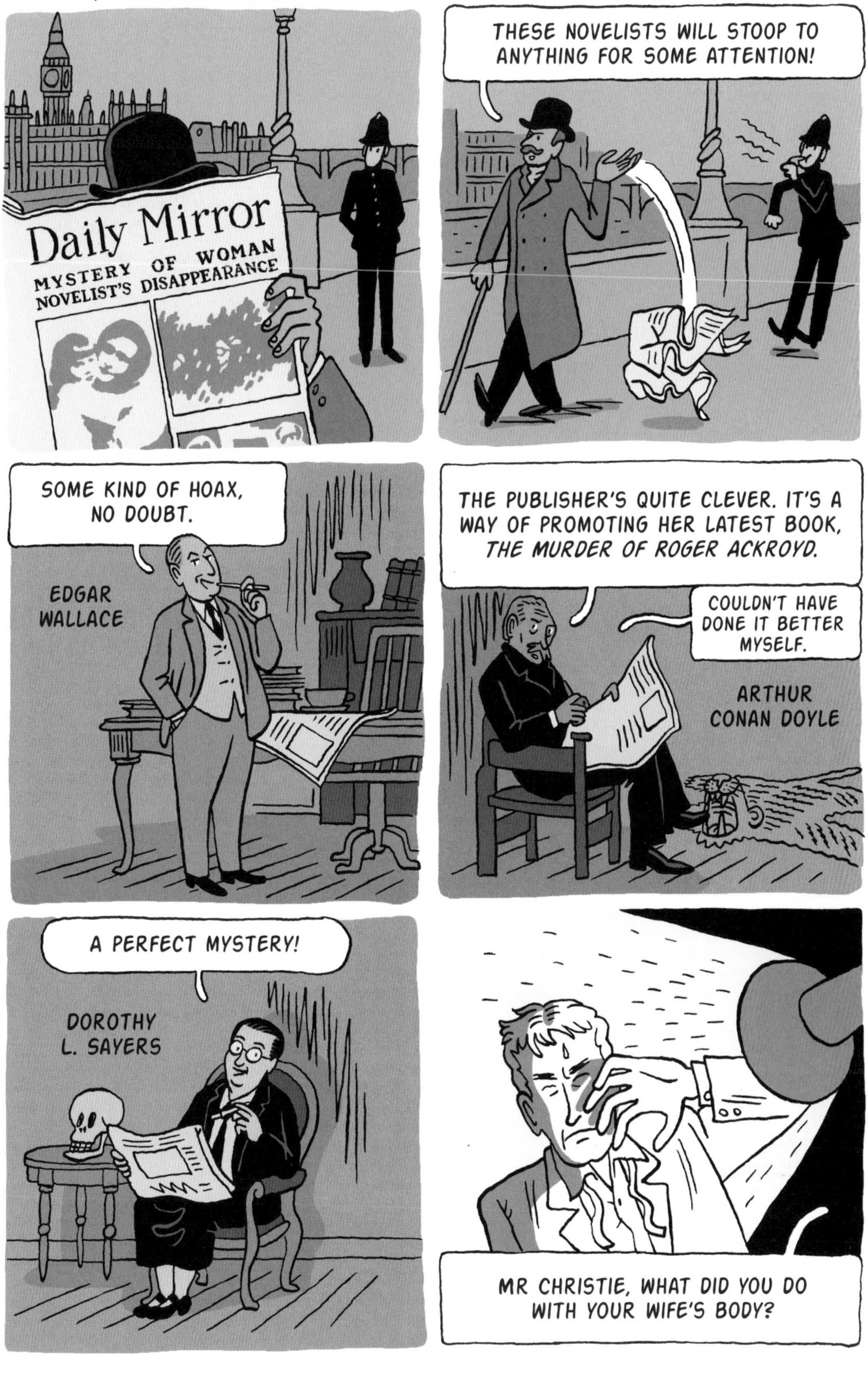
Daily Mirror
MYSTERY OF WOMAN NOVELIST'S DISAPPEARANCE
THESE NOVELISTS WILL STOOP TO ANYTHING FOR SOME ATTENTION!
SOME KIND OF HOAX, NO DOUBT.
EDGAR WALLACE
THE PUBLISHER'S QUITE CLEVER. IT'S A WAY OF PROMOTING HER LATEST BOOK, *THE MURDER OF ROGER ACKROYD.*
COULDN'T HAVE DONE IT BETTER MYSELF.
ARTHUR CONAN DOYLE
A PERFECT MYSTERY!
DOROTHY L. SAYERS
MR CHRISTIE, WHAT DID YOU DO WITH YOUR WIFE'S BODY?

LONDON, HOME OFFICE

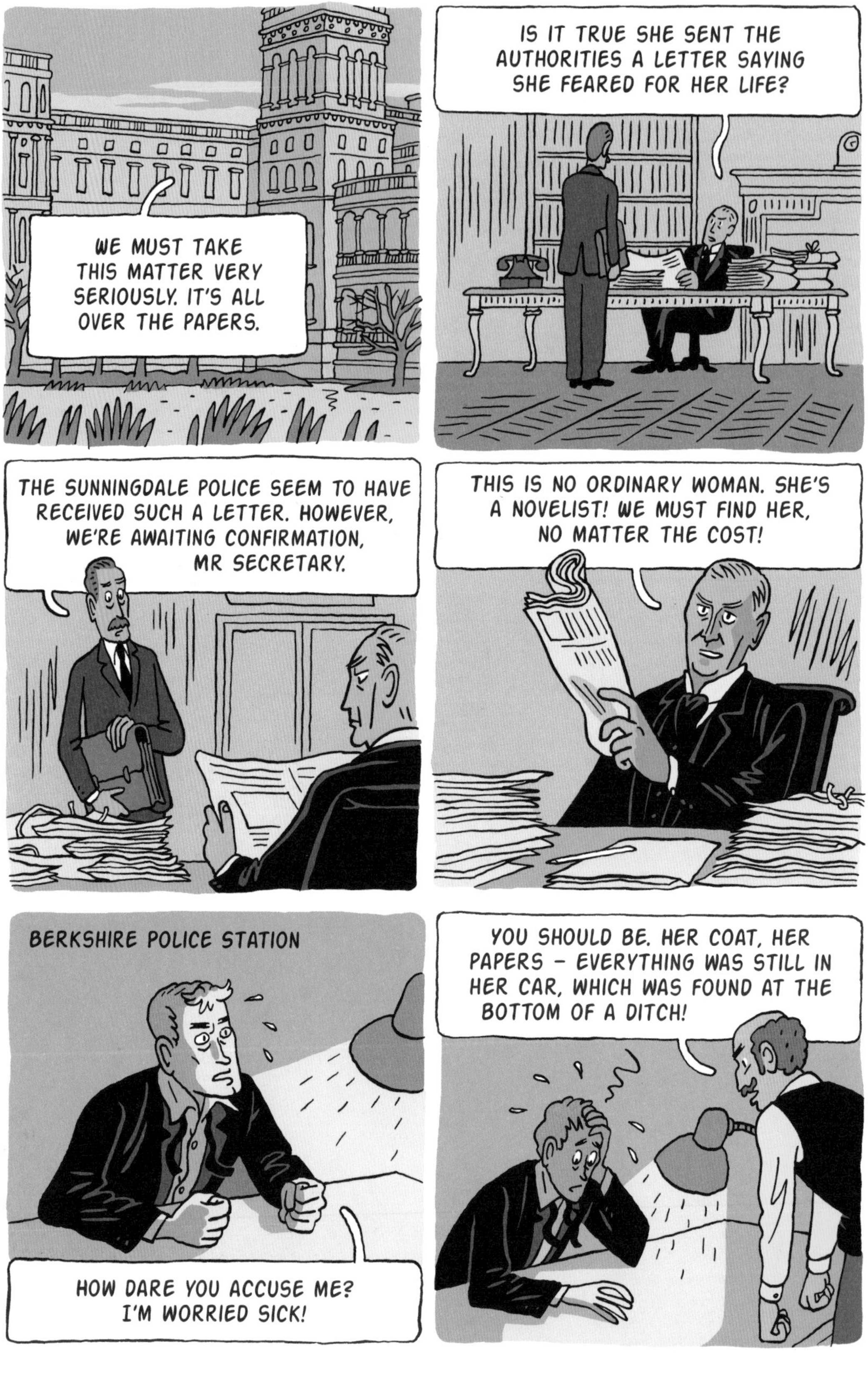
WE MUST TAKE THIS MATTER VERY SERIOUSLY. IT'S ALL OVER THE PAPERS.
IS IT TRUE SHE SENT THE AUTHORITIES A LETTER SAYING SHE FEARED FOR HER LIFE?
THE SUNNINGDALE POLICE SEEM TO HAVE RECEIVED SUCH A LETTER. HOWEVER, WE'RE AWAITING CONFIRMATION, MR SECRETARY.
THIS IS NO ORDINARY WOMAN. SHE'S A NOVELIST! WE MUST FIND HER, NO MATTER THE COST!
BERKSHIRE POLICE STATION
HOW DARE YOU ACCUSE ME? I'M WORRIED SICK!
YOU SHOULD BE. HER COAT, HER PAPERS – EVERYTHING WAS STILL IN HER CAR, WHICH WAS FOUND AT THE BOTTOM OF A DITCH!

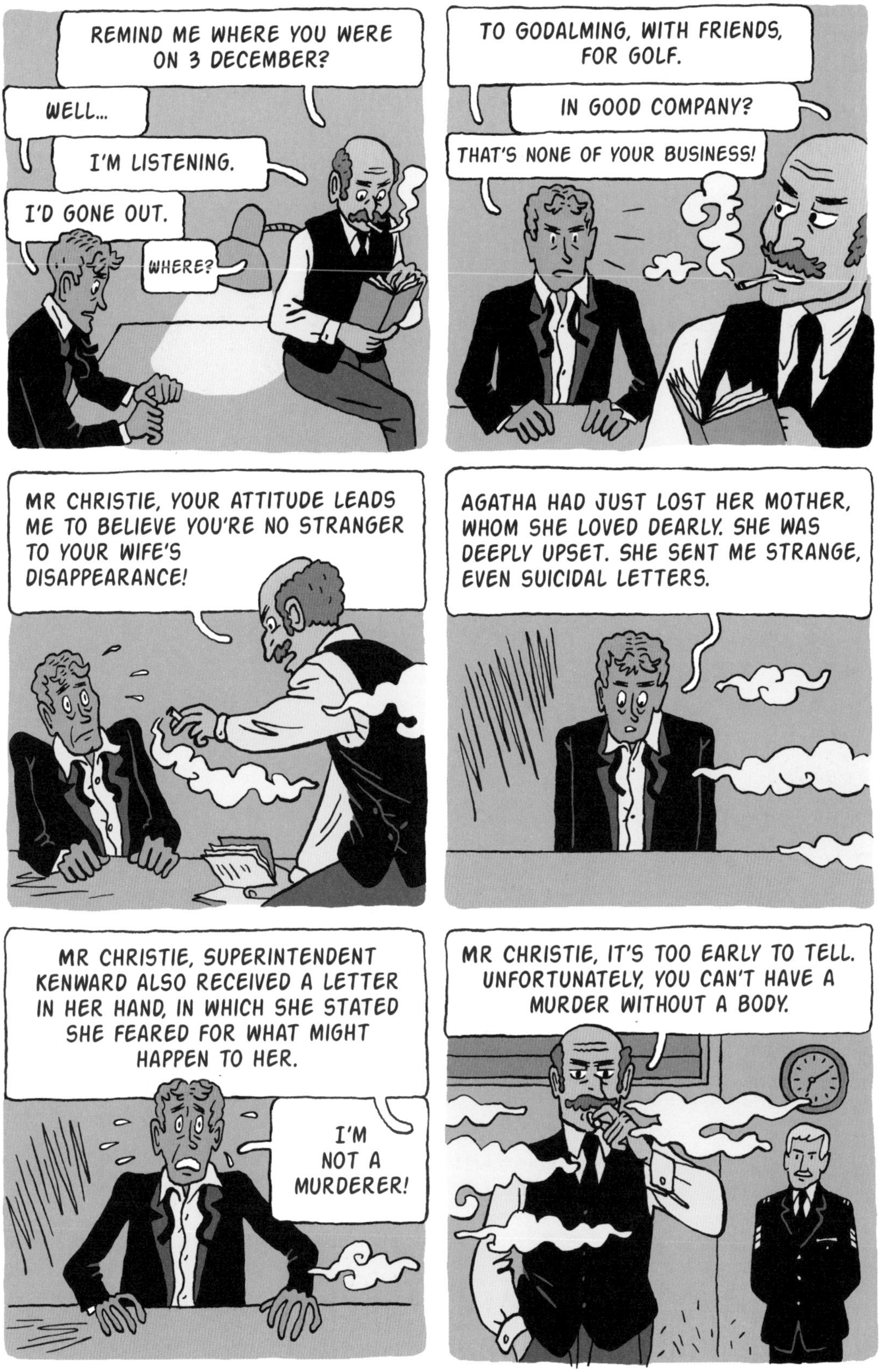
REMIND ME WHERE YOU WERE ON 3 DECEMBER?
WELL...
I'M LISTENING.
I'D GONE OUT.
WHERE?
TO GODALMING, WITH FRIENDS, FOR GOLF.
IN GOOD COMPANY?
THAT'S NONE OF YOUR BUSINESS!
MR CHRISTIE, YOUR ATTITUDE LEADS ME TO BELIEVE YOU'RE NO STRANGER TO YOUR WIFE'S DISAPPEARANCE!
AGATHA HAD JUST LOST HER MOTHER, WHOM SHE LOVED DEARLY. SHE WAS DEEPLY UPSET. SHE SENT ME STRANGE, EVEN SUICIDAL LETTERS.
MR CHRISTIE, SUPERINTENDENT KENWARD ALSO RECEIVED A LETTER IN HER HAND, IN WHICH SHE STATED SHE FEARED FOR WHAT MIGHT HAPPEN TO HER.
I'M NOT A MURDERER!
MR CHRISTIE, IT'S TOO EARLY TO TELL. UNFORTUNATELY, YOU CAN'T HAVE A MURDER WITHOUT A BODY.

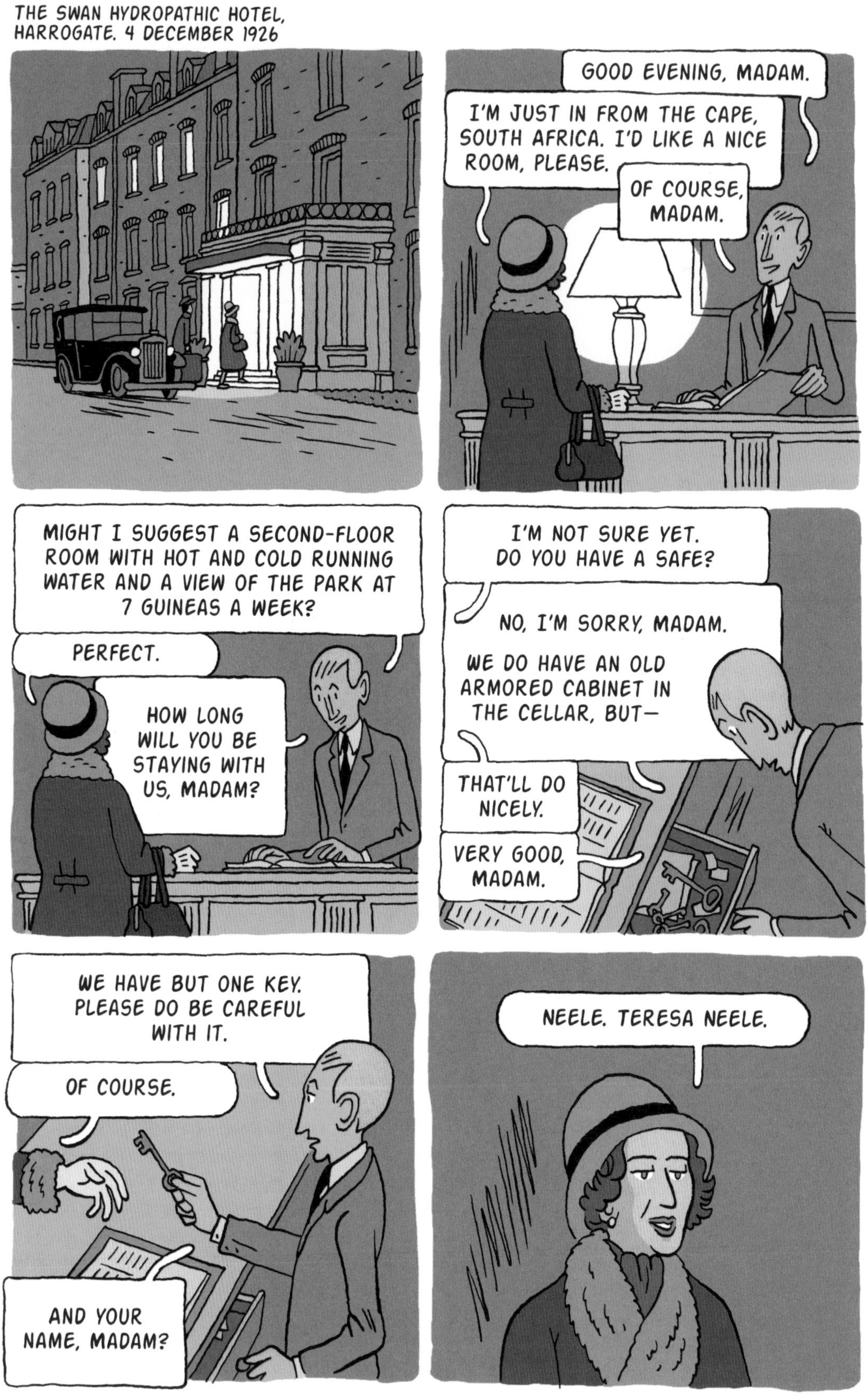
THE SWAN HYDROPATHIC HOTEL, HARROGATE. 4 DECEMBER 1926
GOOD EVENING, MADAM.
I'M JUST IN FROM THE CAPE, SOUTH AFRICA. I'D LIKE A NICE ROOM, PLEASE.
OF COURSE, MADAM.
MIGHT I SUGGEST A SECOND-FLOOR ROOM WITH HOT AND COLD RUNNING WATER AND A VIEW OF THE PARK AT 7 GUINEAS A WEEK?
PERFECT.
HOW LONG WILL YOU BE STAYING WITH US, MADAM?
I'M NOT SURE YET. DO YOU HAVE A SAFE?
NO, I'M SORRY, MADAM.
WE DO HAVE AN OLD ARMORED CABINET IN THE CELLAR, BUT—
THAT'LL DO NICELY.
VERY GOOD, MADAM.
WE HAVE BUT ONE KEY. PLEASE DO BE CAREFUL WITH IT.
OF COURSE.
AND YOUR NAME, MADAM?
NEELE. TERESA NEELE.

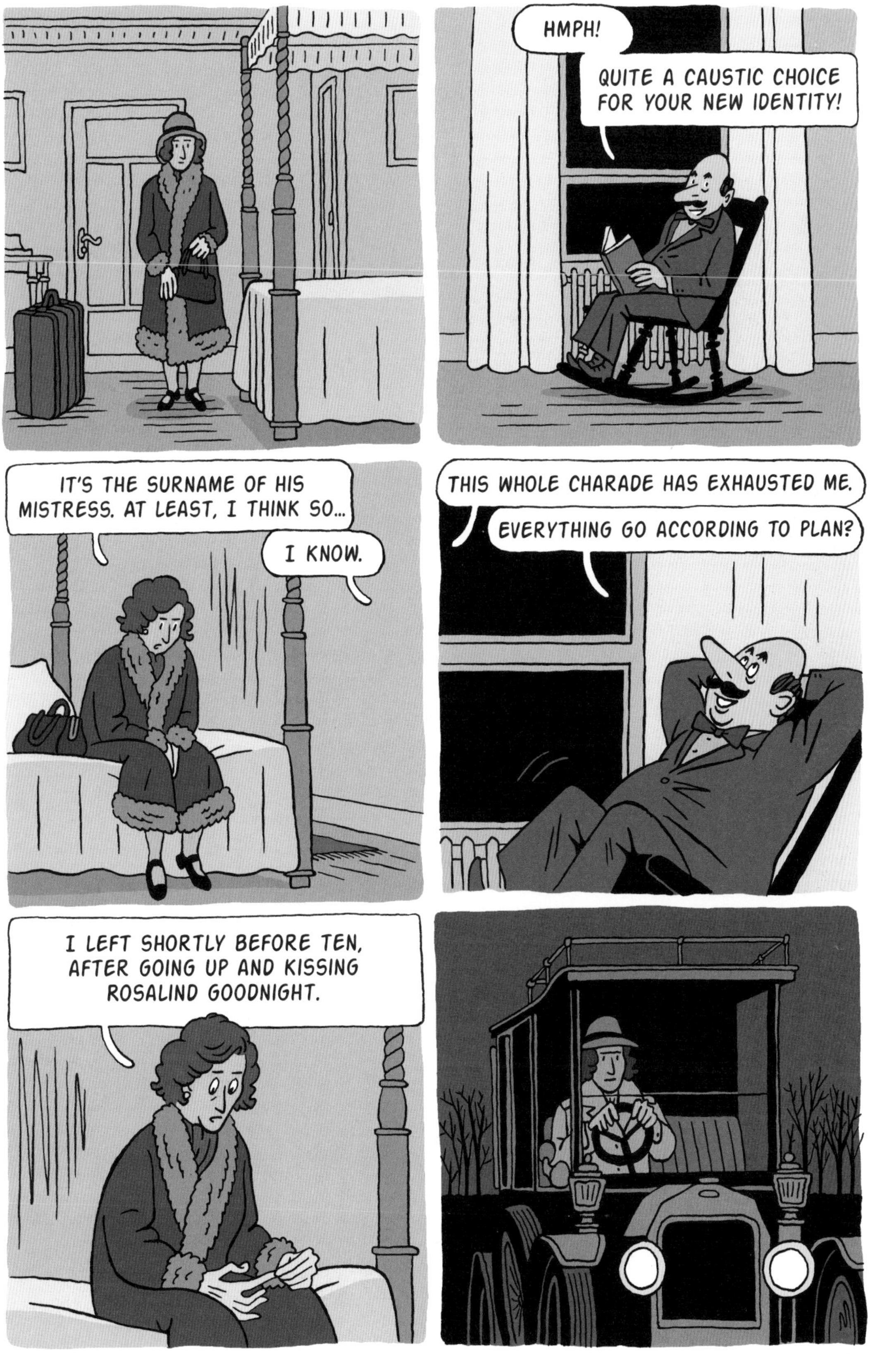
HMPH!
QUITE A CAUSTIC CHOICE FOR YOUR NEW IDENTITY!
IT'S THE SURNAME OF HIS MISTRESS. AT LEAST, I THINK SO...
I KNOW.
THIS WHOLE CHARADE HAS EXHAUSTED ME.
EVERYTHING GO ACCORDING TO PLAN?
I LEFT SHORTLY BEFORE TEN, AFTER GOING UP AND KISSING ROSALIND GOODNIGHT.

I ABANDONED MY CAR BY A LAKE IN SURREY.

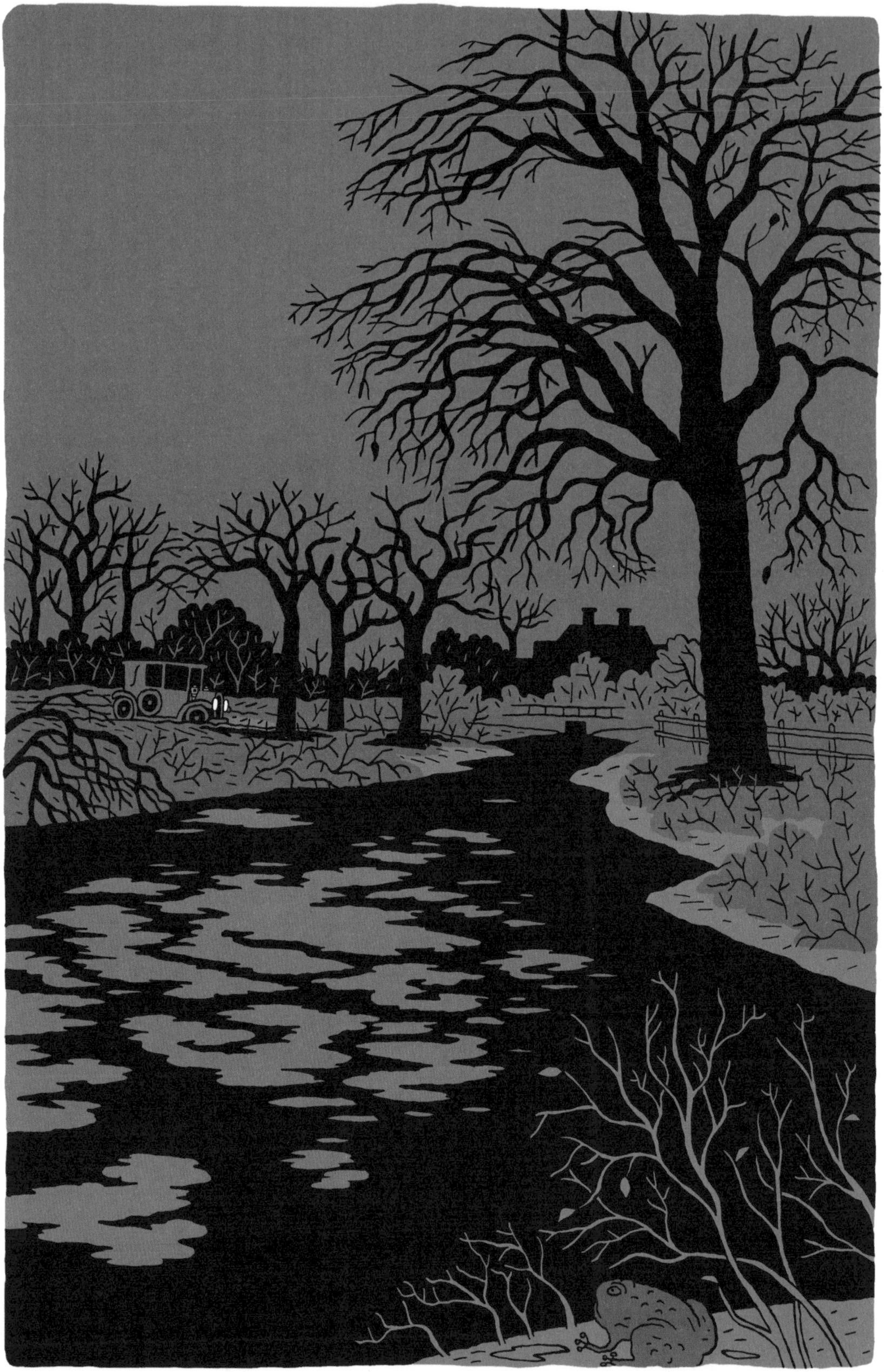

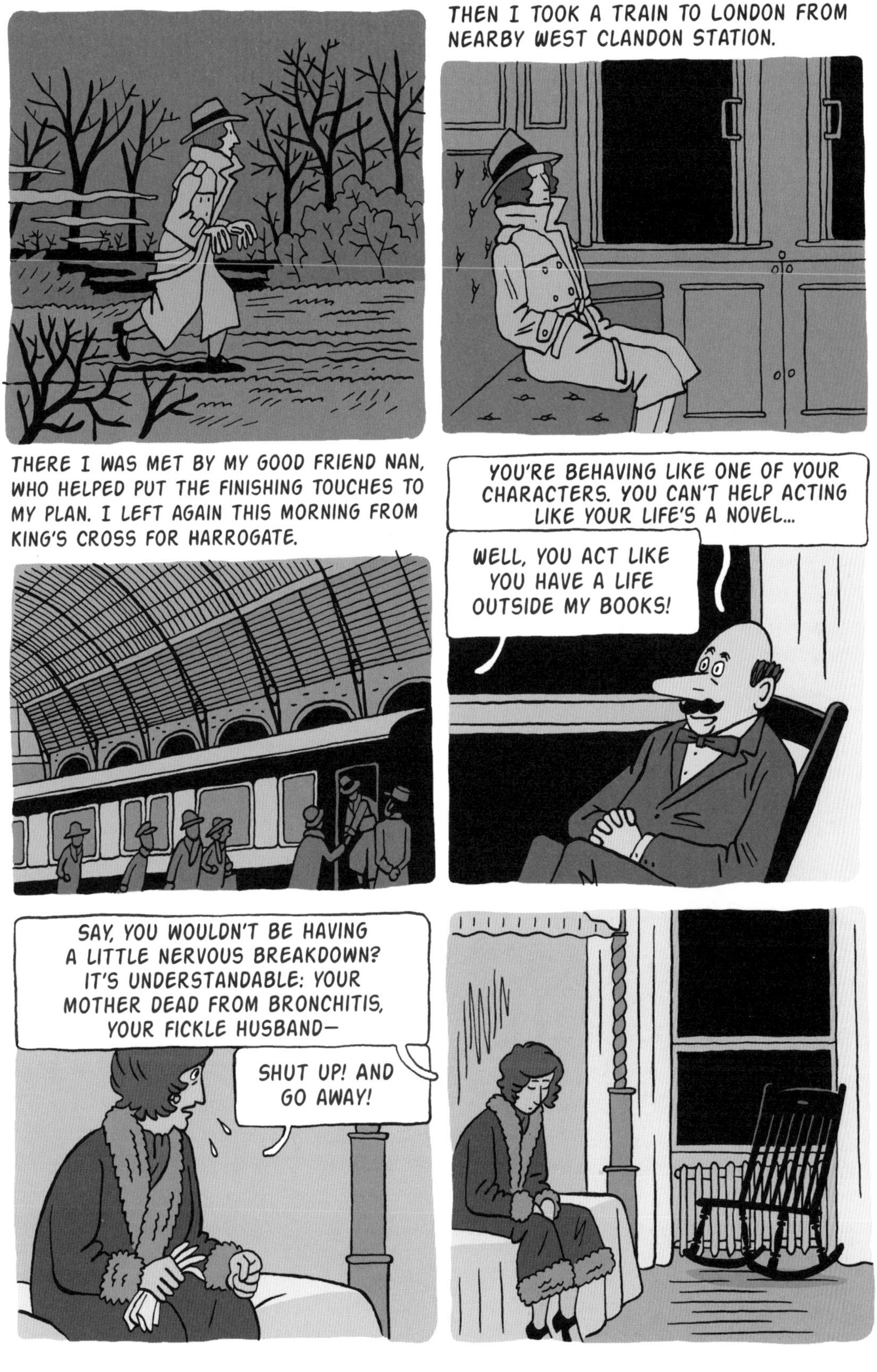
THEN I TOOK A TRAIN TO LONDON FROM NEARBY WEST CLANDON STATION.
THERE I WAS MET BY MY GOOD FRIEND NAN, WHO HELPED PUT THE FINISHING TOUCHES TO MY PLAN. I LEFT AGAIN THIS MORNING FROM KING'S CROSS FOR HARROGATE.
YOU'RE BEHAVING LIKE ONE OF YOUR CHARACTERS. YOU CAN'T HELP ACTING LIKE YOUR LIFE'S A NOVEL...
WELL, YOU ACT LIKE YOU HAVE A LIFE OUTSIDE MY BOOKS!
SAY, YOU WOULDN'T BE HAVING A LITTLE NERVOUS BREAKDOWN? IT'S UNDERSTANDABLE: YOUR MOTHER DEAD FROM BRONCHITIS, YOUR FICKLE HUSBAND—
SHUT UP! AND GO AWAY!

BERKSHIRE POLICE STATION

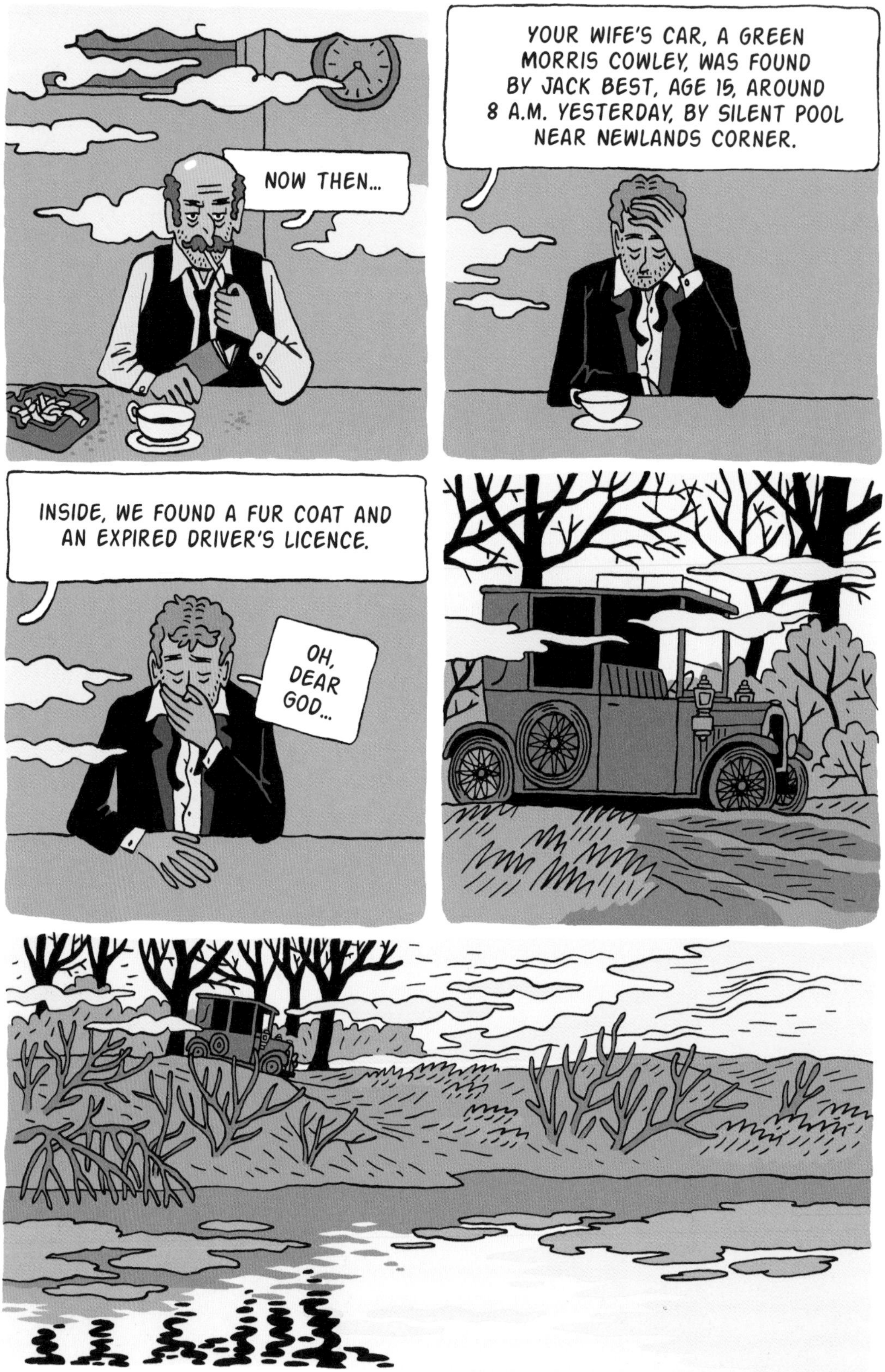
NOW THEN...
YOUR WIFE'S CAR, A GREEN MORRIS COWLEY, WAS FOUND BY JACK BEST, AGE 15, AROUND 8 A.M. YESTERDAY, BY SILENT POOL NEAR NEWLANDS CORNER.
INSIDE, WE FOUND A FUR COAT AND AN EXPIRED DRIVER'S LICENCE.
OH, DEAR GOD...

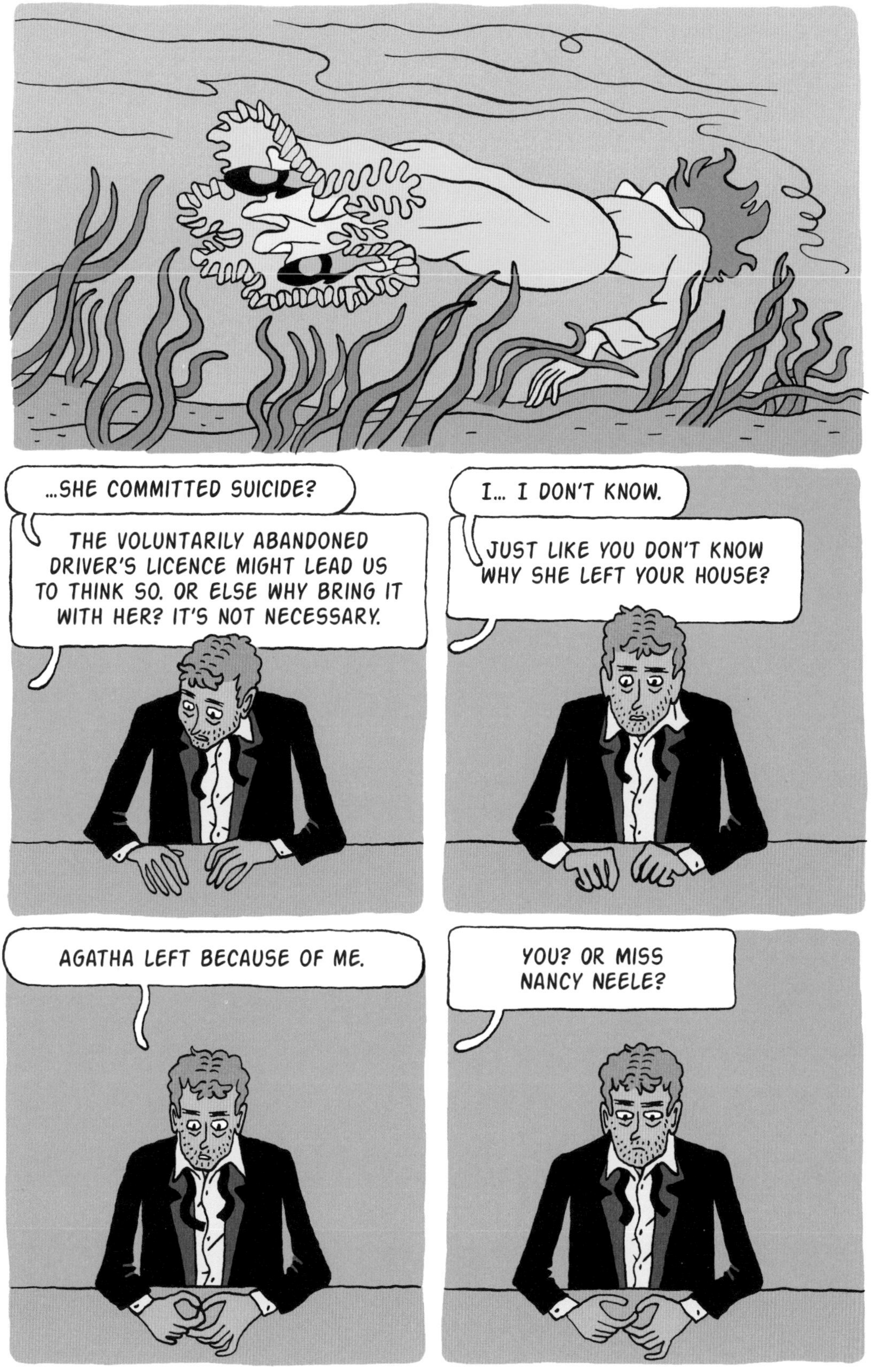
...SHE COMMITTED SUICIDE?
THE VOLUNTARILY ABANDONED DRIVER'S LICENCE MIGHT LEAD US TO THINK SO. OR ELSE WHY BRING IT WITH HER? IT'S NOT NECESSARY.
I... I DON'T KNOW.
JUST LIKE YOU DON'T KNOW WHY SHE LEFT YOUR HOUSE?
AGATHA LEFT BECAUSE OF ME.
YOU? OR MISS NANCY NEELE?

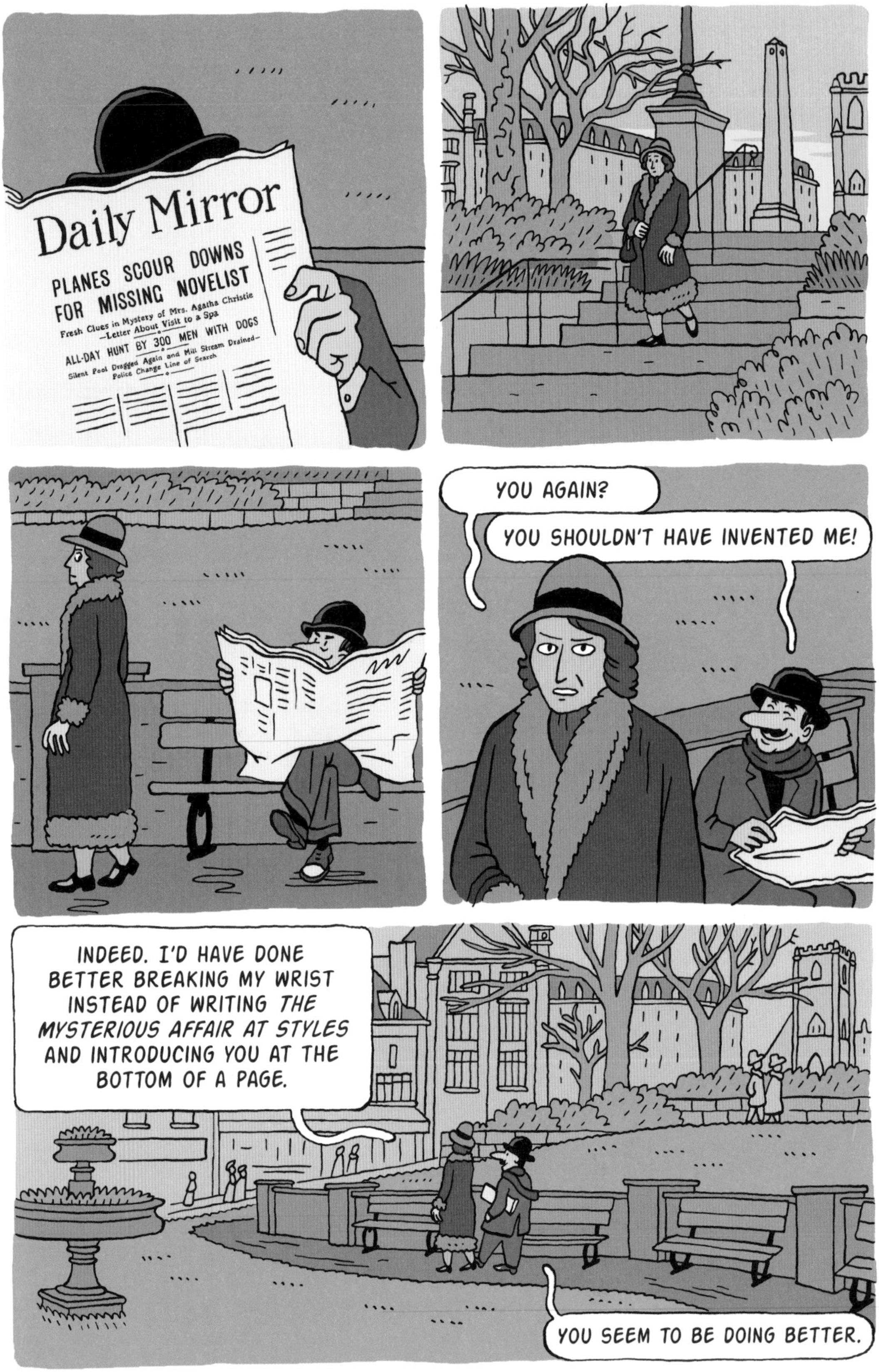

Daily Mirror
PLANES SCOUR DOWNS FOR MISSING NOVELIST
Fresh Clues in Mystery of Mrs. Agatha Christie —Letter About Visit to a Spa
ALL-DAY HUNT BY 300 MEN WITH DOGS
Silent Pool Dragged Again and Mill Stream Drained— Police Change Line of Search
YOU AGAIN?
YOU SHOULDN'T HAVE INVENTED ME!
INDEED. I'D HAVE DONE BETTER BREAKING MY WRIST INSTEAD OF WRITING *THE MYSTERIOUS AFFAIR AT STYLES* AND INTRODUCING YOU AT THE BOTTOM OF A PAGE.
YOU SEEM TO BE DOING BETTER.

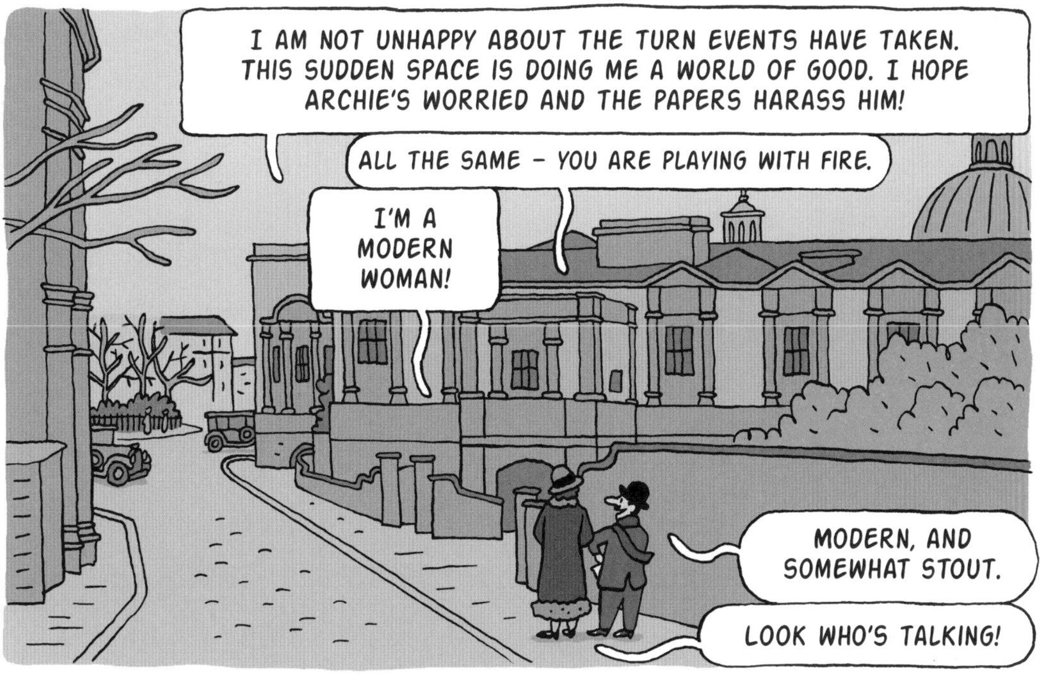
I AM NOT UNHAPPY ABOUT THE TURN EVENTS HAVE TAKEN. THIS SUDDEN SPACE IS DOING ME A WORLD OF GOOD. I HOPE ARCHIE'S WORRIED AND THE PAPERS HARASS HIM!
ALL THE SAME – YOU ARE PLAYING WITH FIRE.
I'M A MODERN WOMAN!
MODERN, AND SOMEWHAT STOUT.
LOOK WHO'S TALKING!

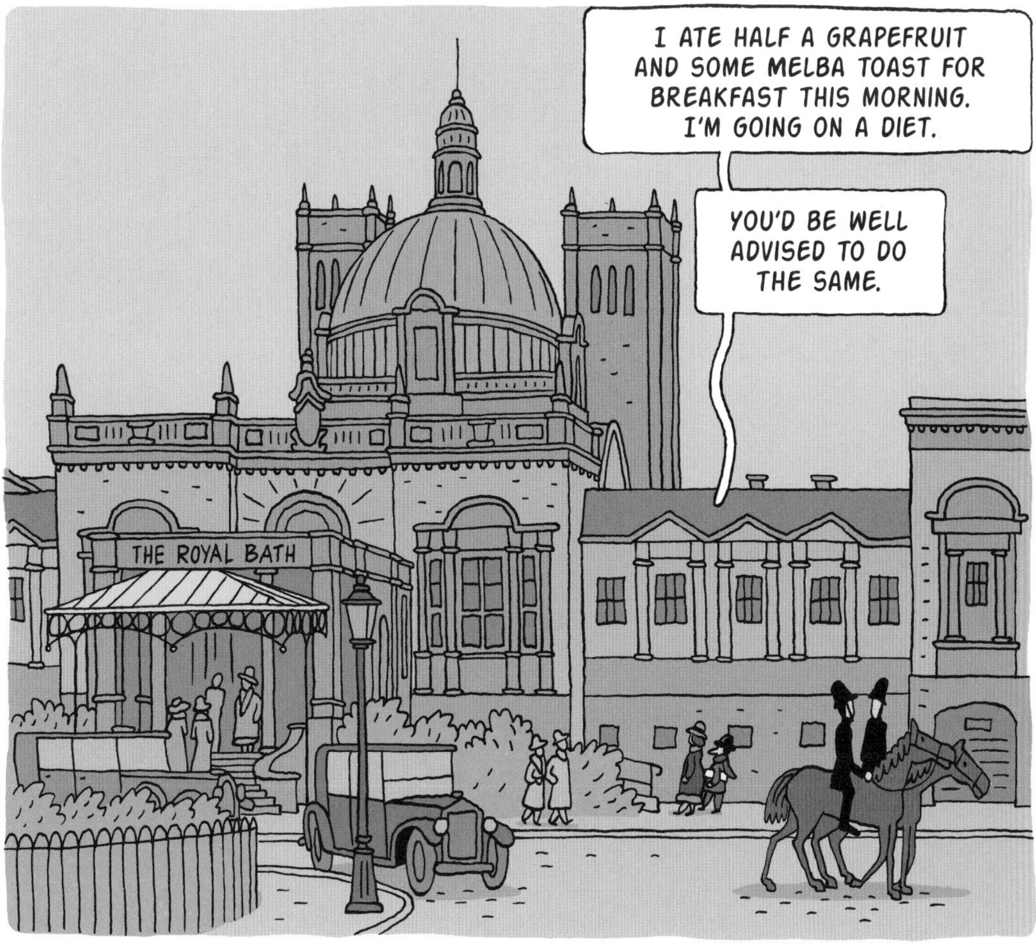
I ATE HALF A GRAPEFRUIT AND SOME MELBA TOAST FOR BREAKFAST THIS MORNING. I'M GOING ON A DIET.
YOU'D BE WELL ADVISED TO DO THE SAME.
THE ROYAL BATH

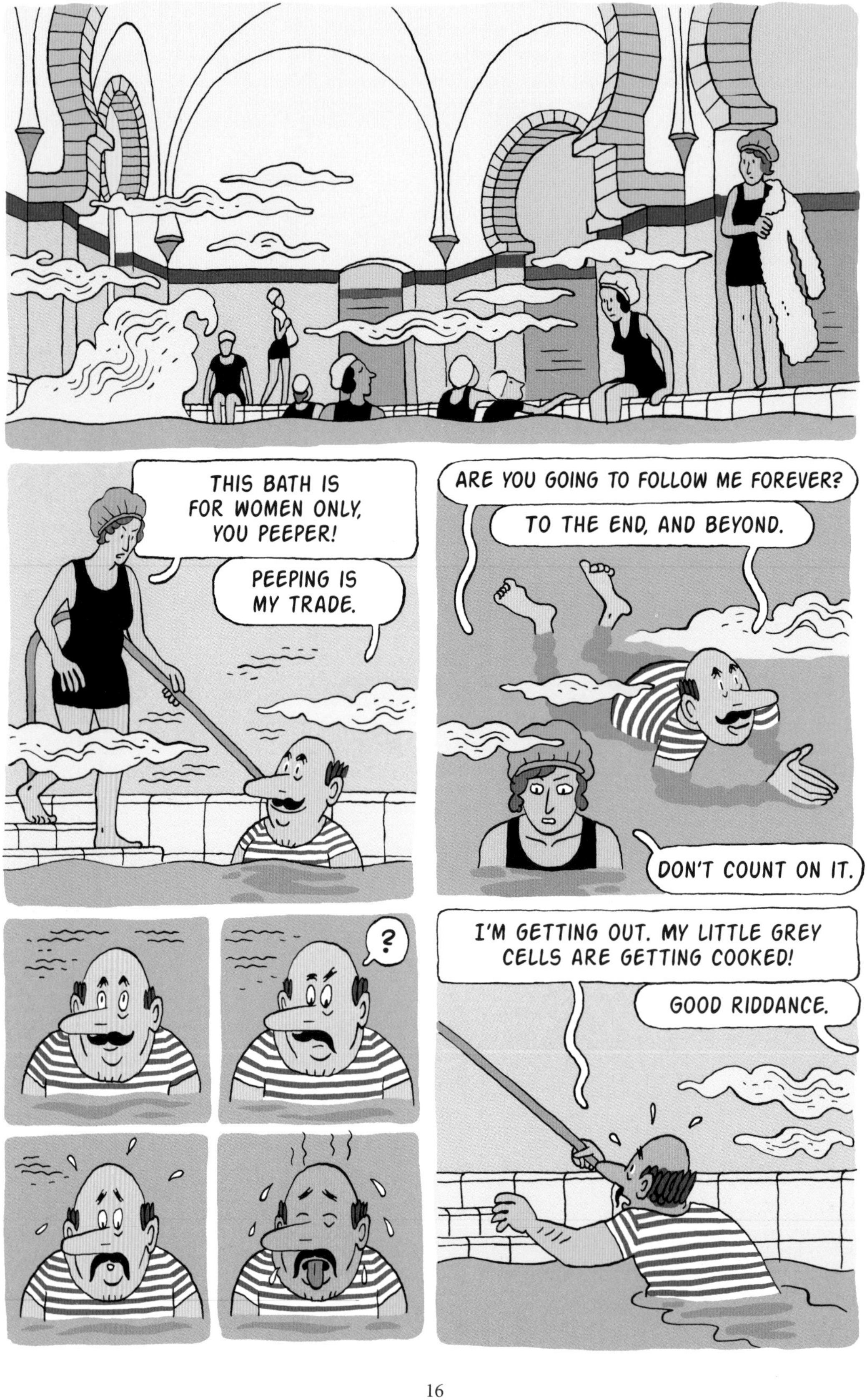
THIS BATH IS FOR WOMEN ONLY, YOU PEEPER!
PEEPING IS MY TRADE.
ARE YOU GOING TO FOLLOW ME FOREVER?
TO THE END, AND BEYOND.
DON'T COUNT ON IT.
?
I'M GETTING OUT. MY LITTLE GREY CELLS ARE GETTING COOKED!
GOOD RIDDANCE.

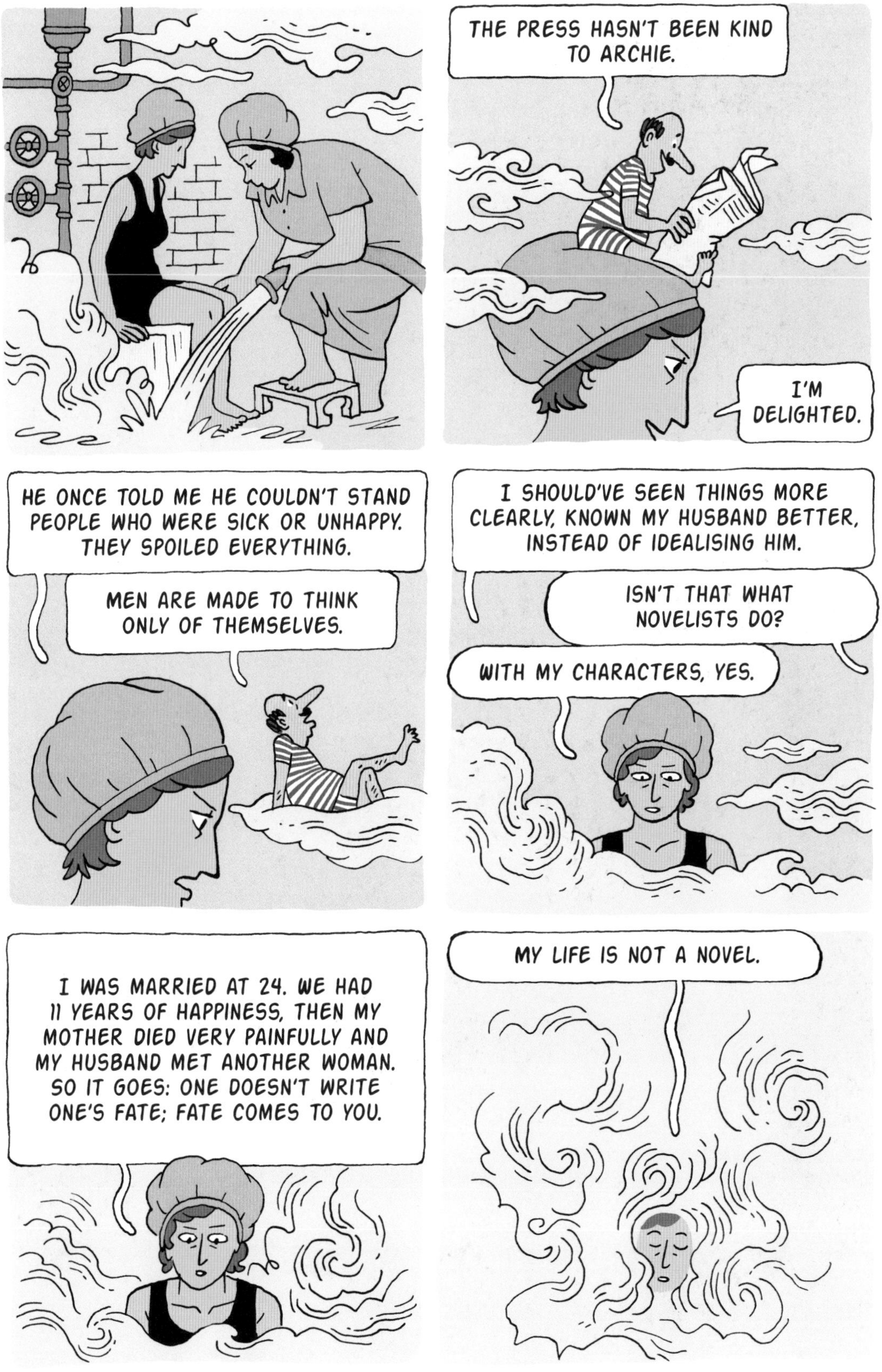
THE PRESS HASN'T BEEN KIND TO ARCHIE.
I'M DELIGHTED.
HE ONCE TOLD ME HE COULDN'T STAND PEOPLE WHO WERE SICK OR UNHAPPY. THEY SPOILED EVERYTHING.
MEN ARE MADE TO THINK ONLY OF THEMSELVES.
I SHOULD'VE SEEN THINGS MORE CLEARLY, KNOWN MY HUSBAND BETTER, INSTEAD OF IDEALISING HIM.
ISN'T THAT WHAT NOVELISTS DO?
WITH MY CHARACTERS, YES.
I WAS MARRIED AT 24. WE HAD 11 YEARS OF HAPPINESS, THEN MY MOTHER DIED VERY PAINFULLY AND MY HUSBAND MET ANOTHER WOMAN. SO IT GOES: ONE DOESN'T WRITE ONE'S FATE; FATE COMES TO YOU.
MY LIFE IS NOT A NOVEL.

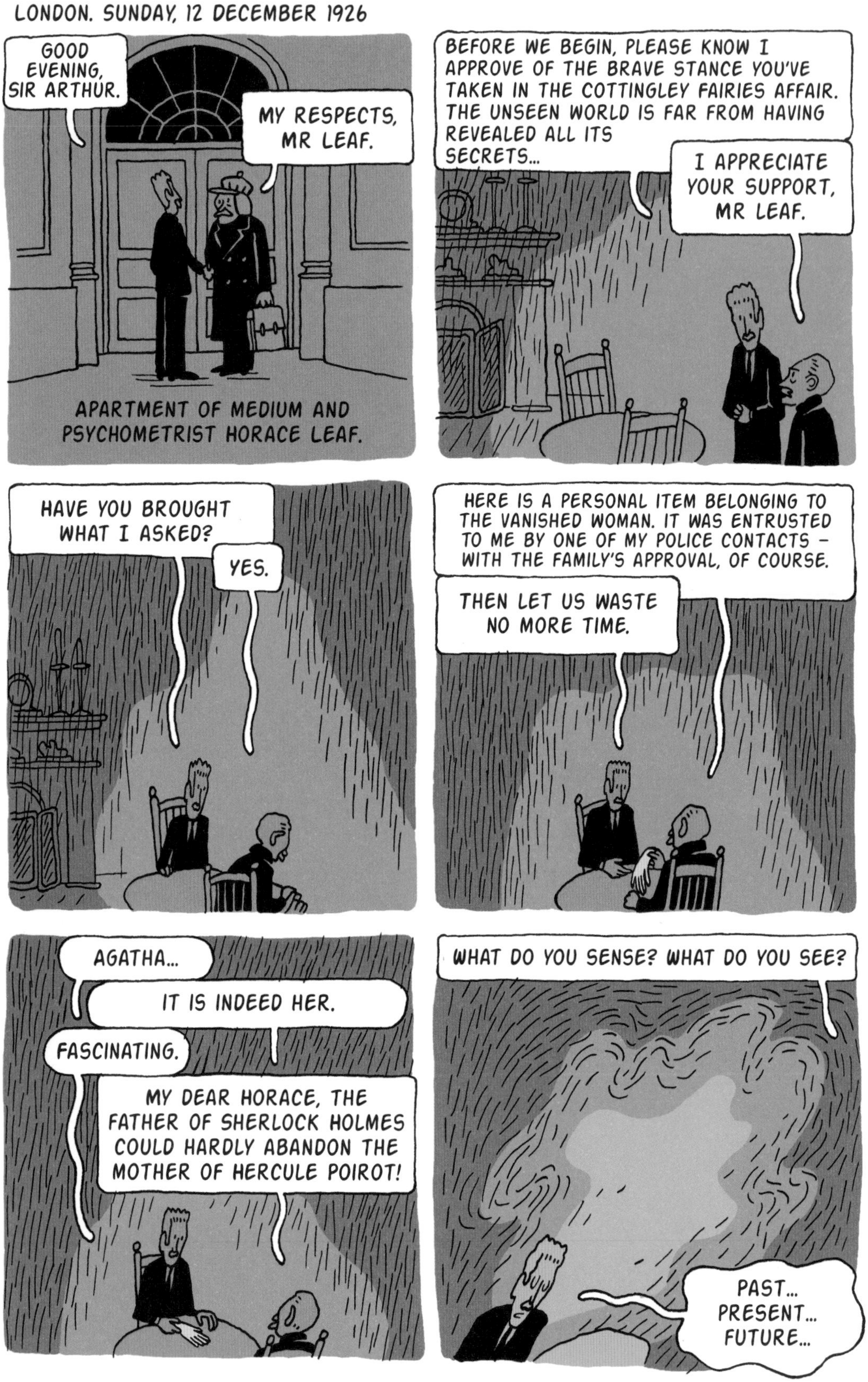
LONDON. SUNDAY, 12 DECEMBER 1926
GOOD EVENING, SIR ARTHUR.
MY RESPECTS, MR LEAF.
APARTMENT OF MEDIUM AND PSYCHOMETRIST HORACE LEAF.
BEFORE WE BEGIN, PLEASE KNOW I APPROVE OF THE BRAVE STANCE YOU'VE TAKEN IN THE COTTINGLEY FAIRIES AFFAIR. THE UNSEEN WORLD IS FAR FROM HAVING REVEALED ALL ITS SECRETS...
I APPRECIATE YOUR SUPPORT, MR LEAF.
HAVE YOU BROUGHT WHAT I ASKED?
YES.
HERE IS A PERSONAL ITEM BELONGING TO THE VANISHED WOMAN. IT WAS ENTRUSTED TO ME BY ONE OF MY POLICE CONTACTS – WITH THE FAMILY'S APPROVAL, OF COURSE.
THEN LET US WASTE NO MORE TIME.
AGATHA...
IT IS INDEED HER.
FASCINATING.
MY DEAR HORACE, THE FATHER OF SHERLOCK HOLMES COULD HARDLY ABANDON THE MOTHER OF HERCULE POIROT!
WHAT DO YOU SENSE? WHAT DO YOU SEE?
PAST... PRESENT... FUTURE...

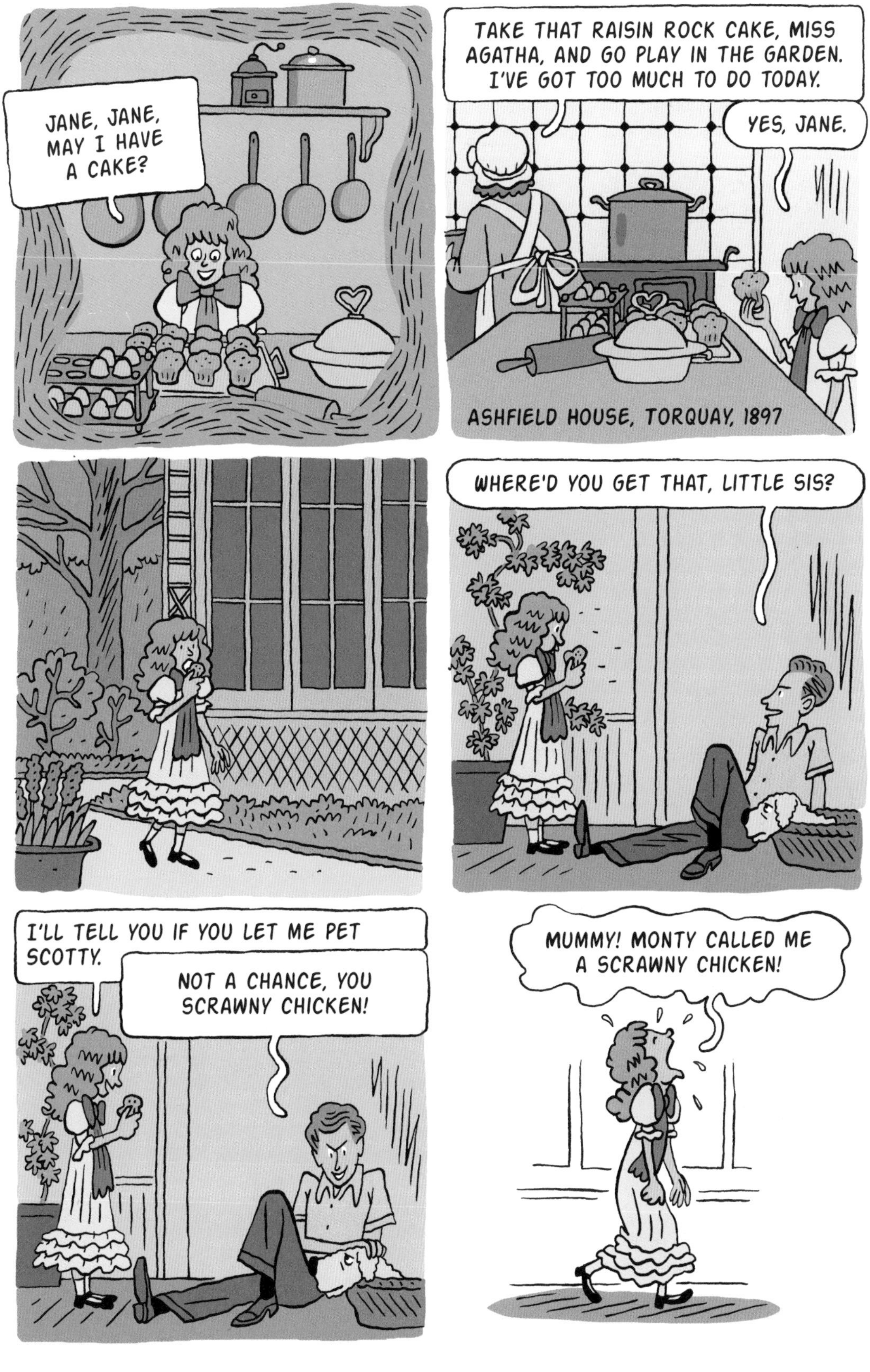
JANE, JANE, MAY I HAVE A CAKE?
TAKE THAT RAISIN ROCK CAKE, MISS AGATHA, AND GO PLAY IN THE GARDEN. I'VE GOT TOO MUCH TO DO TODAY.
YES, JANE.
ASHFIELD HOUSE, TORQUAY, 1897
WHERE'D YOU GET THAT, LITTLE SIS?
I'LL TELL YOU IF YOU LET ME PET SCOTTY.
NOT A CHANCE, YOU SCRAWNY CHICKEN!
MUMMY! MONTY CALLED ME A SCRAWNY CHICKEN!

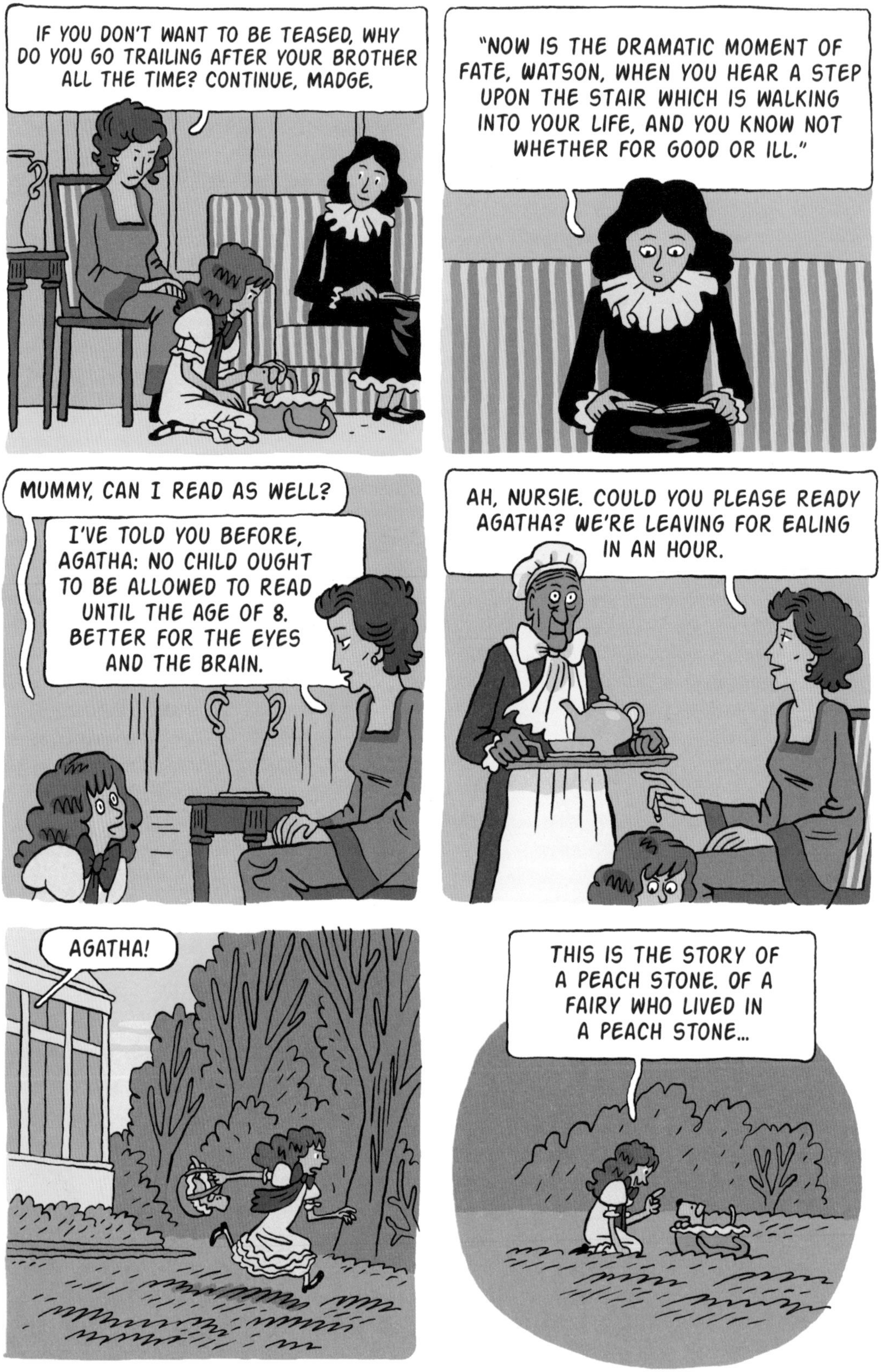
IF YOU DON'T WANT TO BE TEASED, WHY DO YOU GO TRAILING AFTER YOUR BROTHER ALL THE TIME? CONTINUE, MADGE.
"NOW IS THE DRAMATIC MOMENT OF FATE, WATSON, WHEN YOU HEAR A STEP UPON THE STAIR WHICH IS WALKING INTO YOUR LIFE, AND YOU KNOW NOT WHETHER FOR GOOD OR ILL."
MUMMY, CAN I READ AS WELL?
I'VE TOLD YOU BEFORE, AGATHA: NO CHILD OUGHT TO BE ALLOWED TO READ UNTIL THE AGE OF 8. BETTER FOR THE EYES AND THE BRAIN.
AH, NURSIE. COULD YOU PLEASE READY AGATHA? WE'RE LEAVING FOR EALING IN AN HOUR.
AGATHA!
THIS IS THE STORY OF A PEACH STONE. OF A FAIRY WHO LIVED IN A PEACH STONE...

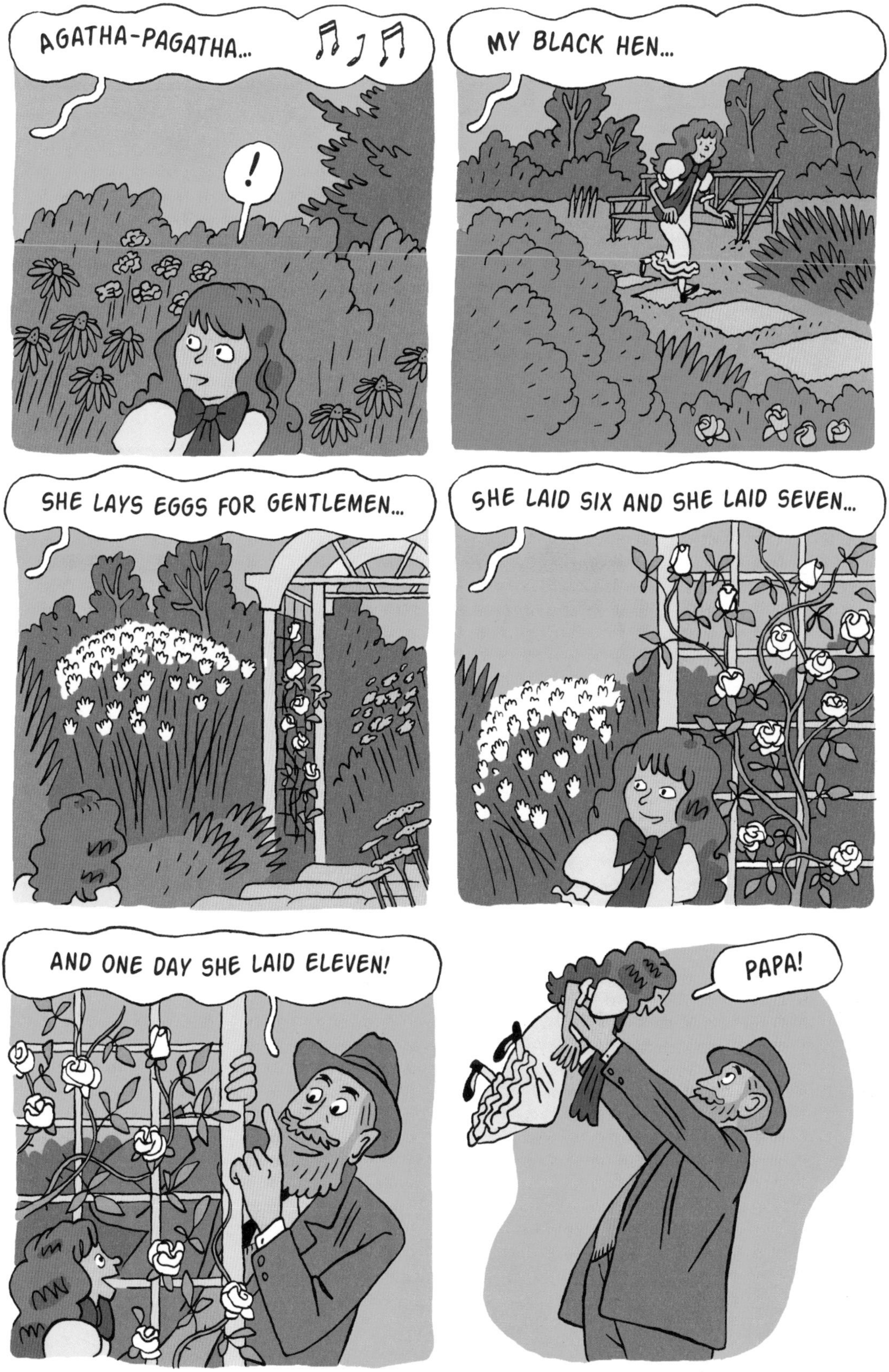
AGATHA-PAGATHA...
!
MY BLACK HEN...
SHE LAYS EGGS FOR GENTLEMEN...
SHE LAID SIX AND SHE LAID SEVEN...
AND ONE DAY SHE LAID ELEVEN!
PAPA!

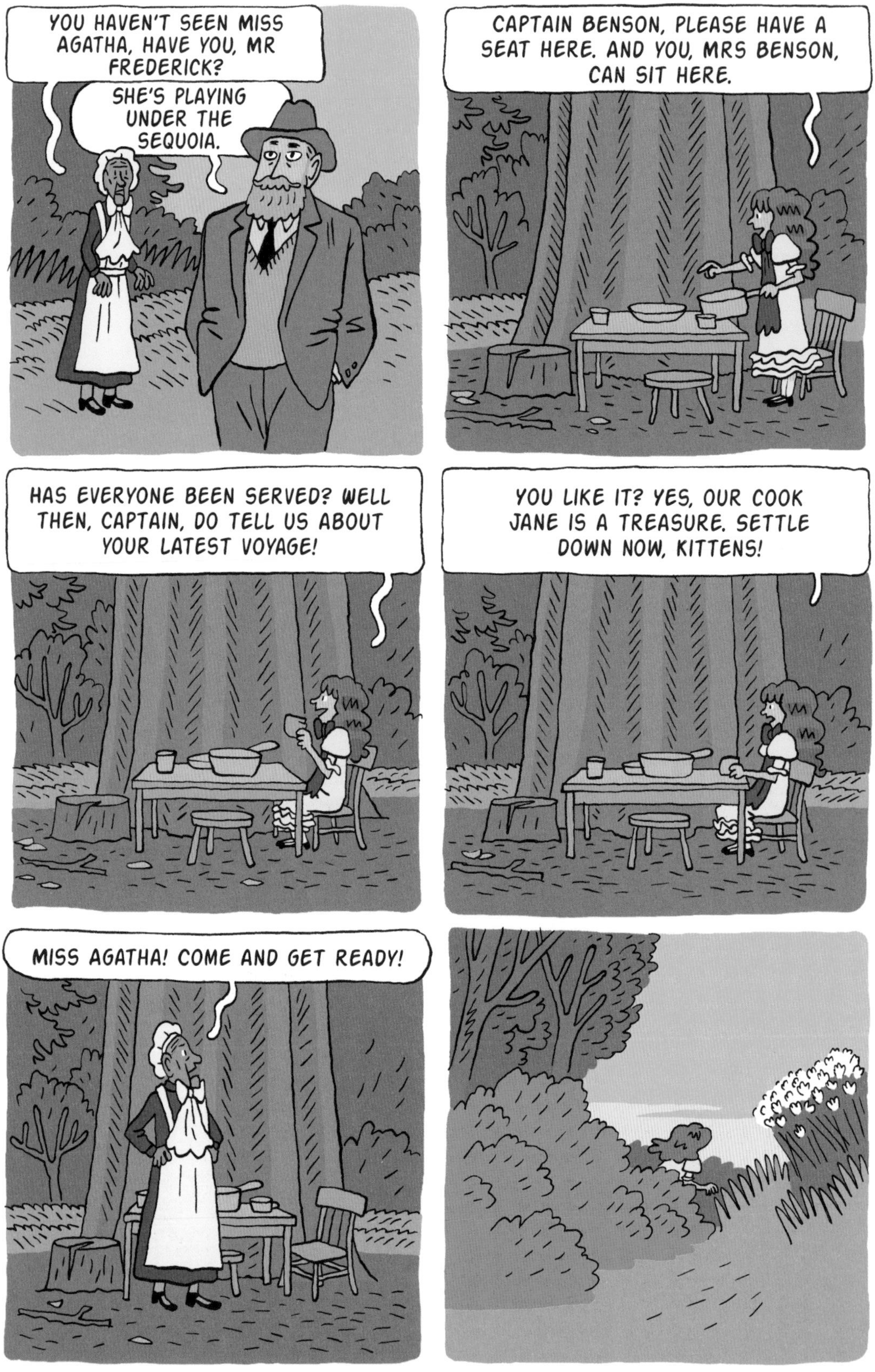
YOU HAVEN'T SEEN MISS AGATHA, HAVE YOU, MR FREDERICK?
SHE'S PLAYING UNDER THE SEQUOIA.
CAPTAIN BENSON, PLEASE HAVE A SEAT HERE. AND YOU, MRS BENSON, CAN SIT HERE.
HAS EVERYONE BEEN SERVED? WELL THEN, CAPTAIN, DO TELL US ABOUT YOUR LATEST VOYAGE!
YOU LIKE IT? YES, OUR COOK JANE IS A TREASURE. SETTLE DOWN NOW, KITTENS!
MISS AGATHA! COME AND GET READY!

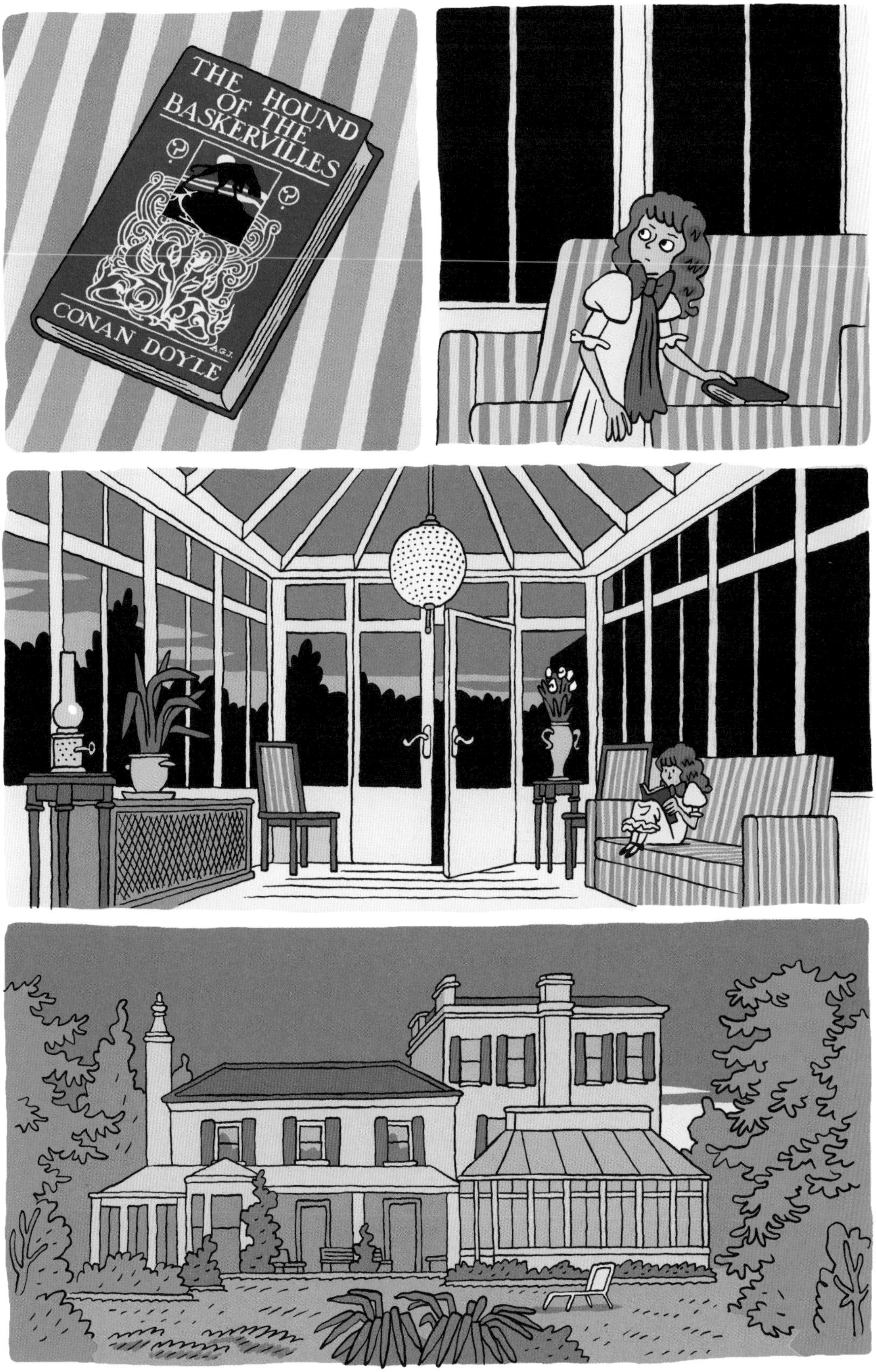
THE HOUND OF THE BASKERVILLES
CONAN DOYLE

EALING, NOVEMBER 1901

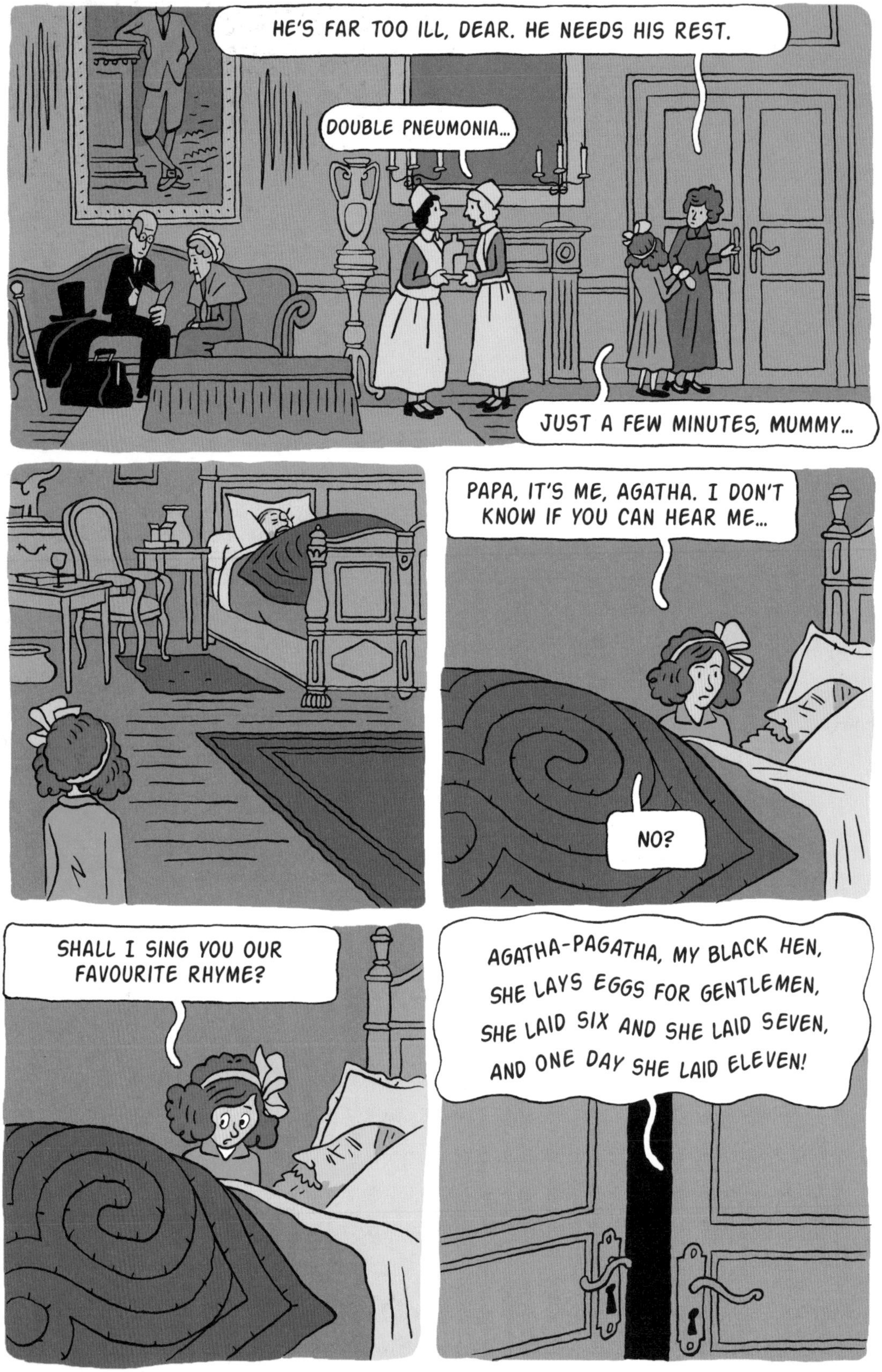
HE'S FAR TOO ILL, DEAR. HE NEEDS HIS REST.
DOUBLE PNEUMONIA...
JUST A FEW MINUTES, MUMMY...
PAPA, IT'S ME, AGATHA. I DON'T KNOW IF YOU CAN HEAR ME...
NO?
SHALL I SING YOU OUR FAVOURITE RHYME?
AGATHA-PAGATHA, MY BLACK HEN,
SHE LAYS EGGS FOR GENTLEMEN,
SHE LAID SIX AND SHE LAID SEVEN,
AND ONE DAY SHE LAID ELEVEN!

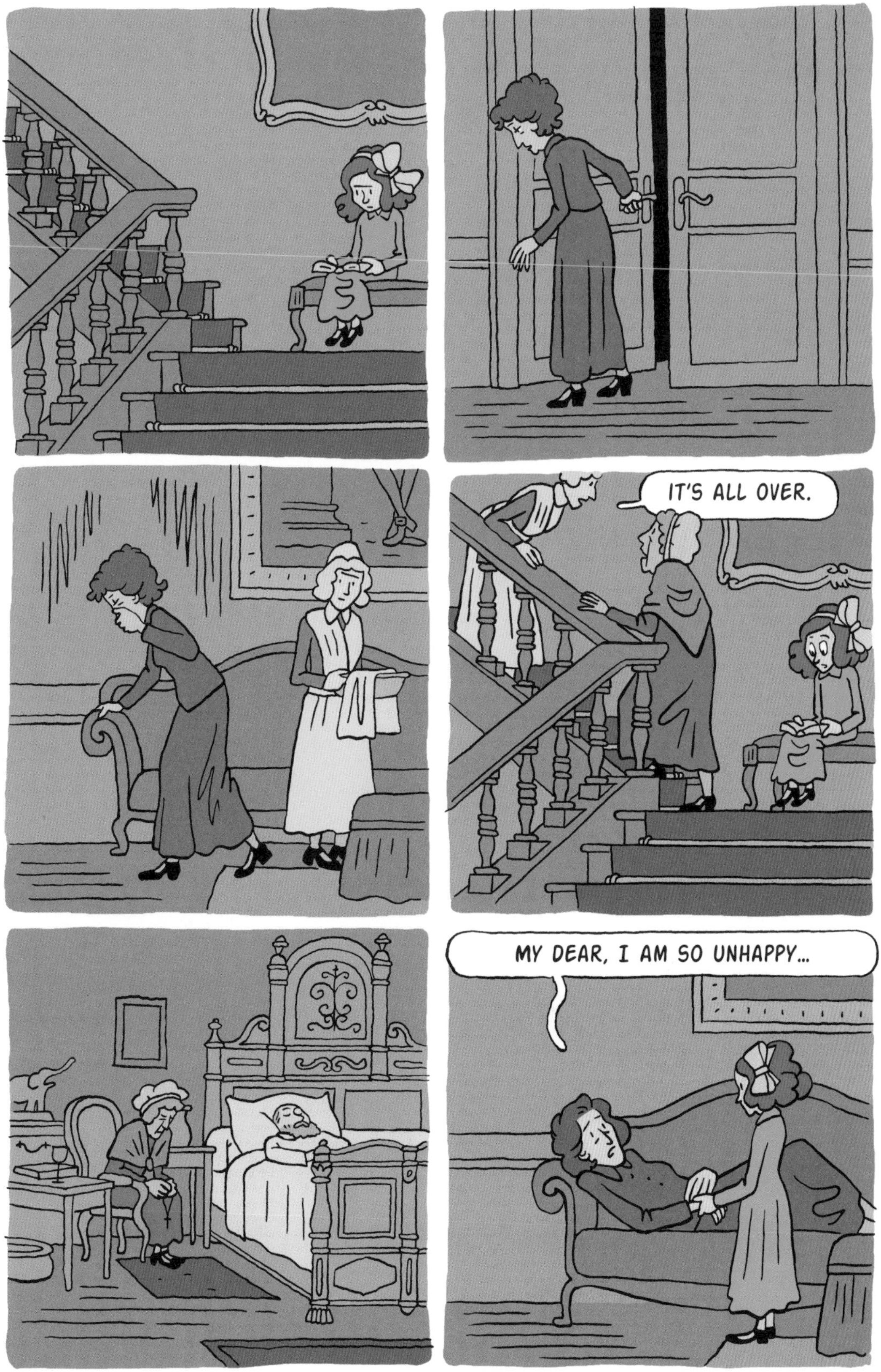
IT'S ALL OVER.
MY DEAR, I AM SO UNHAPPY...

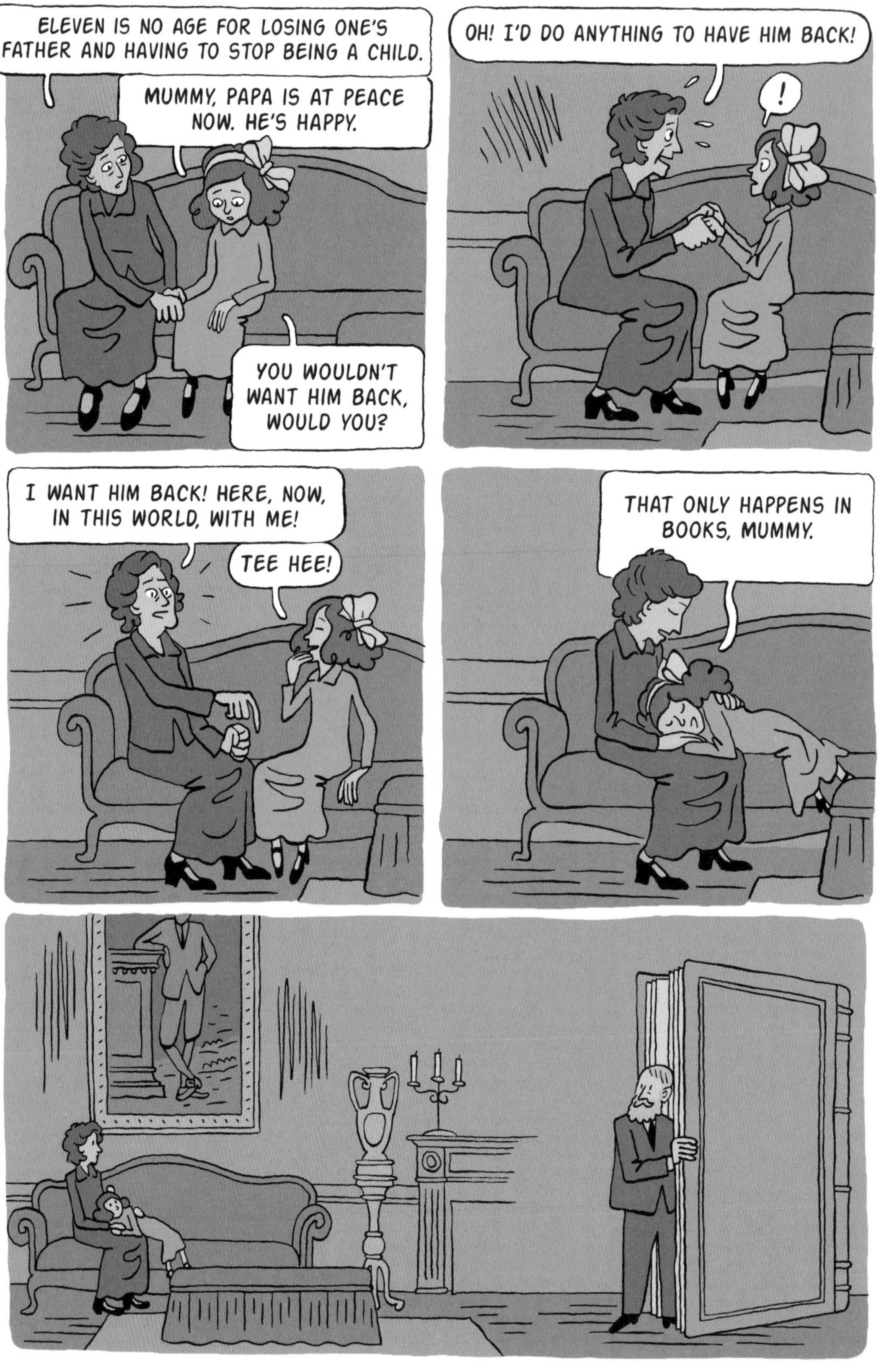
ELEVEN IS NO AGE FOR LOSING ONE'S FATHER AND HAVING TO STOP BEING A CHILD.
MUMMY, PAPA IS AT PEACE NOW. HE'S HAPPY.
YOU WOULDN'T WANT HIM BACK, WOULD YOU?
OH! I'D DO ANYTHING TO HAVE HIM BACK!
!
I WANT HIM BACK! HERE, NOW, IN THIS WORLD, WITH ME!
TEE HEE!
THAT ONLY HAPPENS IN BOOKS, MUMMY.

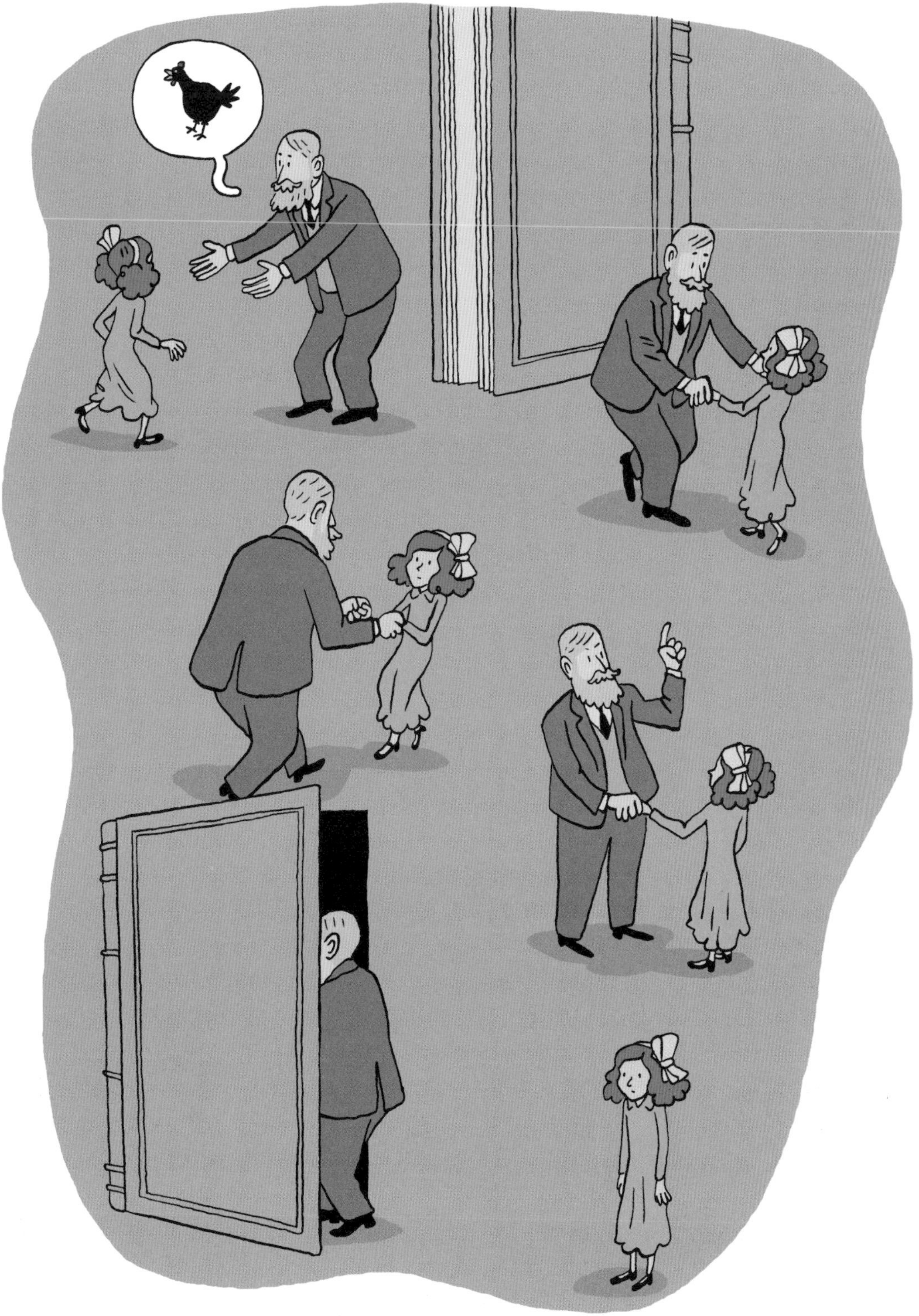

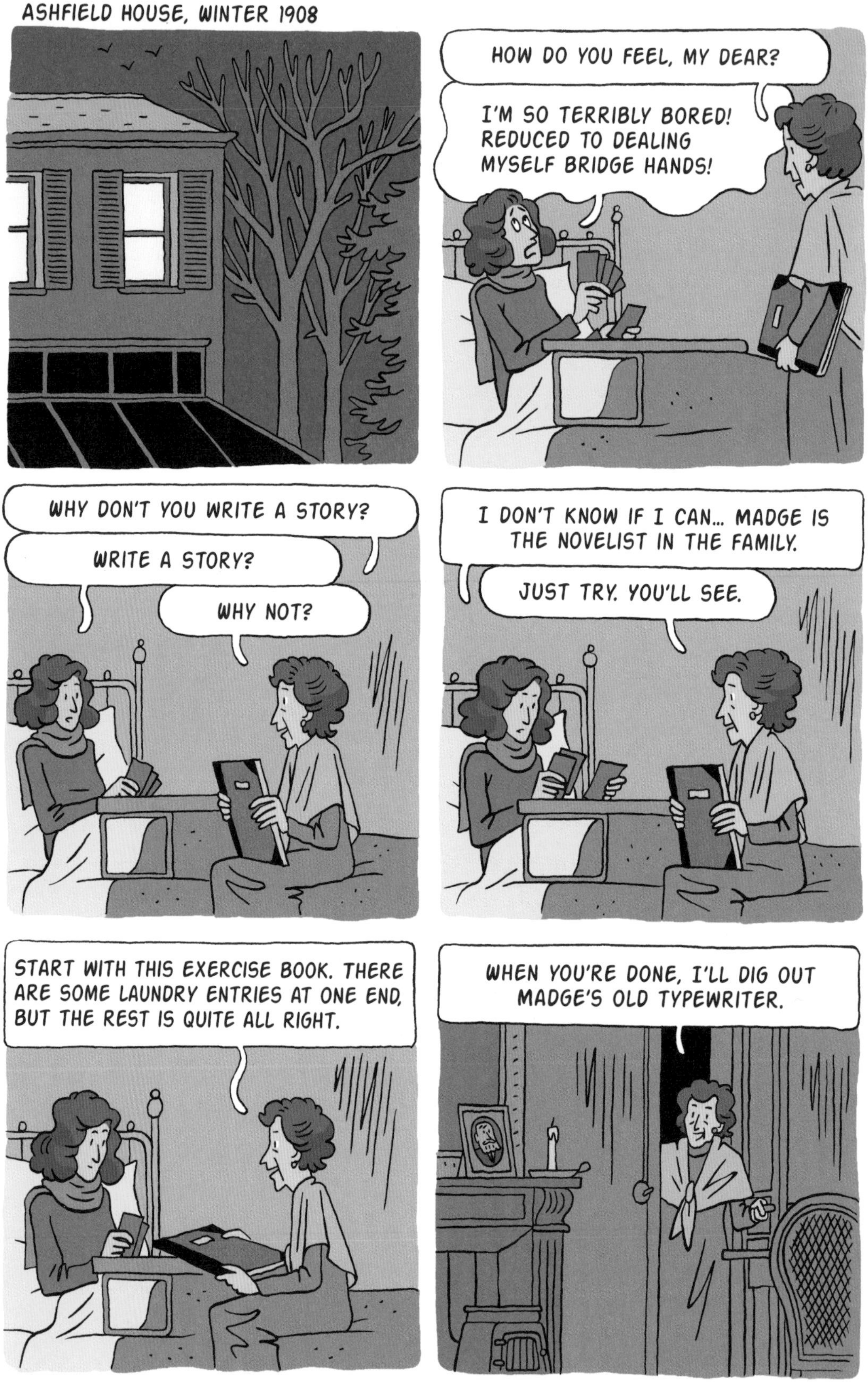
ASHFIELD HOUSE, WINTER 1908
HOW DO YOU FEEL, MY DEAR?
I'M SO TERRIBLY BORED! REDUCED TO DEALING MYSELF BRIDGE HANDS!
WHY DON'T YOU WRITE A STORY?
WRITE A STORY?
WHY NOT?
I DON'T KNOW IF I CAN... MADGE IS THE NOVELIST IN THE FAMILY.
JUST TRY. YOU'LL SEE.
START WITH THIS EXERCISE BOOK. THERE ARE SOME LAUNDRY ENTRIES AT ONE END, BUT THE REST IS QUITE ALL RIGHT.
WHEN YOU'RE DONE, I'LL DIG OUT MADGE'S OLD TYPEWRITER.

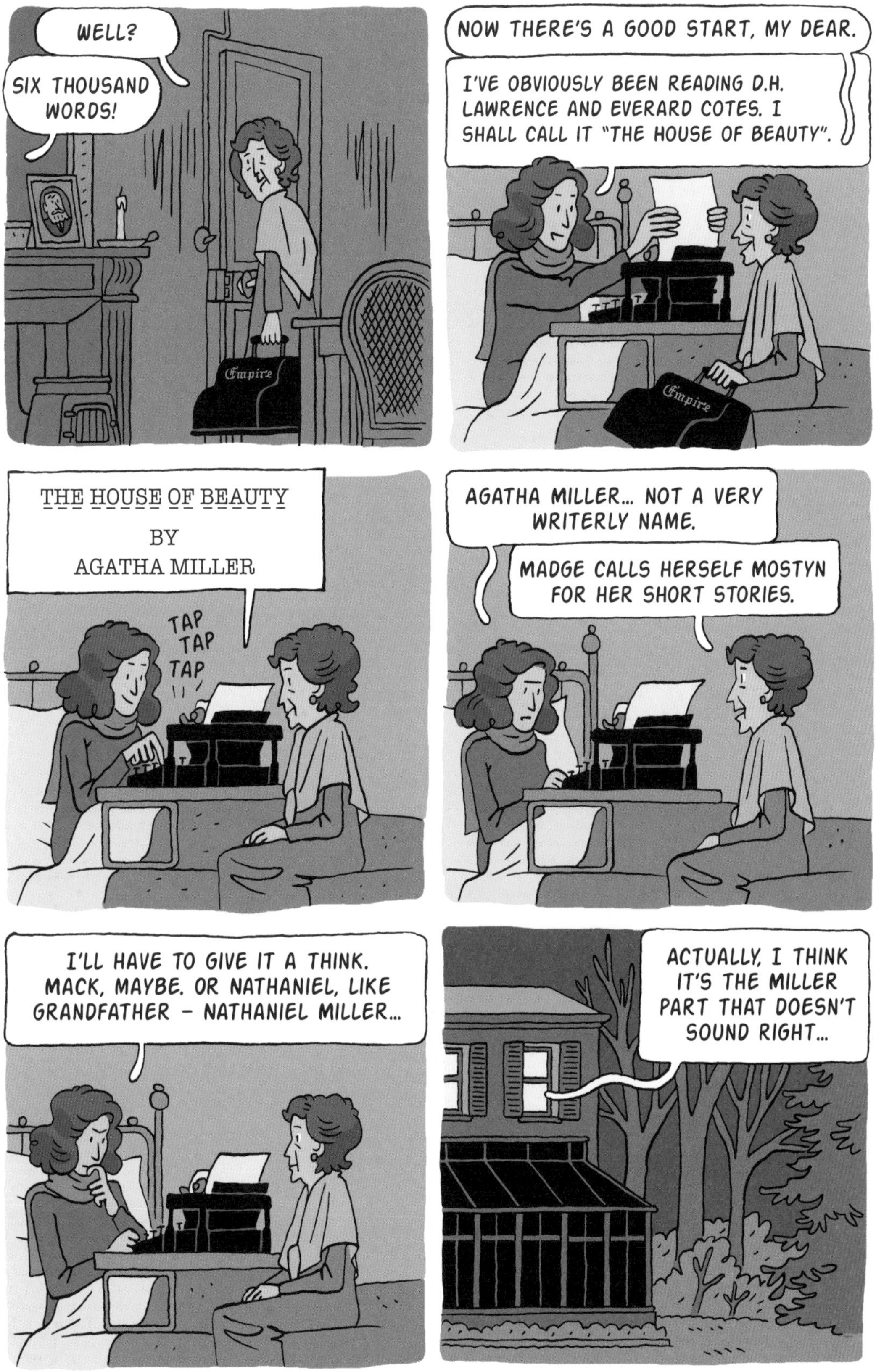
WELL?
SIX THOUSAND WORDS!
NOW THERE'S A GOOD START, MY DEAR.
I'VE OBVIOUSLY BEEN READING D.H. LAWRENCE AND EVERARD COTES. I SHALL CALL IT "THE HOUSE OF BEAUTY".
Empire
THE HOUSE OF BEAUTY
BY
AGATHA MILLER
TAP TAP TAP
AGATHA MILLER... NOT A VERY WRITERLY NAME.
MADGE CALLS HERSELF MOSTYN FOR HER SHORT STORIES.
I'LL HAVE TO GIVE IT A THINK. MACK, MAYBE. OR NATHANIEL, LIKE GRANDFATHER – NATHANIEL MILLER...
ACTUALLY, I THINK IT'S THE MILLER PART THAT DOESN'T SOUND RIGHT...

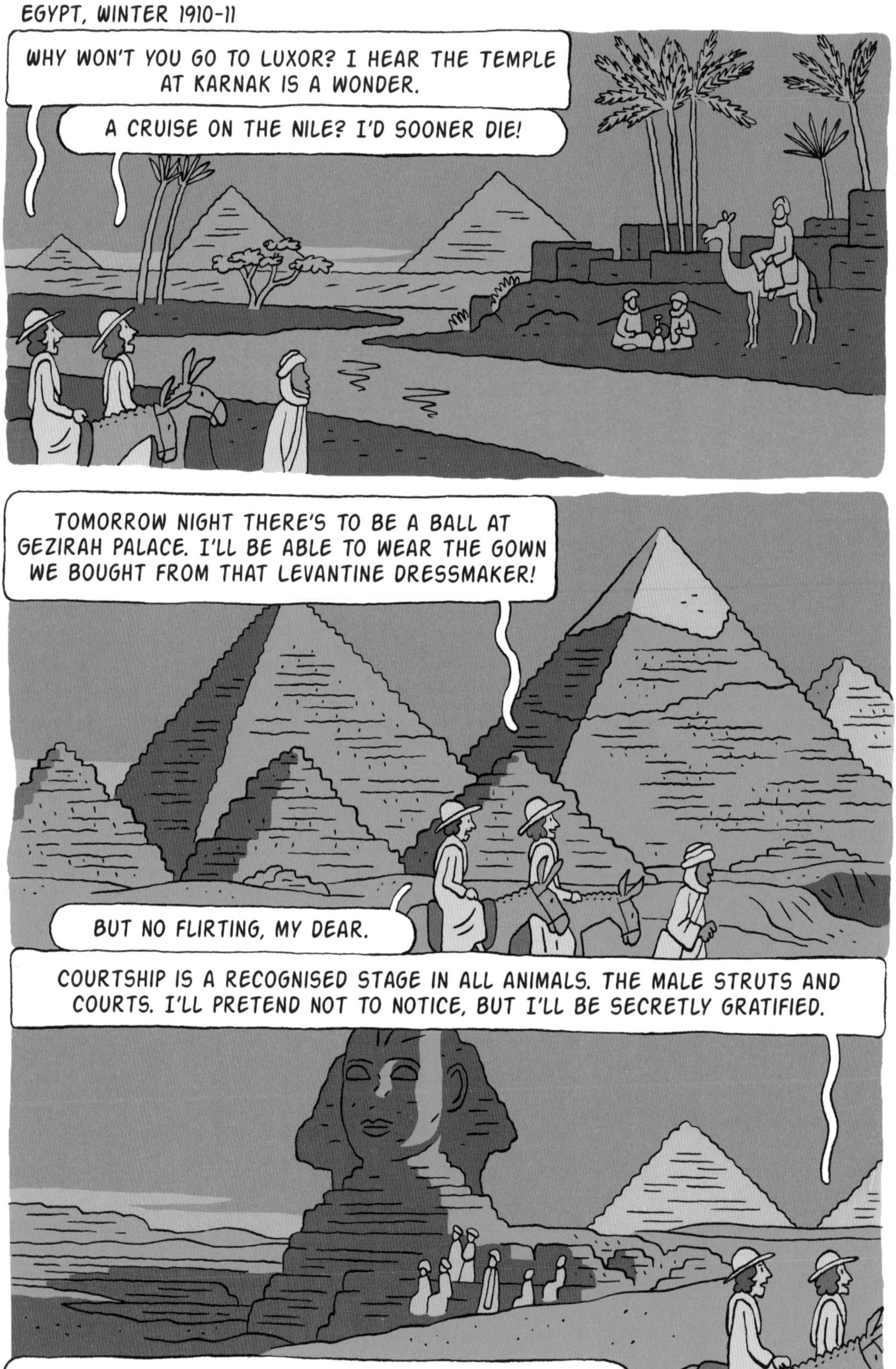
EGYPT, WINTER 1910-11
WHY WON'T YOU GO TO LUXOR? I HEAR THE TEMPLE AT KARNAK IS A WONDER.
A CRUISE ON THE NILE? I'D SOONER DIE!
TOMORROW NIGHT THERE'S TO BE A BALL AT GEZIRAH PALACE. I'LL BE ABLE TO WEAR THE GOWN WE BOUGHT FROM THAT LEVANTINE DRESSMAKER!
BUT NO FLIRTING, MY DEAR.
COURTSHIP IS A RECOGNISED STAGE IN ALL ANIMALS. THE MALE STRUTS AND COURTS. I'LL PRETEND NOT TO NOTICE, BUT I'LL BE SECRETLY GRATIFIED.
DON'T BE SILLY. I HAVEN'T THE MEANS TO MARRY YOU OFF!

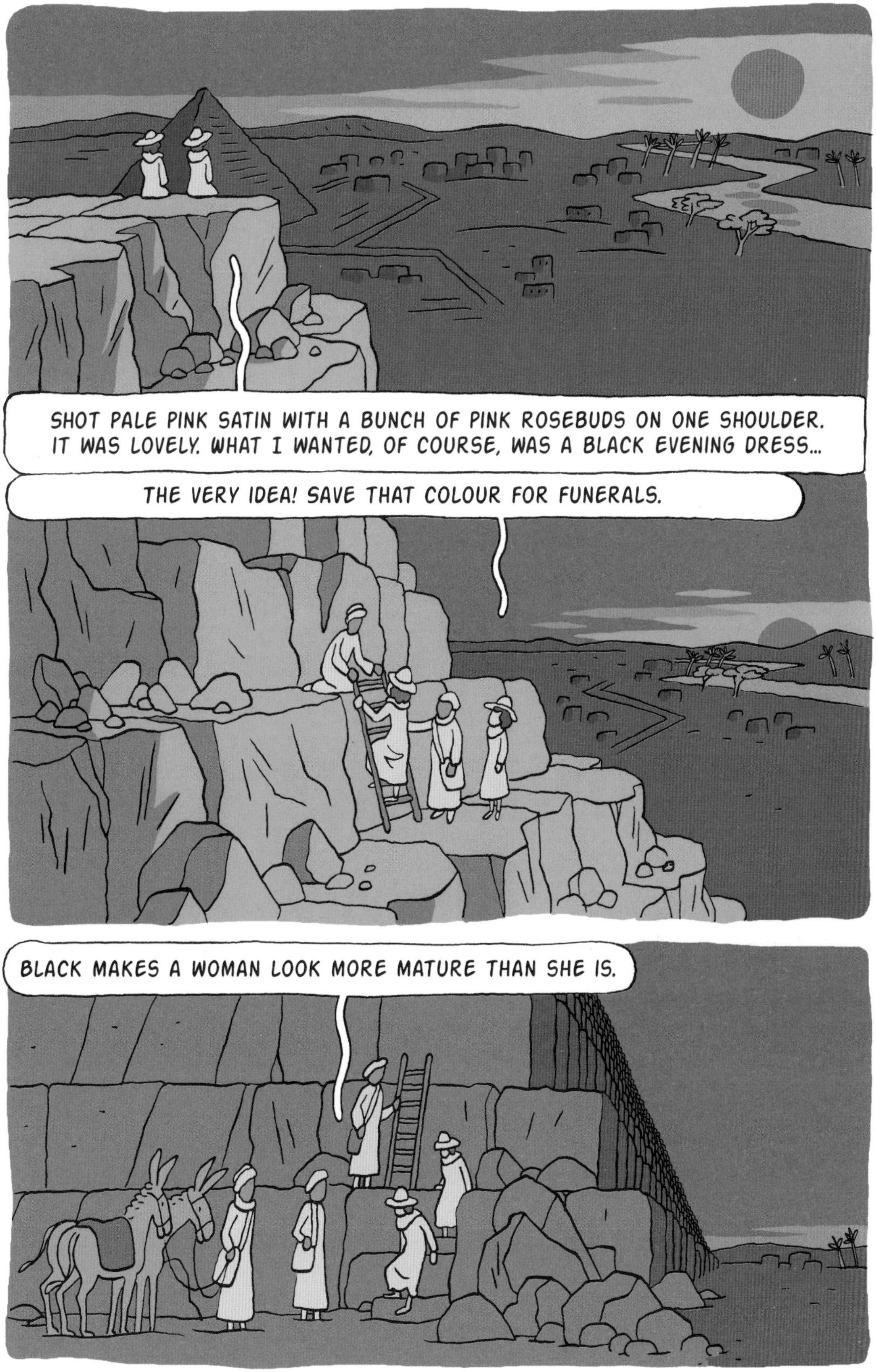
SHOT PALE PINK SATIN WITH A BUNCH OF PINK ROSEBUDS ON ONE SHOULDER. IT WAS LOVELY. WHAT I WANTED, OF COURSE, WAS A BLACK EVENING DRESS...
THE VERY IDEA! SAVE THAT COLOUR FOR FUNERALS.
BLACK MAKES A WOMAN LOOK MORE MATURE THAN SHE IS.

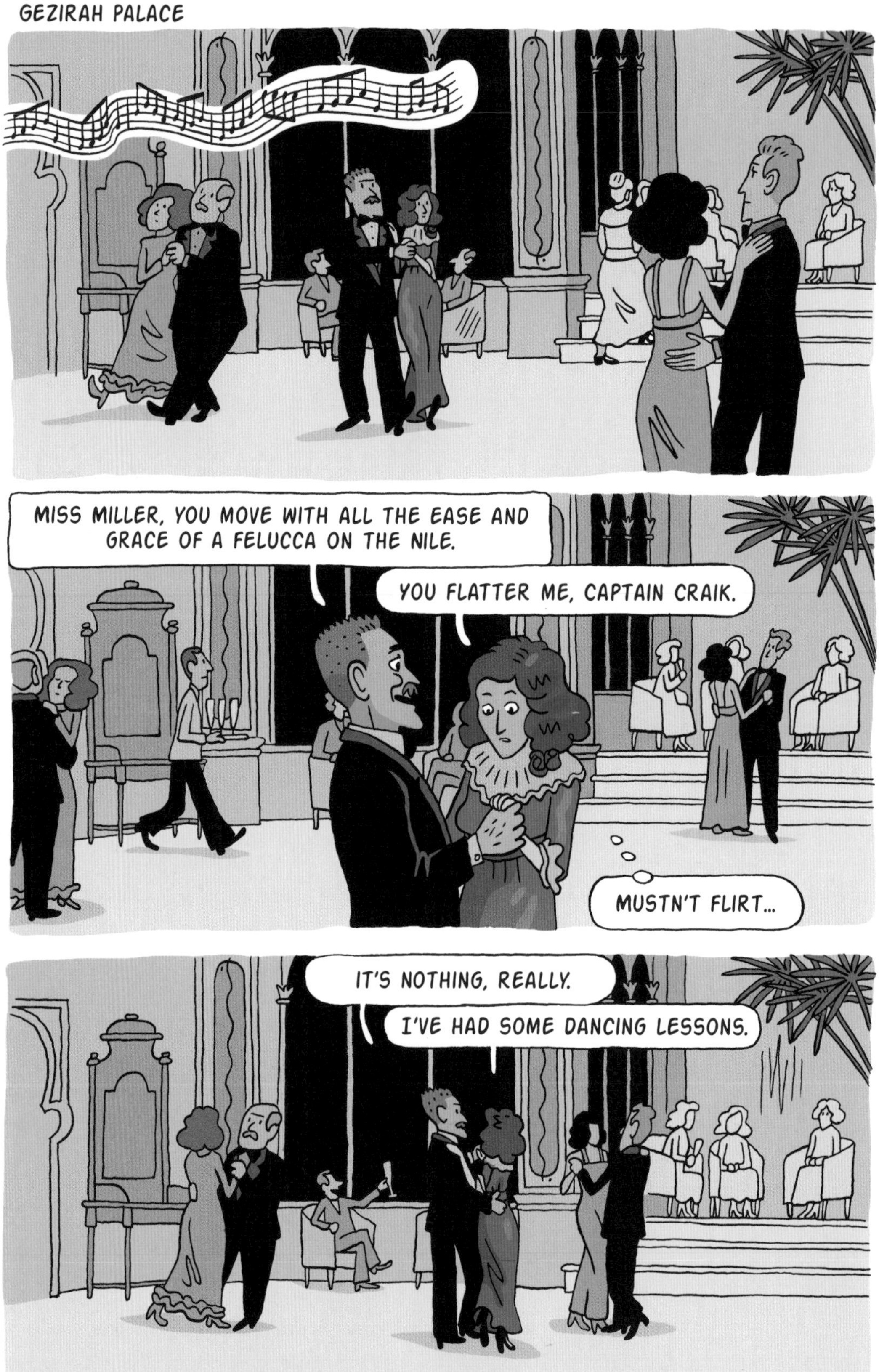
GEZIRAH PALACE
MISS MILLER, YOU MOVE WITH ALL THE EASE AND GRACE OF A FELUCCA ON THE NILE.
YOU FLATTER ME, CAPTAIN CRAIK.
MUSTN'T FLIRT...
IT'S NOTHING, REALLY.
I'VE HAD SOME DANCING LESSONS.

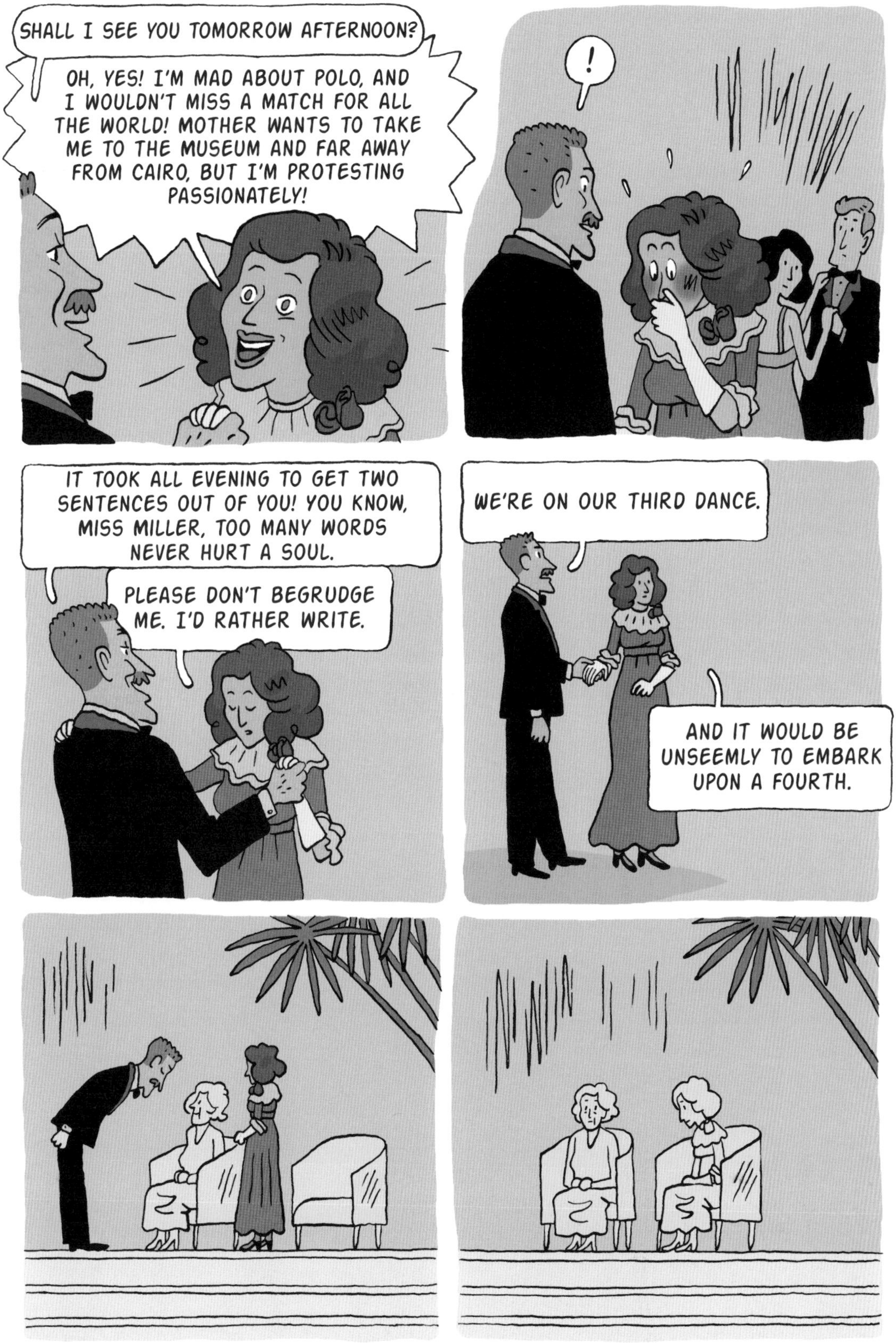
SHALL I SEE YOU TOMORROW AFTERNOON?
OH, YES! I'M MAD ABOUT POLO, AND I WOULDN'T MISS A MATCH FOR ALL THE WORLD! MOTHER WANTS TO TAKE ME TO THE MUSEUM AND FAR AWAY FROM CAIRO, BUT I'M PROTESTING PASSIONATELY!
!
IT TOOK ALL EVENING TO GET TWO SENTENCES OUT OF YOU! YOU KNOW, MISS MILLER, TOO MANY WORDS NEVER HURT A SOUL.
PLEASE DON'T BEGRUDGE ME. I'D RATHER WRITE.
WE'RE ON OUR THIRD DANCE.
AND IT WOULD BE UNSEEMLY TO EMBARK UPON A FOURTH.

THE ENGLISH COUNTRYSIDE, 10 MAY 1911

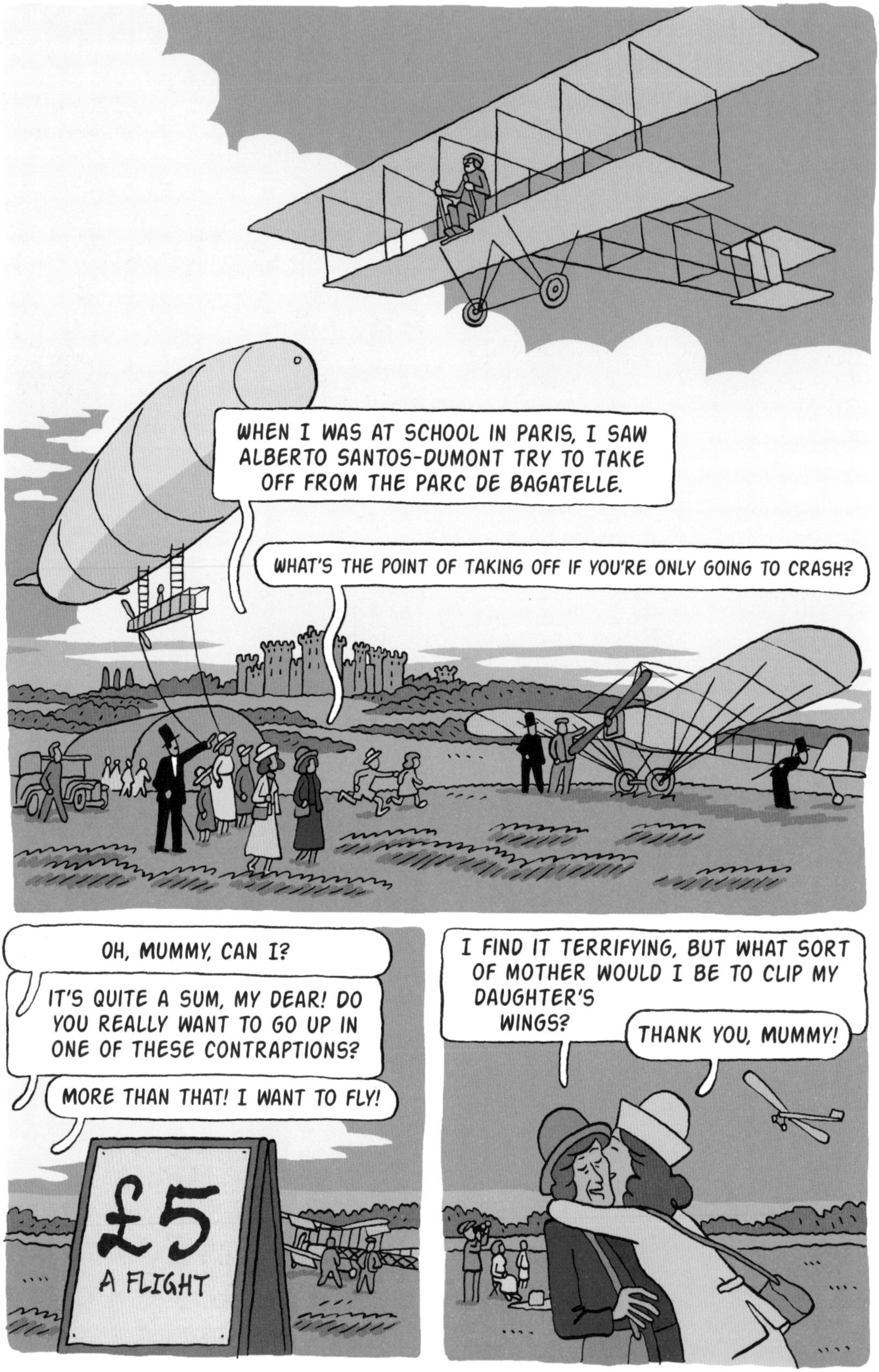

WHEN I WAS AT SCHOOL IN PARIS, I SAW ALBERTO SANTOS-DUMONT TRY TO TAKE OFF FROM THE PARC DE BAGATELLE.
WHAT'S THE POINT OF TAKING OFF IF YOU'RE ONLY GOING TO CRASH?
OH, MUMMY, CAN I?
IT'S QUITE A SUM, MY DEAR! DO YOU REALLY WANT TO GO UP IN ONE OF THESE CONTRAPTIONS?
MORE THAN THAT! I WANT TO FLY!
£5 A FLIGHT
I FIND IT TERRIFYING, BUT WHAT SORT OF MOTHER WOULD I BE TO CLIP MY DAUGHTER'S WINGS?
THANK YOU, MUMMY!

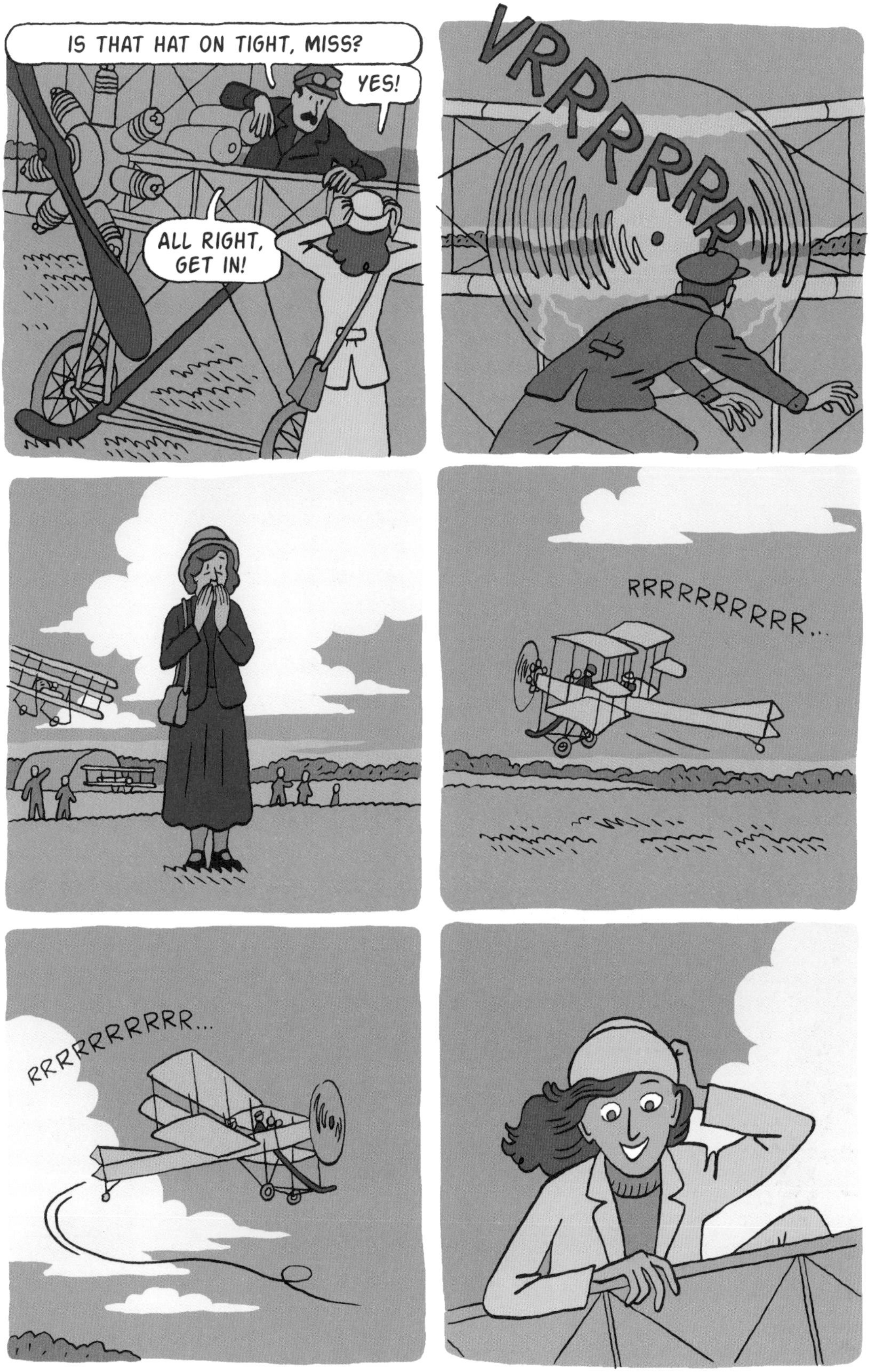
IS THAT HAT ON TIGHT, MISS?
YES!
ALL RIGHT, GET IN!
VRRRRRRR
RRRRRRRRRR...
RRRRRRRRRR...

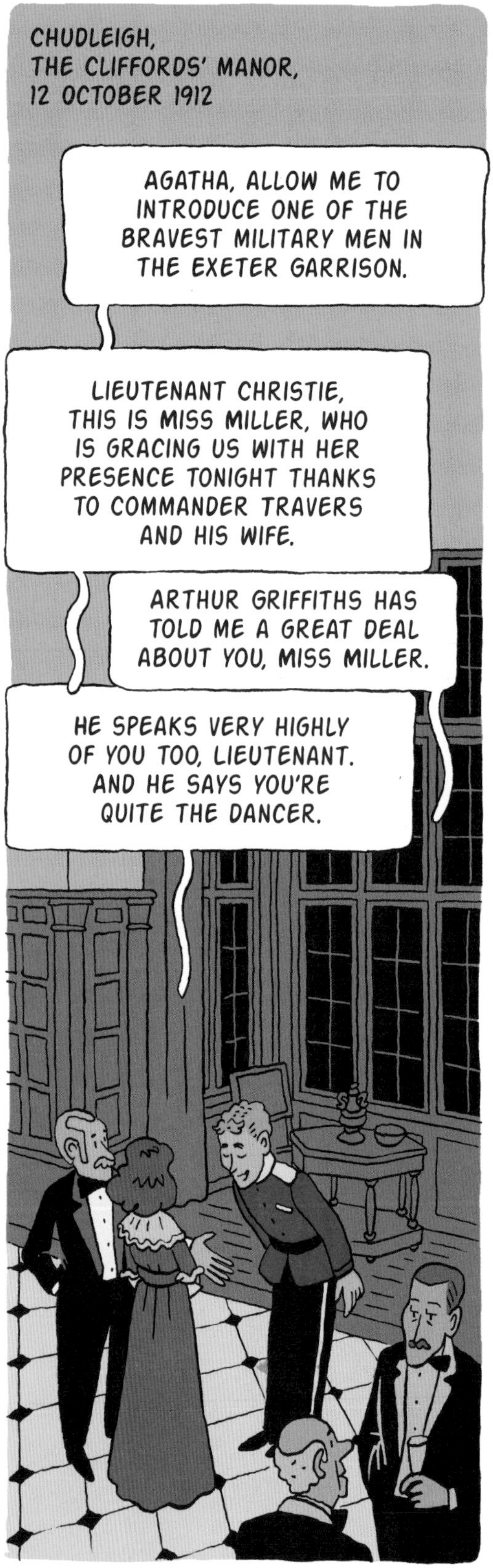
CHUDLEIGH, THE CLIFFORDS' MANOR, 12 OCTOBER 1912
AGATHA, ALLOW ME TO INTRODUCE ONE OF THE BRAVEST MILITARY MEN IN THE EXETER GARRISON.
LIEUTENANT CHRISTIE, THIS IS MISS MILLER, WHO IS GRACING US WITH HER PRESENCE TONIGHT THANKS TO COMMANDER TRAVERS AND HIS WIFE.
ARTHUR GRIFFITHS HAS TOLD ME A GREAT DEAL ABOUT YOU, MISS MILLER.
HE SPEAKS VERY HIGHLY OF YOU TOO, LIEUTENANT. AND HE SAYS YOU'RE QUITE THE DANCER.

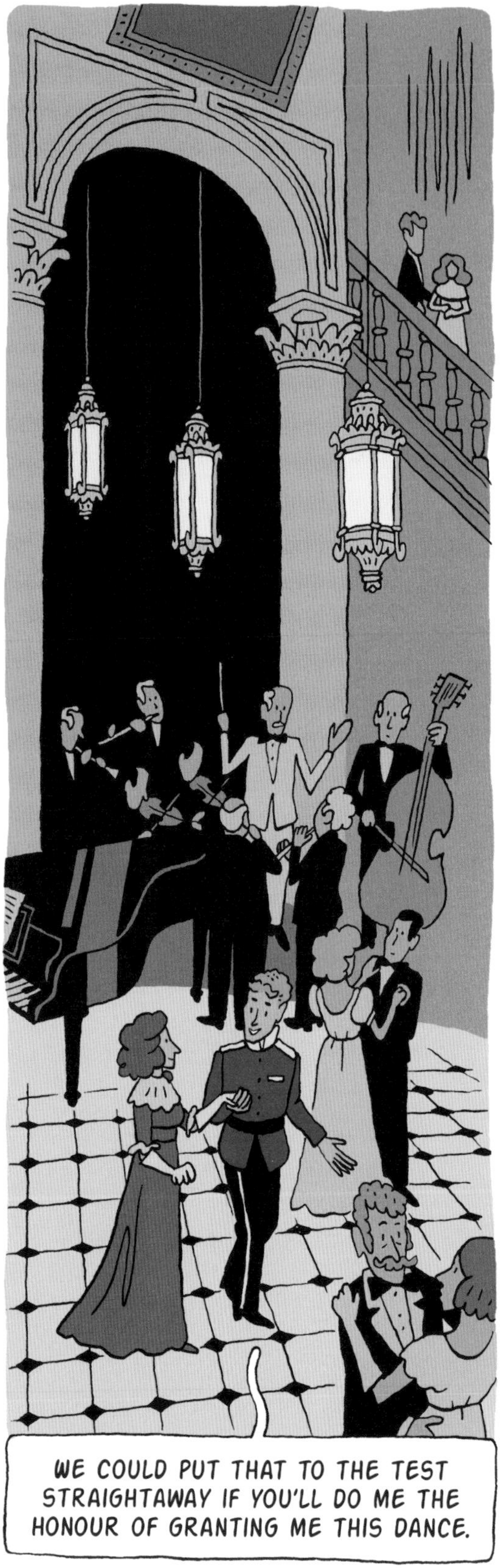
WE COULD PUT THAT TO THE TEST STRAIGHTAWAY IF YOU'LL DO ME THE HONOUR OF GRANTING ME THIS DANCE.

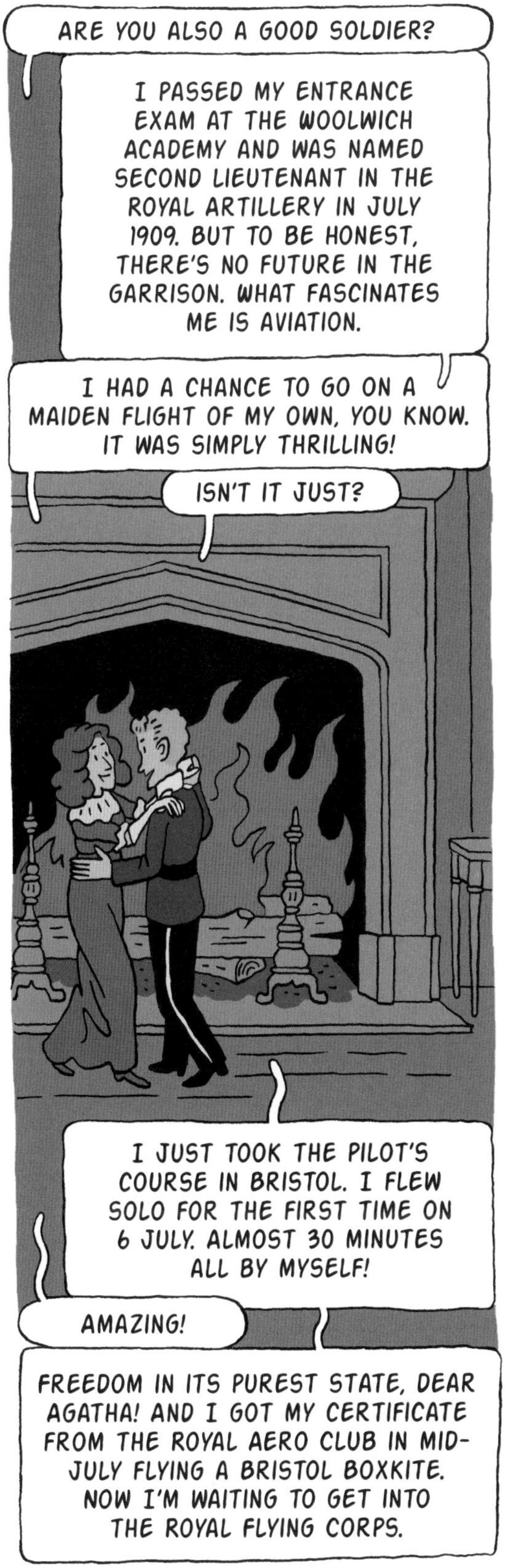
ARE YOU ALSO A GOOD SOLDIER?
I PASSED MY ENTRANCE EXAM AT THE WOOLWICH ACADEMY AND WAS NAMED SECOND LIEUTENANT IN THE ROYAL ARTILLERY IN JULY 1909. BUT TO BE HONEST, THERE'S NO FUTURE IN THE GARRISON. WHAT FASCINATES ME IS AVIATION.
I HAD A CHANCE TO GO ON A MAIDEN FLIGHT OF MY OWN, YOU KNOW. IT WAS SIMPLY THRILLING!
ISN'T IT JUST?
I JUST TOOK THE PILOT'S COURSE IN BRISTOL. I FLEW SOLO FOR THE FIRST TIME ON 6 JULY. ALMOST 30 MINUTES ALL BY MYSELF!
AMAZING!
FREEDOM IN ITS PUREST STATE, DEAR AGATHA! AND I GOT MY CERTIFICATE FROM THE ROYAL AERO CLUB IN MID-JULY FLYING A BRISTOL BOXKITE. NOW I'M WAITING TO GET INTO THE ROYAL FLYING CORPS.
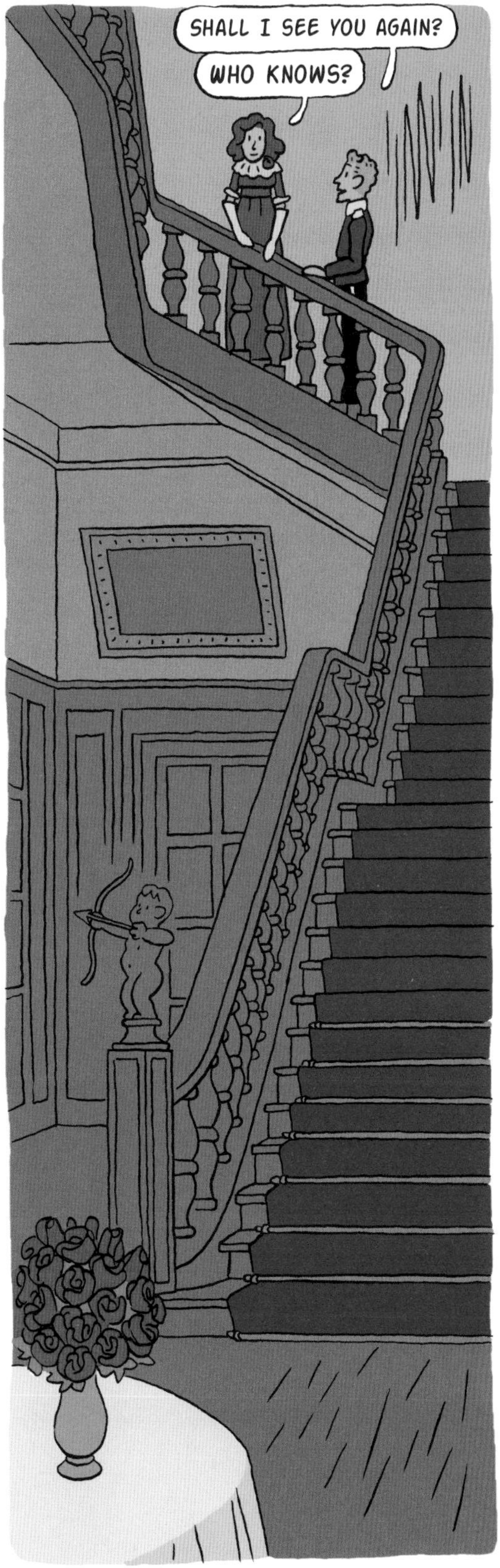
SHALL I SEE YOU AGAIN?
WHO KNOWS?

CLIFTON, A SUBURB OF BRISTOL. AT ARCHIBALD CHRISTIE'S PARENTS' HOUSE, 23 DECEMBER 1914

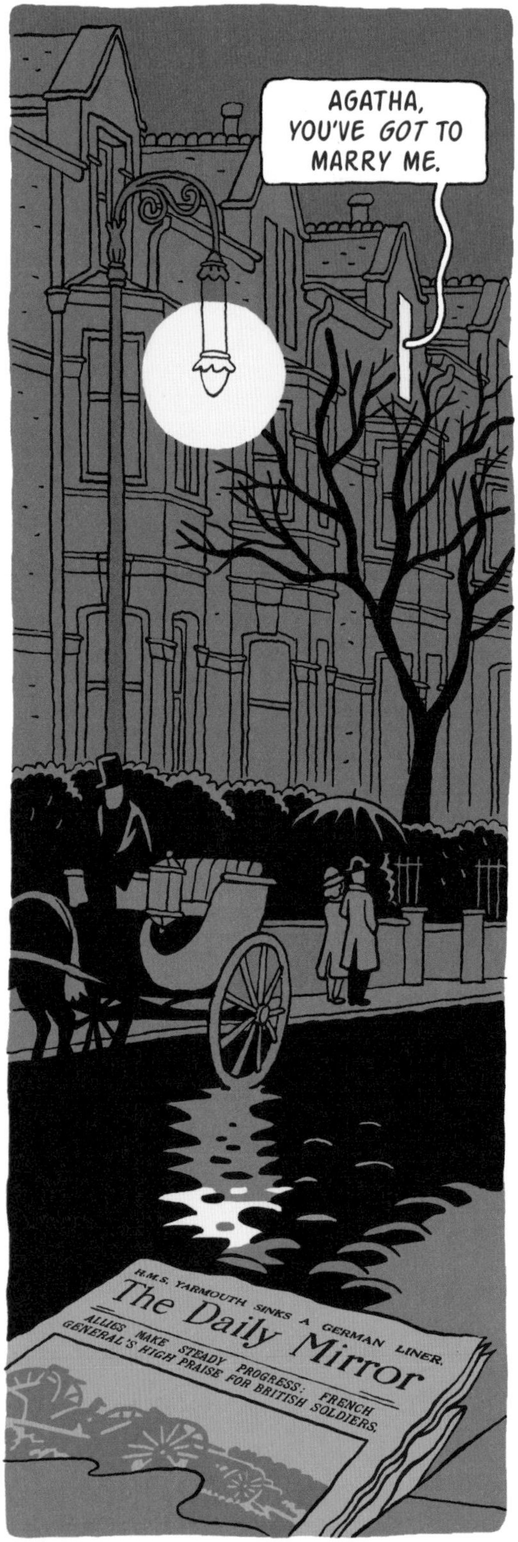
AGATHA, YOU'VE *GOT* TO MARRY ME.
H.M.S. YARMOUTH SINKS A GERMAN LINER.
The Daily Mirror
ALLIES MAKE STEADY PROGRESS: FRENCH GENERAL'S HIGH PRAISE FOR BRITISH SOLDIERS.

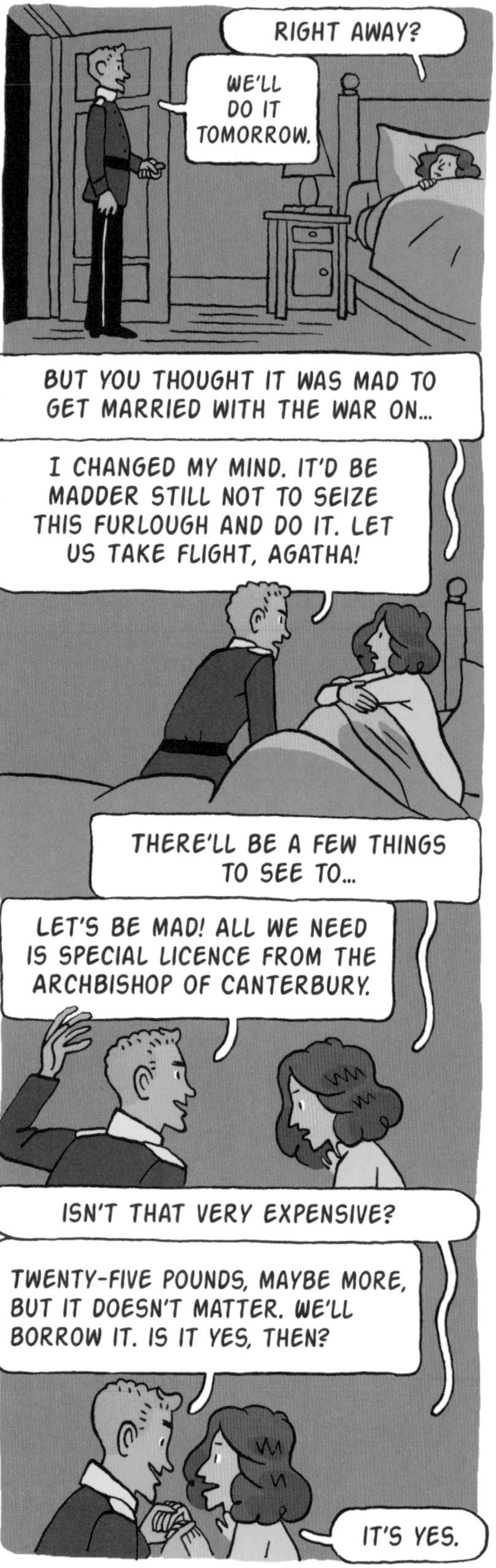
RIGHT AWAY?
WE'LL DO IT TOMORROW.
BUT YOU THOUGHT IT WAS MAD TO GET MARRIED WITH THE WAR ON...
I CHANGED MY MIND. IT'D BE MADDER STILL NOT TO SEIZE THIS FURLOUGH AND DO IT. LET US TAKE FLIGHT, AGATHA!
THERE'LL BE A FEW THINGS TO SEE TO...
LET'S BE MAD! ALL WE NEED IS SPECIAL LICENCE FROM THE ARCHBISHOP OF CANTERBURY.
ISN'T THAT VERY EXPENSIVE?
TWENTY-FIVE POUNDS, MAYBE MORE, BUT IT DOESN'T MATTER. WE'LL BORROW IT. IS IT YES, THEN?
IT'S YES.

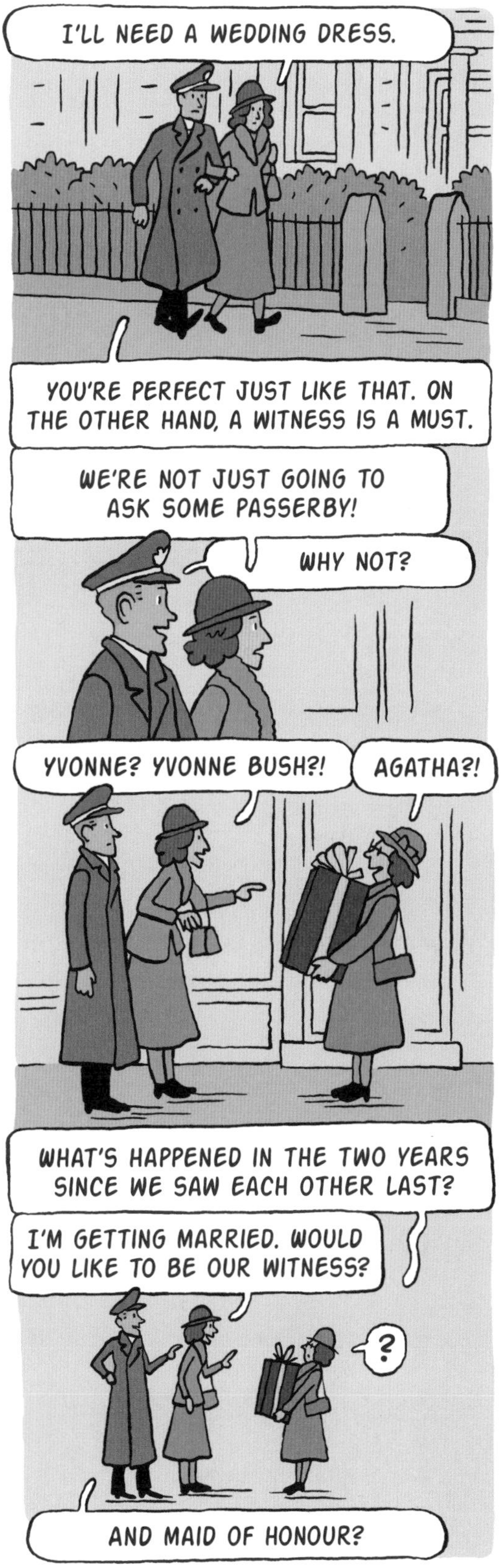
I'LL NEED A WEDDING DRESS.
YOU'RE PERFECT JUST LIKE THAT. ON THE OTHER HAND, A WITNESS IS A MUST.
WE'RE NOT JUST GOING TO ASK SOME PASSERBY!
WHY NOT?
YVONNE? YVONNE BUSH?!
AGATHA?!
WHAT'S HAPPENED IN THE TWO YEARS SINCE WE SAW EACH OTHER LAST?
I'M GETTING MARRIED. WOULD YOU LIKE TO BE OUR WITNESS?
?
AND MAID OF HONOUR?

ST EMMANUEL CHURCH,
24 DECEMBER 1914

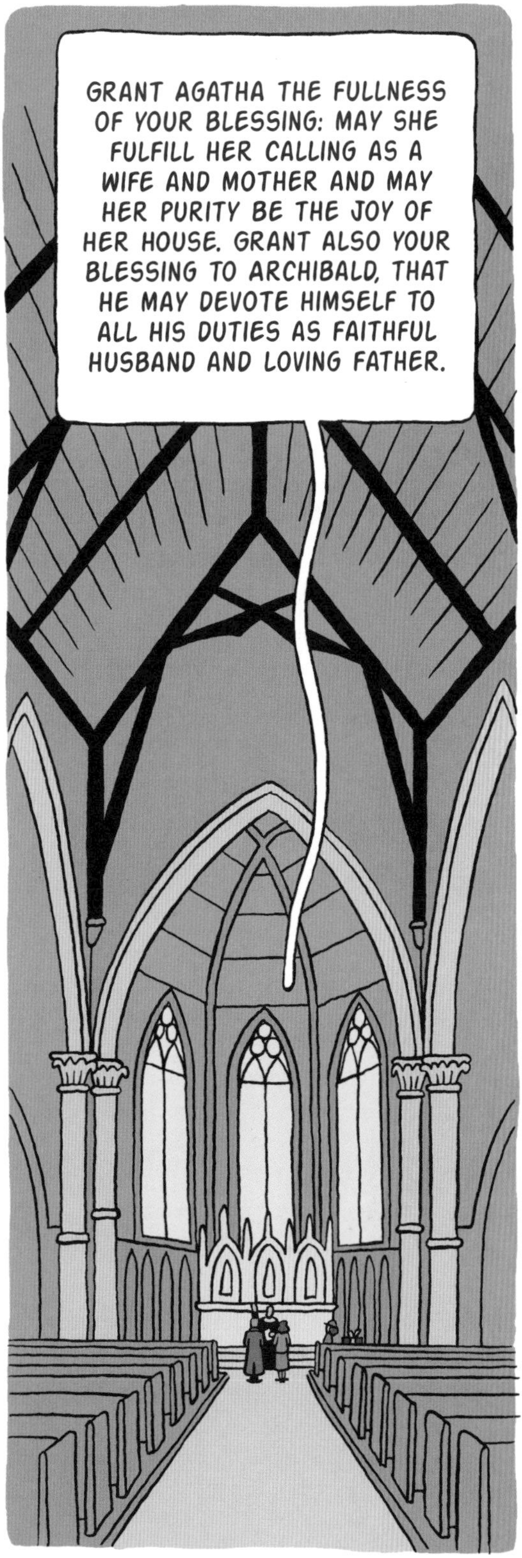
GRANT AGATHA THE FULLNESS OF YOUR BLESSING: MAY SHE FULFILL HER CALLING AS A WIFE AND MOTHER AND MAY HER PURITY BE THE JOY OF HER HOUSE. GRANT ALSO YOUR BLESSING TO ARCHIBALD, THAT HE MAY DEVOTE HIMSELF TO ALL HIS DUTIES AS FAITHFUL HUSBAND AND LOVING FATHER.

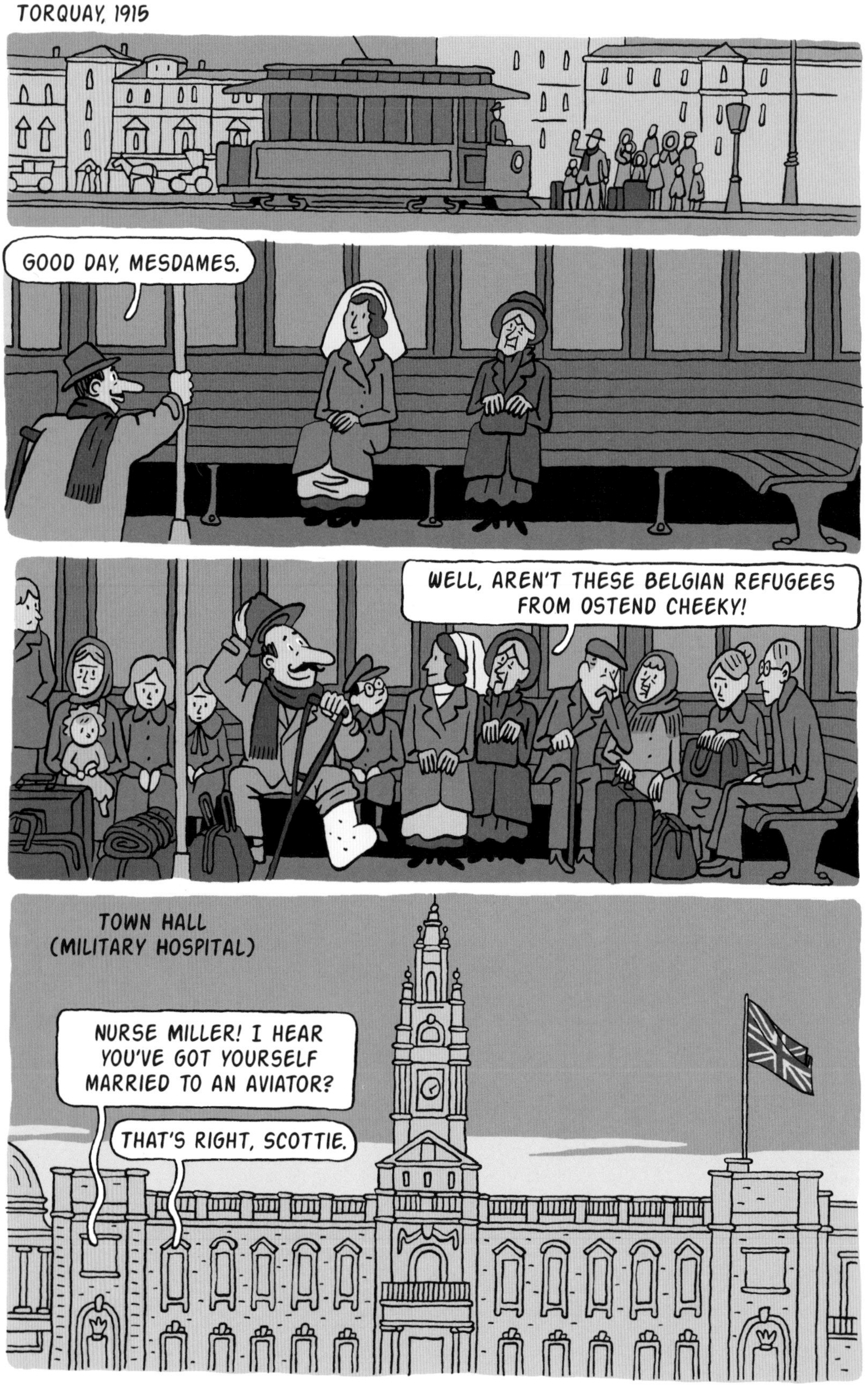
TORQUAY, 1915
GOOD DAY, MESDAMES.
WELL, AREN'T THESE BELGIAN REFUGEES FROM OSTEND CHEEKY!
TOWN HALL (MILITARY HOSPITAL)
NURSE MILLER! I HEAR YOU'VE GOT YOURSELF MARRIED TO AN AVIATOR?
THAT'S RIGHT, SCOTTIE.

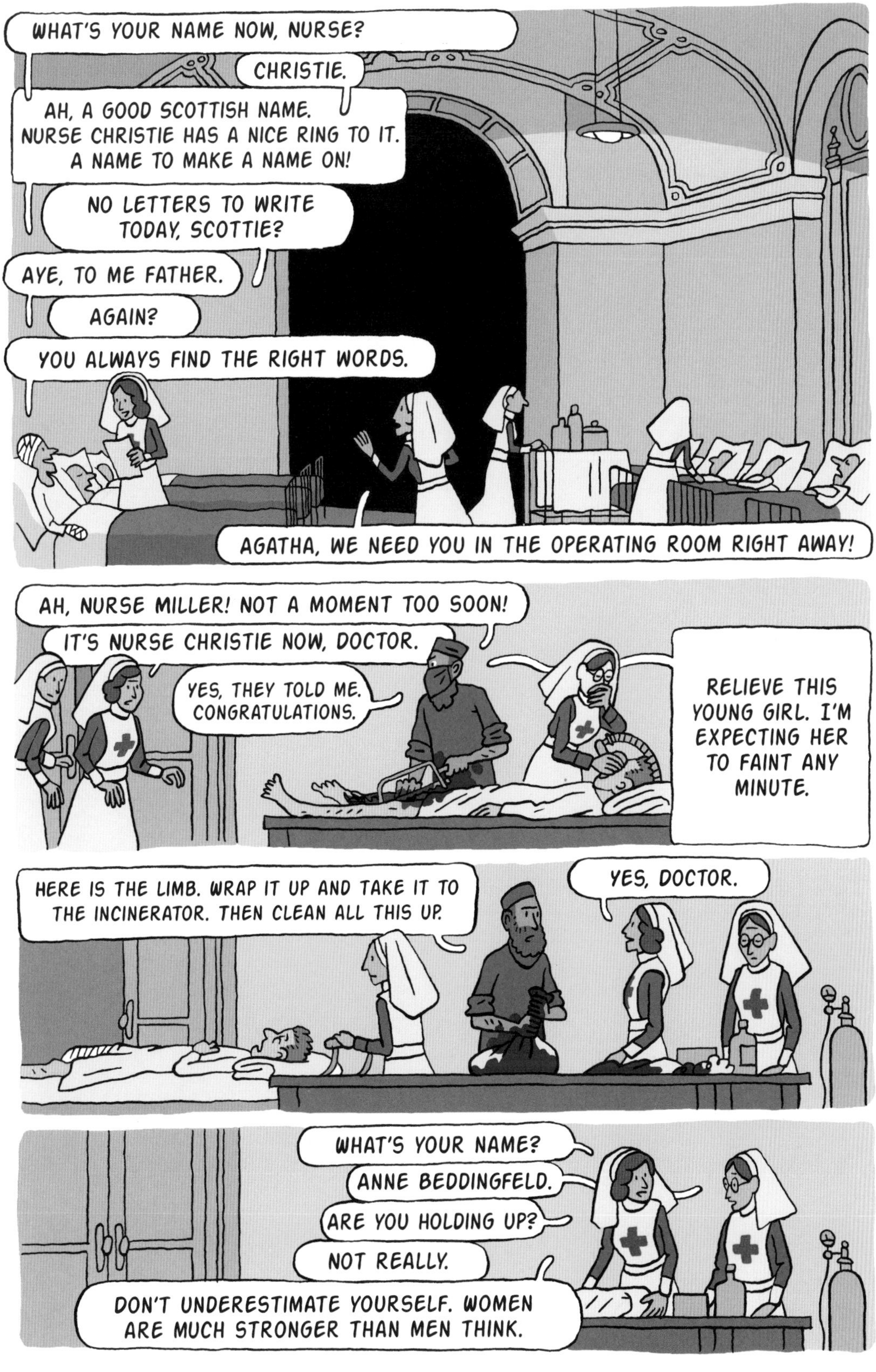
WHAT'S YOUR NAME NOW, NURSE?
CHRISTIE.
AH, A GOOD SCOTTISH NAME. NURSE CHRISTIE HAS A NICE RING TO IT. A NAME TO MAKE A NAME ON!
NO LETTERS TO WRITE TODAY, SCOTTIE?
AYE, TO ME FATHER.
AGAIN?
YOU ALWAYS FIND THE RIGHT WORDS.
AGATHA, WE NEED YOU IN THE OPERATING ROOM RIGHT AWAY!
AH, NURSE MILLER! NOT A MOMENT TOO SOON!
IT'S NURSE CHRISTIE NOW, DOCTOR.
YES, THEY TOLD ME. CONGRATULATIONS.
RELIEVE THIS YOUNG GIRL. I'M EXPECTING HER TO FAINT ANY MINUTE.
HERE IS THE LIMB. WRAP IT UP AND TAKE IT TO THE INCINERATOR. THEN CLEAN ALL THIS UP.
YES, DOCTOR.
WHAT'S YOUR NAME?
ANNE BEDDINGFELD.
ARE YOU HOLDING UP?
NOT REALLY.
DON'T UNDERESTIMATE YOURSELF. WOMEN ARE MUCH STRONGER THAN MEN THINK.

1917

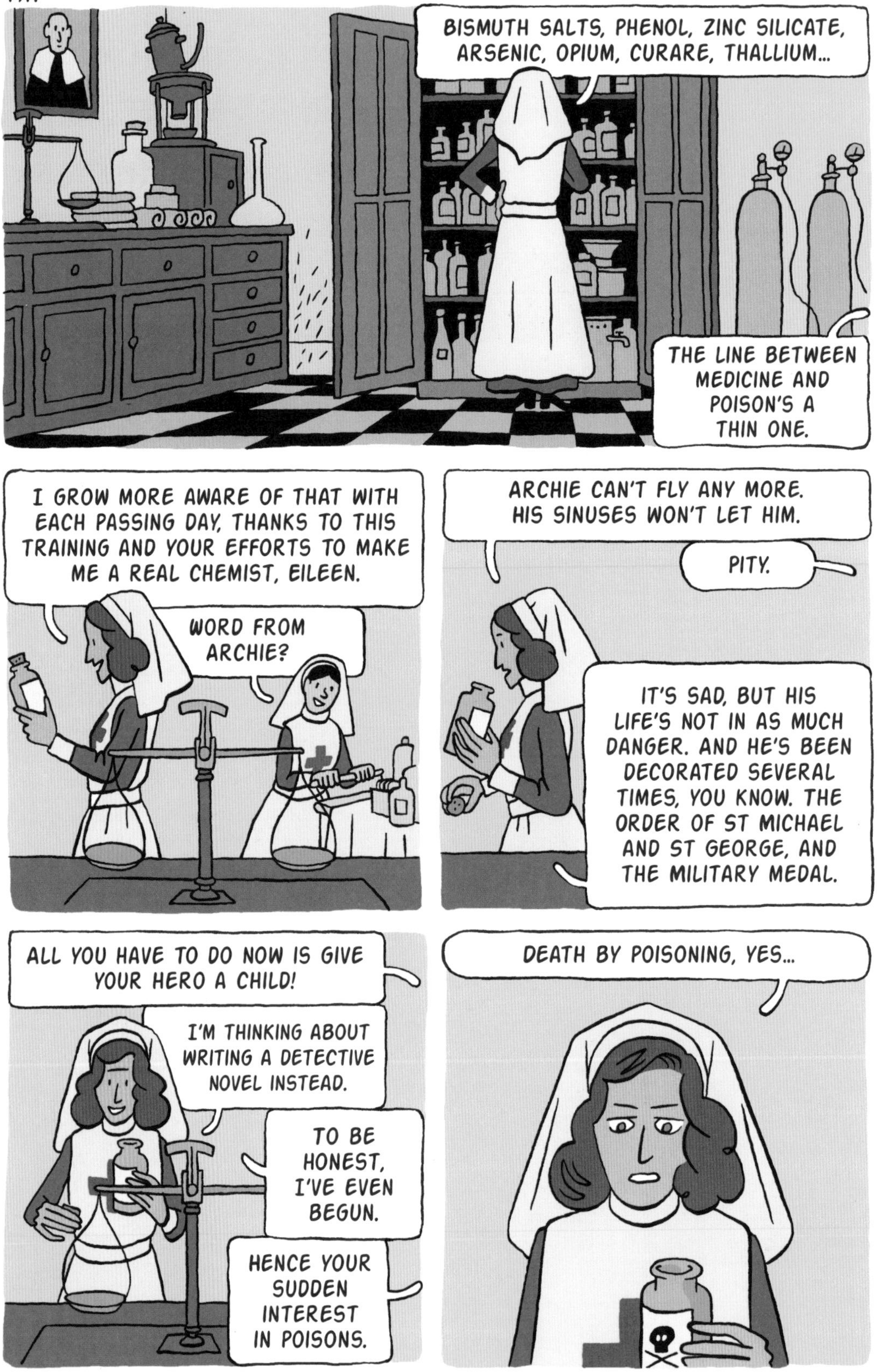

BISMUTH SALTS, PHENOL, ZINC SILICATE, ARSENIC, OPIUM, CURARE, THALLIUM...
THE LINE BETWEEN MEDICINE AND POISON'S A THIN ONE.
I GROW MORE AWARE OF THAT WITH EACH PASSING DAY, THANKS TO THIS TRAINING AND YOUR EFFORTS TO MAKE ME A REAL CHEMIST, EILEEN.
WORD FROM ARCHIE?
ARCHIE CAN'T FLY ANY MORE. HIS SINUSES WON'T LET HIM.
PITY.
IT'S SAD, BUT HIS LIFE'S NOT IN AS MUCH DANGER. AND HE'S BEEN DECORATED SEVERAL TIMES, YOU KNOW. THE ORDER OF ST MICHAEL AND ST GEORGE, AND THE MILITARY MEDAL.
ALL YOU HAVE TO DO NOW IS GIVE YOUR HERO A CHILD!
I'M THINKING ABOUT WRITING A DETECTIVE NOVEL INSTEAD.
TO BE HONEST, I'VE EVEN BEGUN.
HENCE YOUR SUDDEN INTEREST IN POISONS.
DEATH BY POISONING, YES...

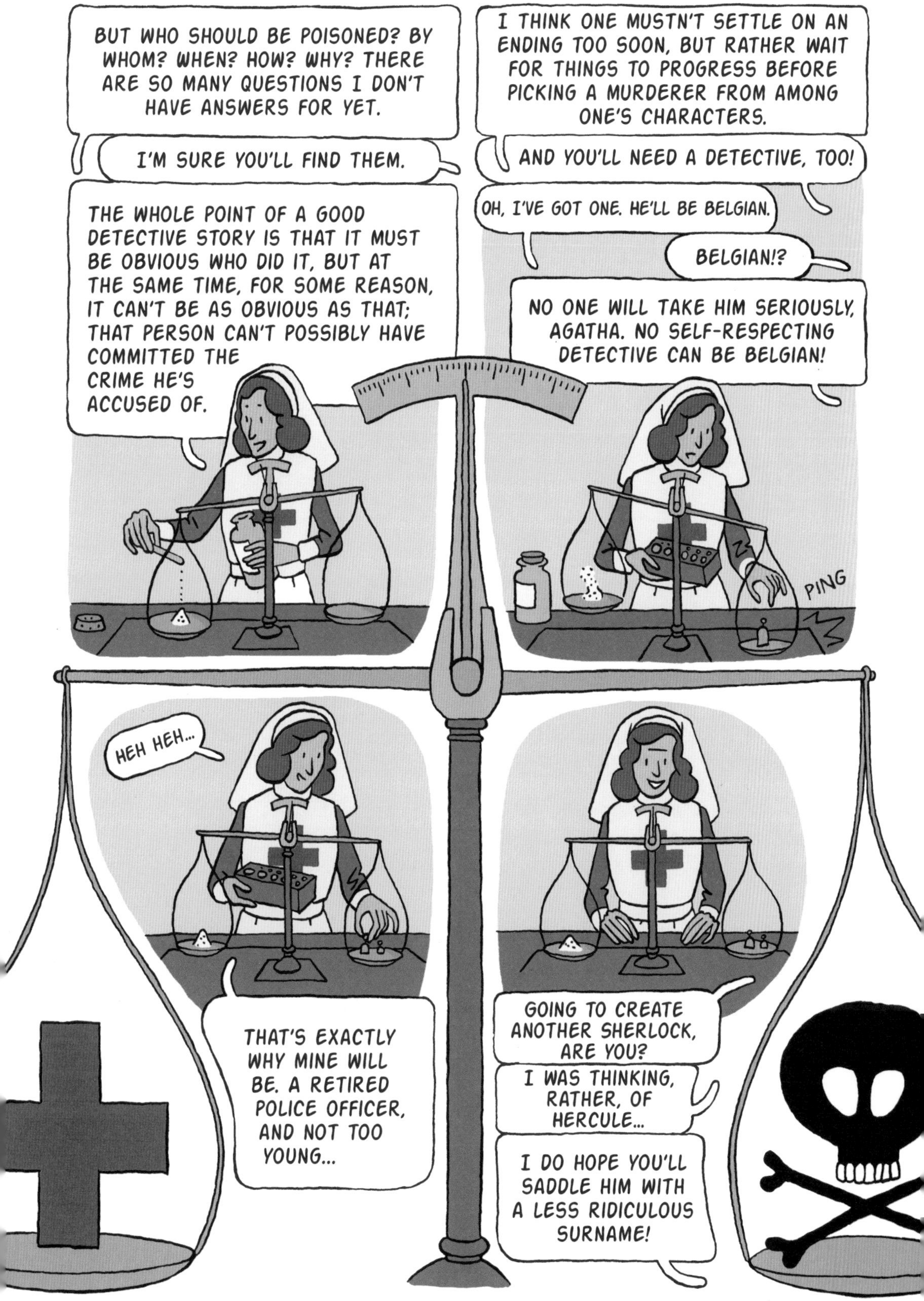

BUT WHO SHOULD BE POISONED? BY WHOM? WHEN? HOW? WHY? THERE ARE SO MANY QUESTIONS I DON'T HAVE ANSWERS FOR YET.
I'M SURE YOU'LL FIND THEM.
THE WHOLE POINT OF A GOOD DETECTIVE STORY IS THAT IT MUST BE OBVIOUS WHO DID IT, BUT AT THE SAME TIME, FOR SOME REASON, IT CAN'T BE AS OBVIOUS AS THAT; THAT PERSON CAN'T POSSIBLY HAVE COMMITTED THE CRIME HE'S ACCUSED OF.
I THINK ONE MUSTN'T SETTLE ON AN ENDING TOO SOON, BUT RATHER WAIT FOR THINGS TO PROGRESS BEFORE PICKING A MURDERER FROM AMONG ONE'S CHARACTERS.
AND YOU'LL NEED A DETECTIVE, TOO!
OH, I'VE GOT ONE. HE'LL BE BELGIAN.
BELGIAN!?
NO ONE WILL TAKE HIM SERIOUSLY, AGATHA. NO SELF-RESPECTING DETECTIVE CAN BE BELGIAN!
PING
HEH HEH...
THAT'S EXACTLY WHY MINE WILL BE. A RETIRED POLICE OFFICER, AND NOT TOO YOUNG...
GOING TO CREATE ANOTHER SHERLOCK, ARE YOU?
I WAS THINKING, RATHER, OF HERCULE...
I DO HOPE YOU'LL SADDLE HIM WITH A LESS RIDICULOUS SURNAME!

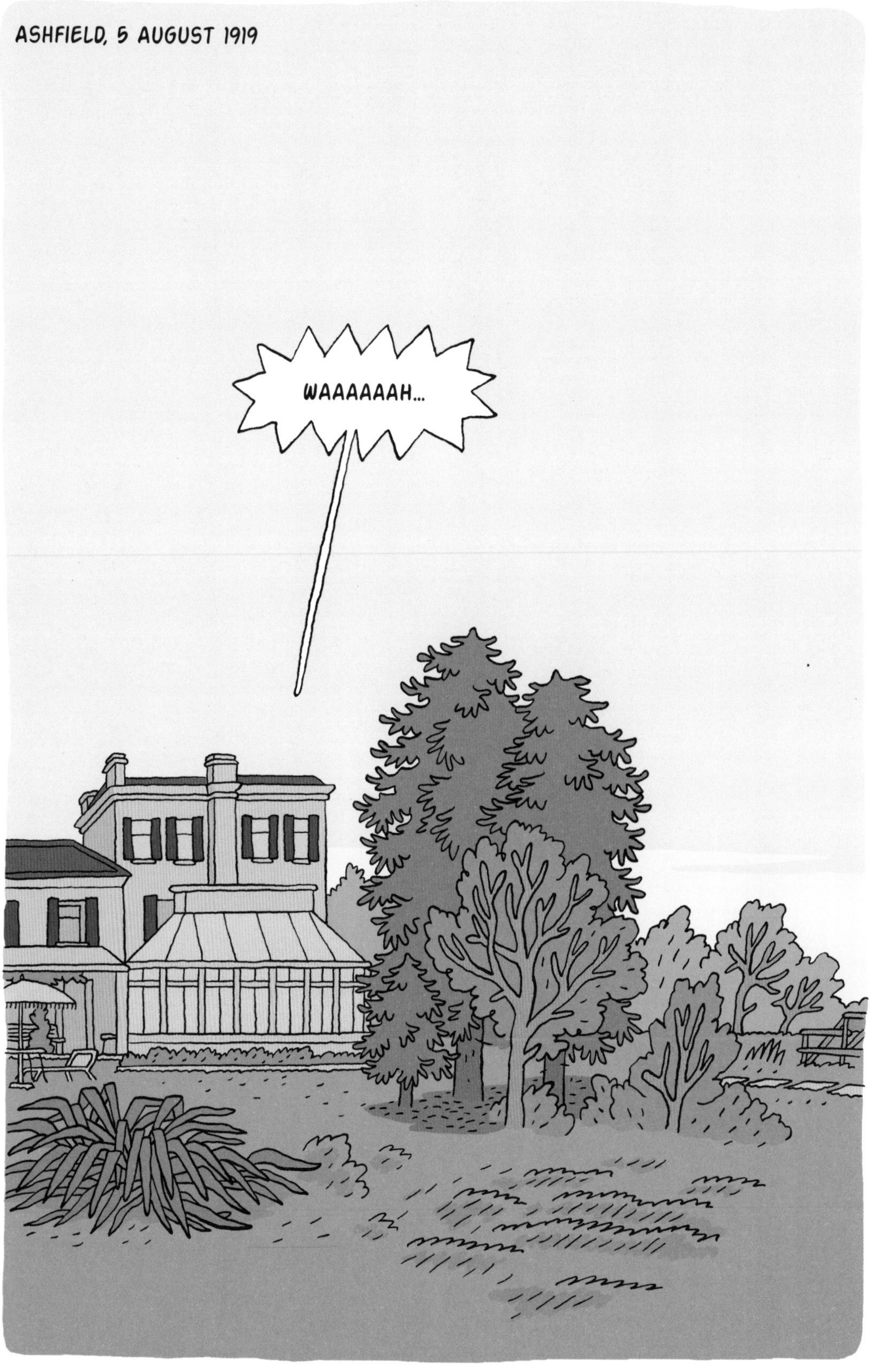
ASHFIELD, 5 AUGUST 1919
WAAAAAAH...

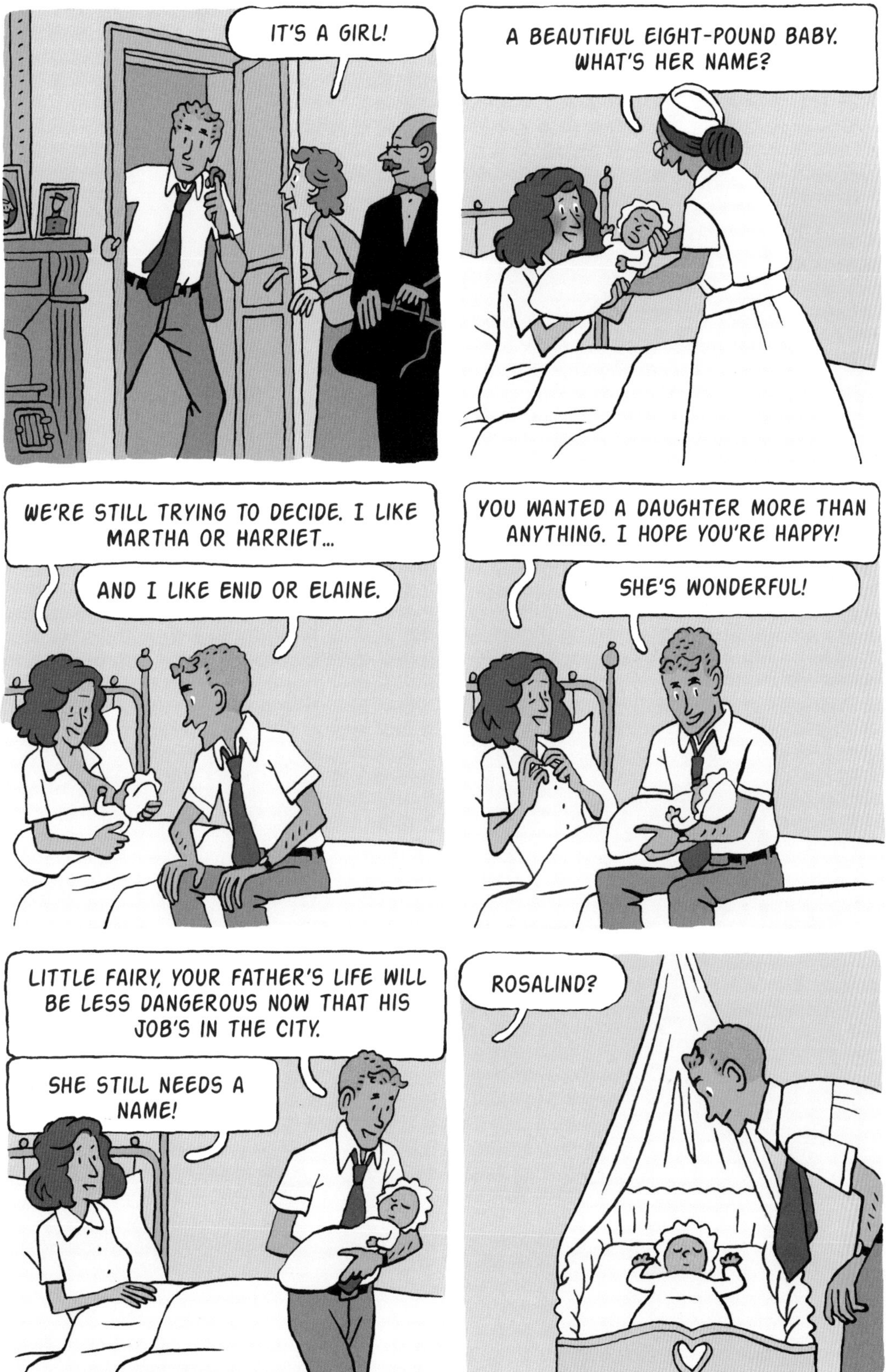
IT'S A GIRL!
A BEAUTIFUL EIGHT-POUND BABY. WHAT'S HER NAME?
WE'RE STILL TRYING TO DECIDE. I LIKE MARTHA OR HARRIET...
AND I LIKE ENID OR ELAINE.
YOU WANTED A DAUGHTER MORE THAN ANYTHING. I HOPE YOU'RE HAPPY!
SHE'S WONDERFUL!
LITTLE FAIRY, YOUR FATHER'S LIFE WILL BE LESS DANGEROUS NOW THAT HIS JOB'S IN THE CITY.
SHE STILL NEEDS A NAME!
ROSALIND?

THE BODLEY HEAD, PUBLISHERS, LONDON, 1919

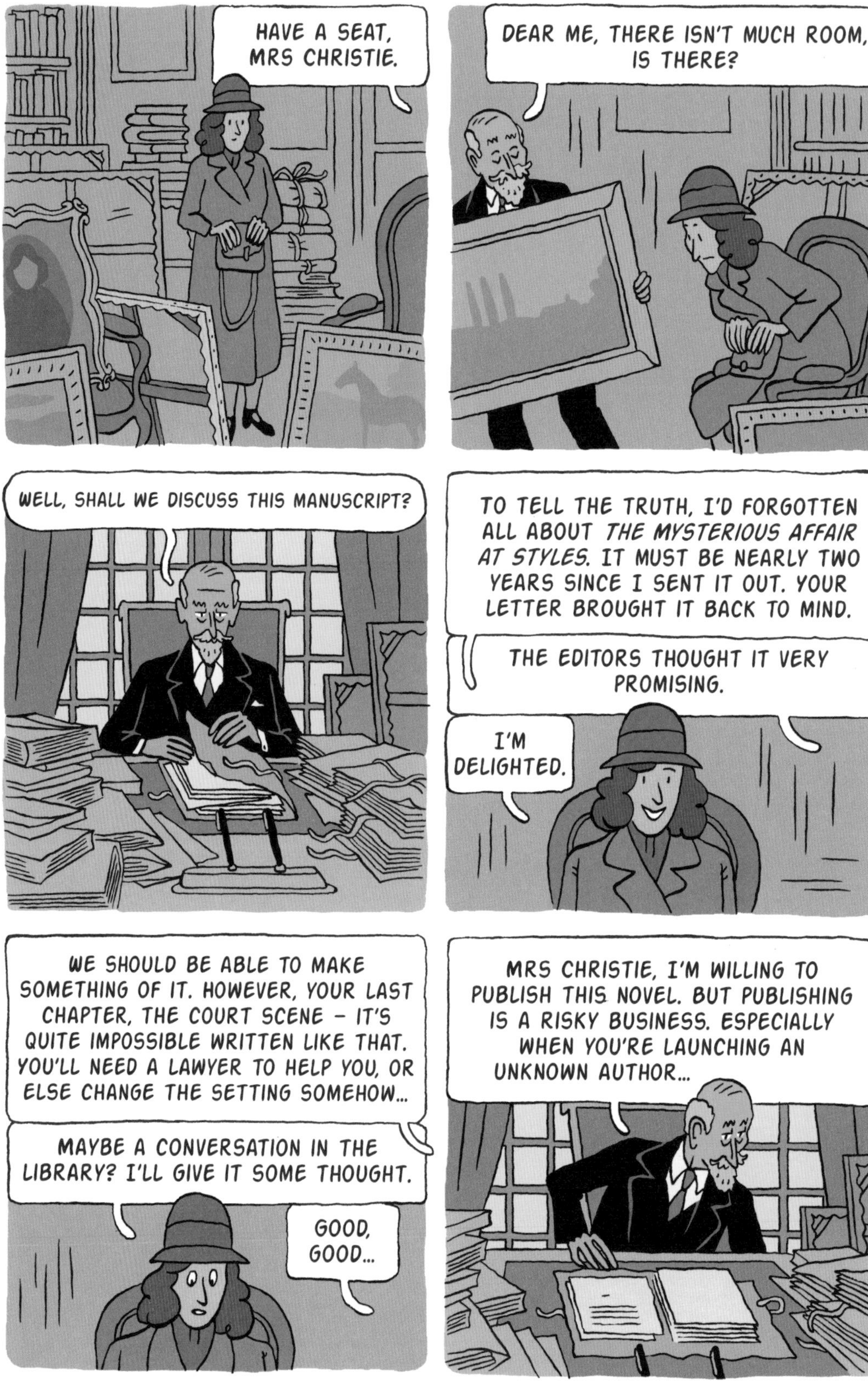

HAVE A SEAT, MRS CHRISTIE.
DEAR ME, THERE ISN'T MUCH ROOM, IS THERE?
WELL, SHALL WE DISCUSS THIS MANUSCRIPT?
TO TELL THE TRUTH, I'D FORGOTTEN ALL ABOUT *THE MYSTERIOUS AFFAIR AT STYLES*. IT MUST BE NEARLY TWO YEARS SINCE I SENT IT OUT. YOUR LETTER BROUGHT IT BACK TO MIND.
THE EDITORS THOUGHT IT VERY PROMISING.
I'M DELIGHTED.
WE SHOULD BE ABLE TO MAKE SOMETHING OF IT. HOWEVER, YOUR LAST CHAPTER, THE COURT SCENE – IT'S QUITE IMPOSSIBLE WRITTEN LIKE THAT. YOU'LL NEED A LAWYER TO HELP YOU, OR ELSE CHANGE THE SETTING SOMEHOW...
MAYBE A CONVERSATION IN THE LIBRARY? I'LL GIVE IT SOME THOUGHT.
GOOD, GOOD...
MRS CHRISTIE, I'M WILLING TO PUBLISH THIS NOVEL. BUT PUBLISHING IS A RISKY BUSINESS. ESPECIALLY WHEN YOU'RE LAUNCHING AN UNKNOWN AUTHOR...

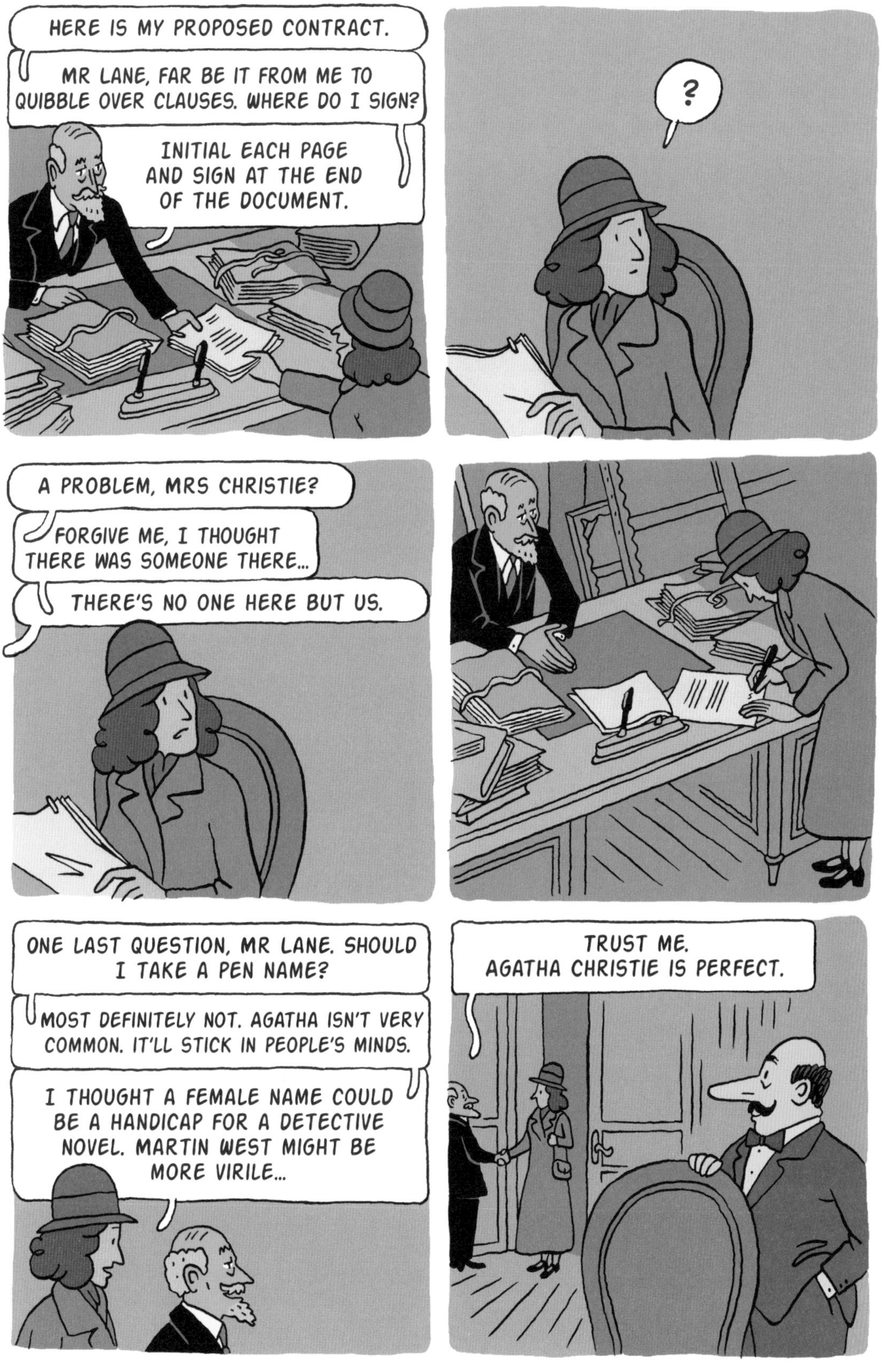
HERE IS MY PROPOSED CONTRACT.
MR LANE, FAR BE IT FROM ME TO QUIBBLE OVER CLAUSES. WHERE DO I SIGN?
INITIAL EACH PAGE AND SIGN AT THE END OF THE DOCUMENT.
?
A PROBLEM, MRS CHRISTIE?
FORGIVE ME, I THOUGHT THERE WAS SOMEONE THERE...
THERE'S NO ONE HERE BUT US.
ONE LAST QUESTION, MR LANE. SHOULD I TAKE A PEN NAME?
MOST DEFINITELY NOT. AGATHA ISN'T VERY COMMON. IT'LL STICK IN PEOPLE'S MINDS.
I THOUGHT A FEMALE NAME COULD BE A HANDICAP FOR A DETECTIVE NOVEL. MARTIN WEST MIGHT BE MORE VIRILE...
TRUST ME. AGATHA CHRISTIE IS PERFECT.

EAST CROYDON, 1922

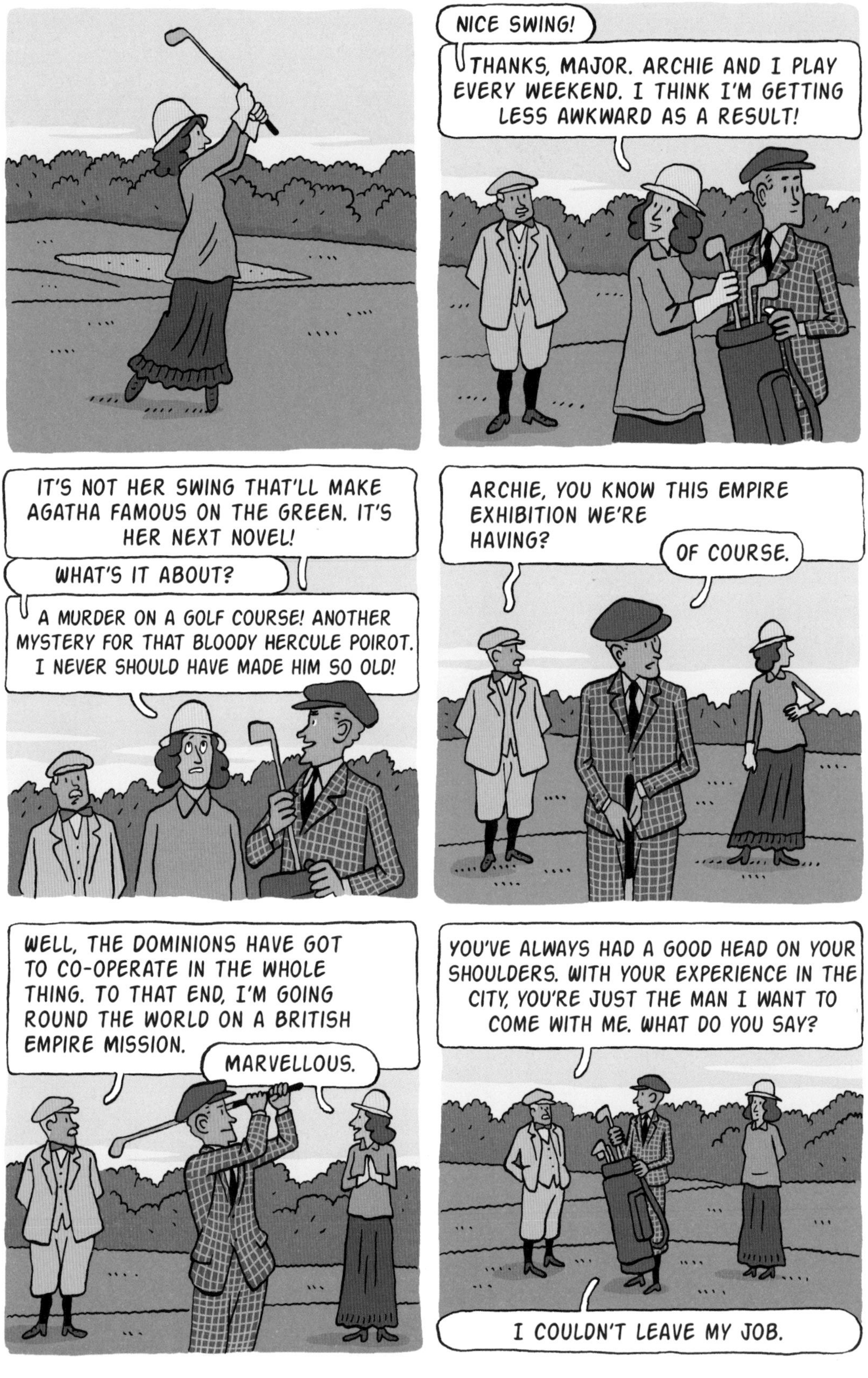
NICE SWING!
THANKS, MAJOR. ARCHIE AND I PLAY EVERY WEEKEND. I THINK I'M GETTING LESS AWKWARD AS A RESULT!
IT'S NOT HER SWING THAT'LL MAKE AGATHA FAMOUS ON THE GREEN. IT'S HER NEXT NOVEL!
WHAT'S IT ABOUT?
A MURDER ON A GOLF COURSE! ANOTHER MYSTERY FOR THAT BLOODY HERCULE POIROT. I NEVER SHOULD HAVE MADE HIM SO OLD!
ARCHIE, YOU KNOW THIS EMPIRE EXHIBITION WE'RE HAVING?
OF COURSE.
WELL, THE DOMINIONS HAVE GOT TO CO-OPERATE IN THE WHOLE THING. TO THAT END, I'M GOING ROUND THE WORLD ON A BRITISH EMPIRE MISSION.
MARVELLOUS.
YOU'VE ALWAYS HAD A GOOD HEAD ON YOUR SHOULDERS. WITH YOUR EXPERIENCE IN THE CITY, YOU'RE JUST THE MAN I WANT TO COME WITH ME. WHAT DO YOU SAY?
I COULDN'T LEAVE MY JOB.

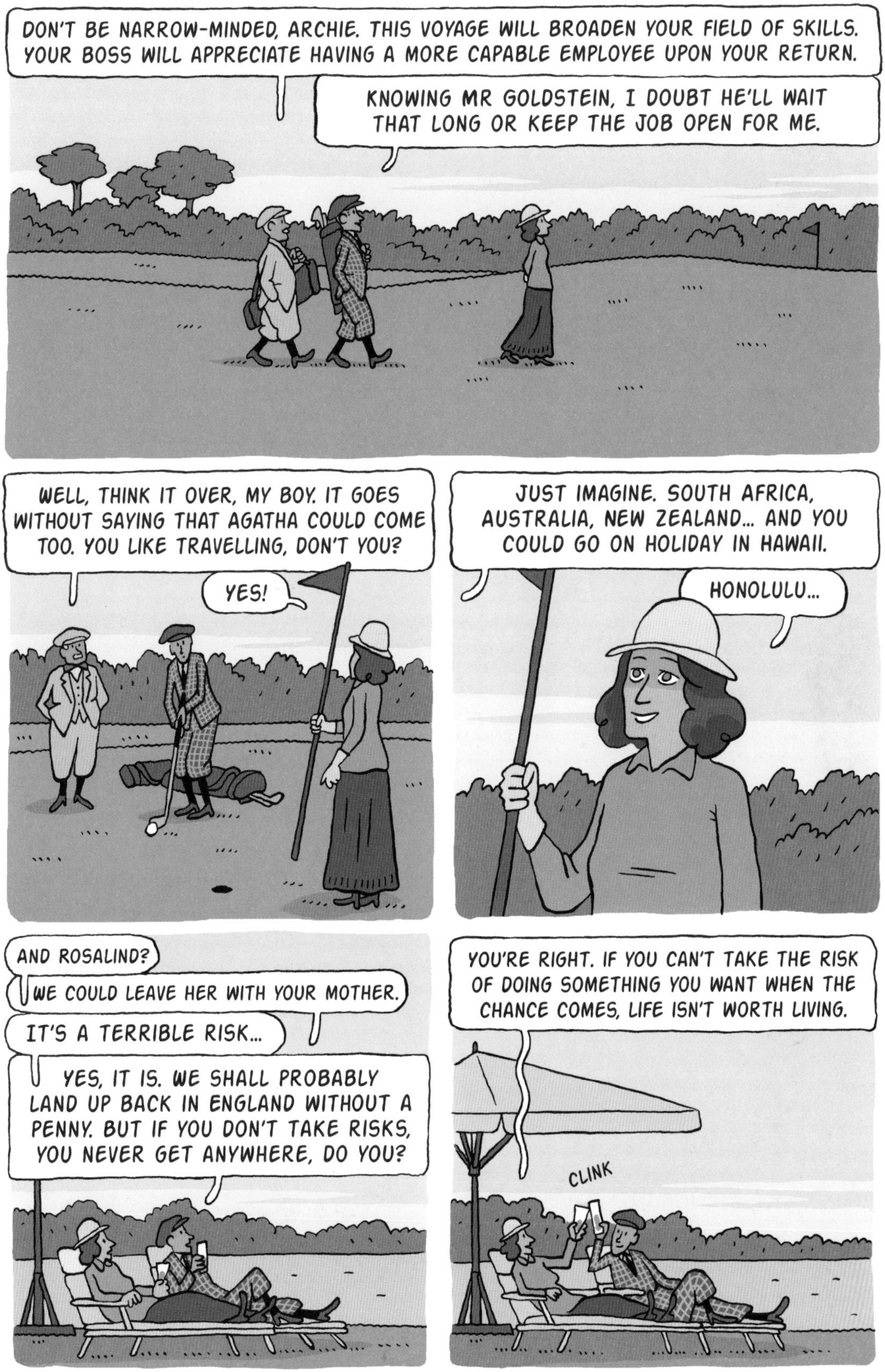

DON'T BE NARROW-MINDED, ARCHIE. THIS VOYAGE WILL BROADEN YOUR FIELD OF SKILLS. YOUR BOSS WILL APPRECIATE HAVING A MORE CAPABLE EMPLOYEE UPON YOUR RETURN.
KNOWING MR GOLDSTEIN, I DOUBT HE'LL WAIT THAT LONG OR KEEP THE JOB OPEN FOR ME.
WELL, THINK IT OVER, MY BOY. IT GOES WITHOUT SAYING THAT AGATHA COULD COME TOO. YOU LIKE TRAVELLING, DON'T YOU?
YES!
JUST IMAGINE. SOUTH AFRICA, AUSTRALIA, NEW ZEALAND... AND YOU COULD GO ON HOLIDAY IN HAWAII.
HONOLULU...
AND ROSALIND?
WE COULD LEAVE HER WITH YOUR MOTHER.
IT'S A TERRIBLE RISK...
YES, IT IS. WE SHALL PROBABLY LAND UP BACK IN ENGLAND WITHOUT A PENNY. BUT IF YOU DON'T TAKE RISKS, YOU NEVER GET ANYWHERE, DO YOU?
YOU'RE RIGHT. IF YOU CAN'T TAKE THE RISK OF DOING SOMETHING YOU WANT WHEN THE CHANCE COMES, LIFE ISN'T WORTH LIVING.
CLINK

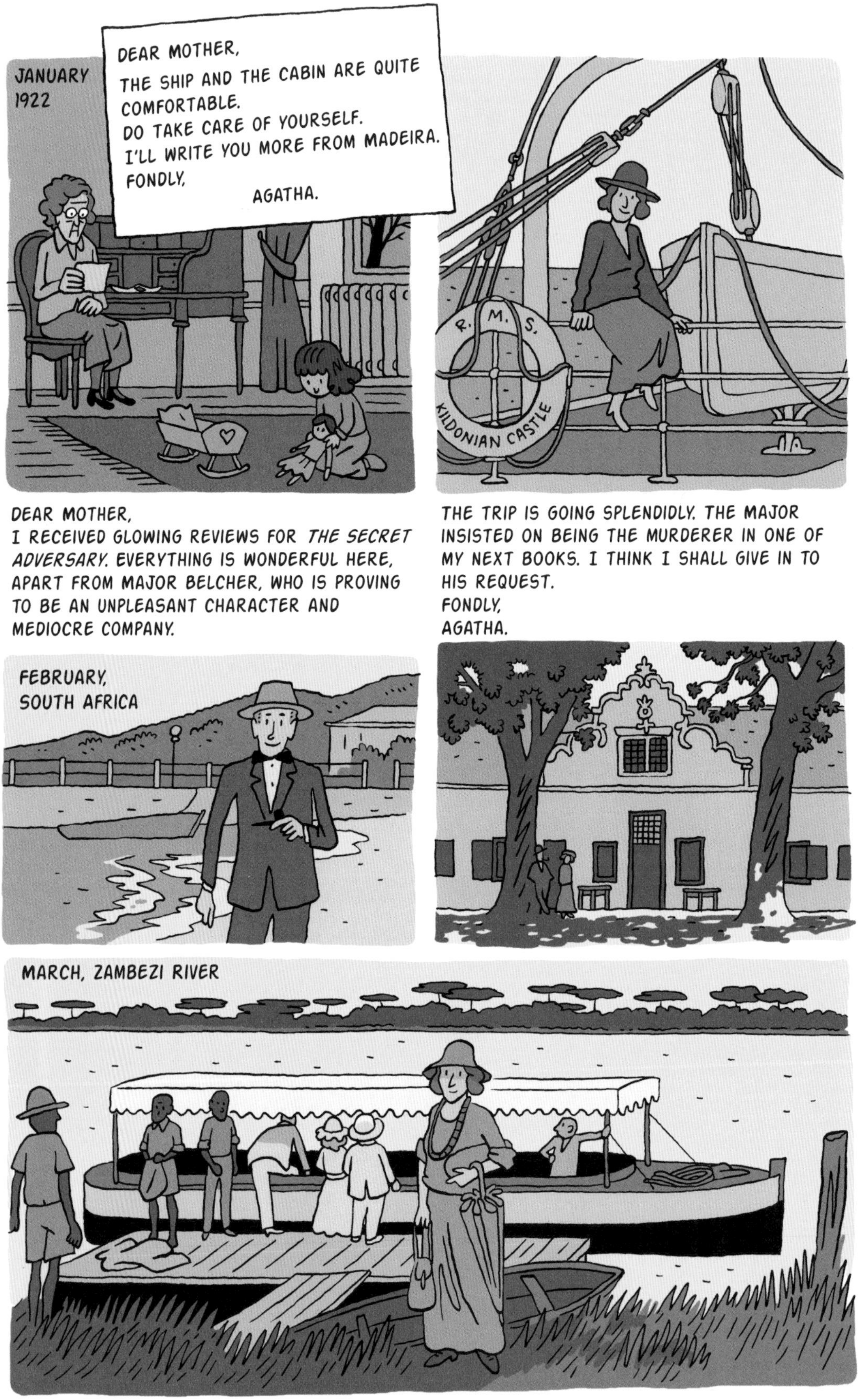
JANUARY 1922
DEAR MOTHER,
THE SHIP AND THE CABIN ARE QUITE COMFORTABLE.
DO TAKE CARE OF YOURSELF.
I'LL WRITE YOU MORE FROM MADEIRA.
FONDLY,
AGATHA.
R. M. S.
KILDONIAN CASTLE
DEAR MOTHER,
I RECEIVED GLOWING REVIEWS FOR *THE SECRET ADVERSARY*. EVERYTHING IS WONDERFUL HERE, APART FROM MAJOR BELCHER, WHO IS PROVING TO BE AN UNPLEASANT CHARACTER AND MEDIOCRE COMPANY.
THE TRIP IS GOING SPLENDIDLY. THE MAJOR INSISTED ON BEING THE MURDERER IN ONE OF MY NEXT BOOKS. I THINK I SHALL GIVE IN TO HIS REQUEST.
FONDLY,
AGATHA.
FEBRUARY, SOUTH AFRICA
MARCH, ZAMBEZI RIVER

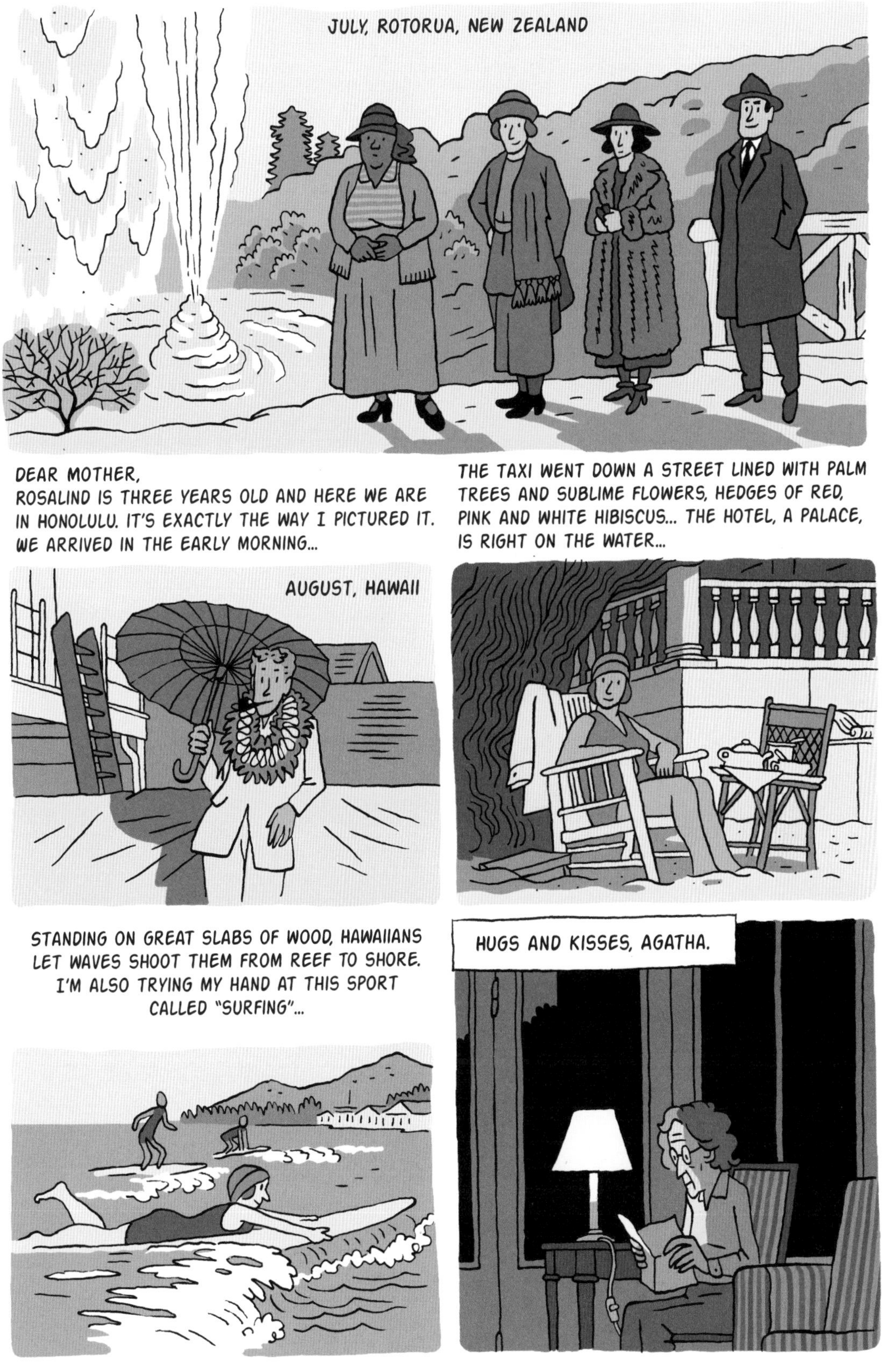
JULY, ROTORUA, NEW ZEALAND
DEAR MOTHER,
ROSALIND IS THREE YEARS OLD AND HERE WE ARE IN HONOLULU. IT'S EXACTLY THE WAY I PICTURED IT. WE ARRIVED IN THE EARLY MORNING...
AUGUST, HAWAII
THE TAXI WENT DOWN A STREET LINED WITH PALM TREES AND SUBLIME FLOWERS, HEDGES OF RED, PINK AND WHITE HIBISCUS... THE HOTEL, A PALACE, IS RIGHT ON THE WATER...
STANDING ON GREAT SLABS OF WOOD, HAWAIIANS LET WAVES SHOOT THEM FROM REEF TO SHORE. I'M ALSO TRYING MY HAND AT THIS SPORT CALLED "SURFING"...
HUGS AND KISSES, AGATHA.

CHELSEA, LONDON, 1923

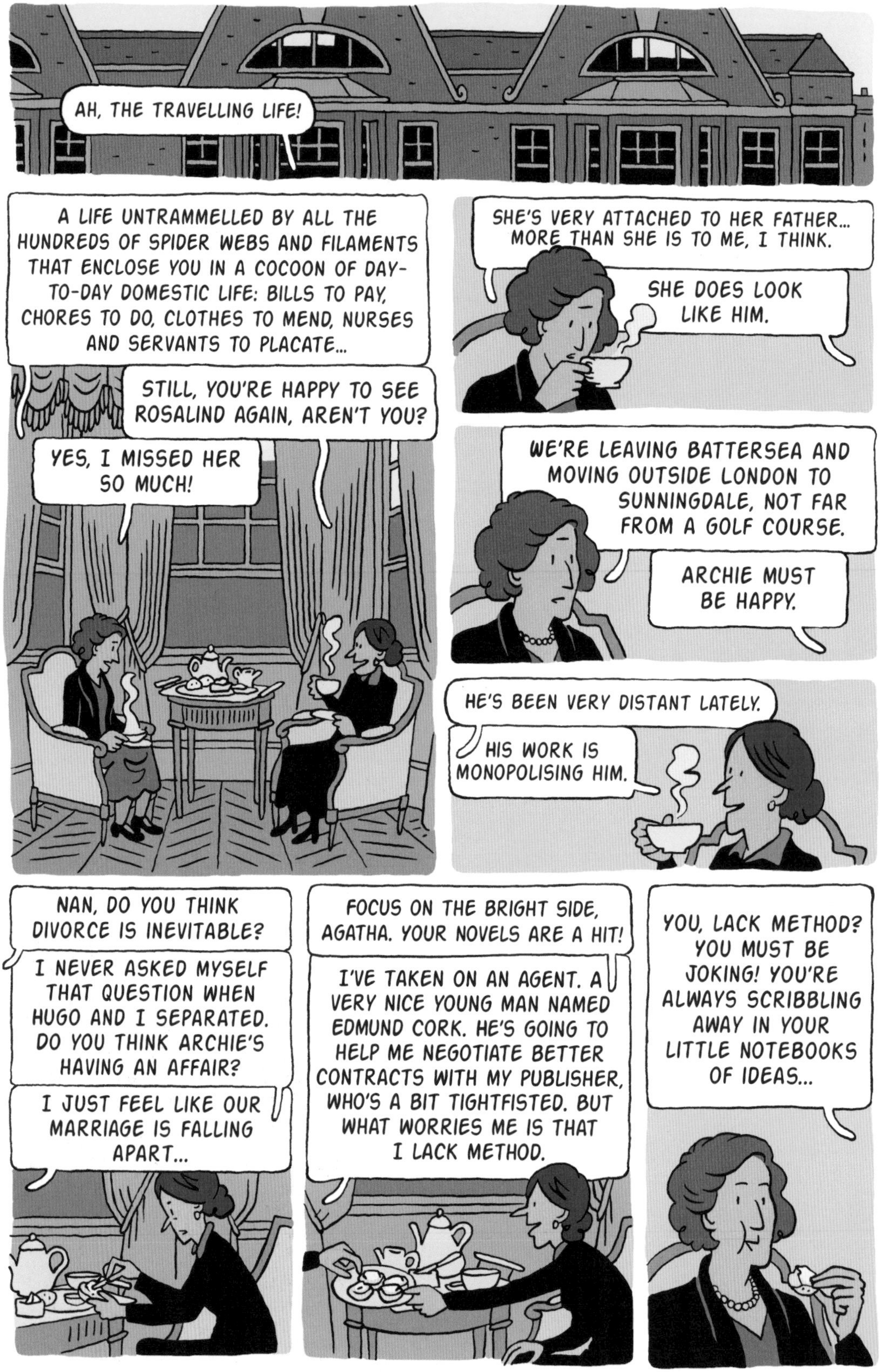
AH, THE TRAVELLING LIFE!
A LIFE UNTRAMMELLED BY ALL THE HUNDREDS OF SPIDER WEBS AND FILAMENTS THAT ENCLOSE YOU IN A COCOON OF DAY-TO-DAY DOMESTIC LIFE: BILLS TO PAY, CHORES TO DO, CLOTHES TO MEND, NURSES AND SERVANTS TO PLACATE...
STILL, YOU'RE HAPPY TO SEE ROSALIND AGAIN, AREN'T YOU?
YES, I MISSED HER SO MUCH!
SHE'S VERY ATTACHED TO HER FATHER... MORE THAN SHE IS TO ME, I THINK.
SHE DOES LOOK LIKE HIM.
WE'RE LEAVING BATTERSEA AND MOVING OUTSIDE LONDON TO SUNNINGDALE, NOT FAR FROM A GOLF COURSE.
ARCHIE MUST BE HAPPY.
HE'S BEEN VERY DISTANT LATELY.
HIS WORK IS MONOPOLISING HIM.
NAN, DO YOU THINK DIVORCE IS INEVITABLE?
I NEVER ASKED MYSELF THAT QUESTION WHEN HUGO AND I SEPARATED. DO YOU THINK ARCHIE'S HAVING AN AFFAIR?
I JUST FEEL LIKE OUR MARRIAGE IS FALLING APART...
FOCUS ON THE BRIGHT SIDE, AGATHA. YOUR NOVELS ARE A HIT!
I'VE TAKEN ON AN AGENT. A VERY NICE YOUNG MAN NAMED EDMUND CORK. HE'S GOING TO HELP ME NEGOTIATE BETTER CONTRACTS WITH MY PUBLISHER, WHO'S A BIT TIGHTFISTED. BUT WHAT WORRIES ME IS THAT I LACK METHOD.
YOU, LACK METHOD? YOU MUST BE JOKING! YOU'RE ALWAYS SCRIBBLING AWAY IN YOUR LITTLE NOTEBOOKS OF IDEAS...

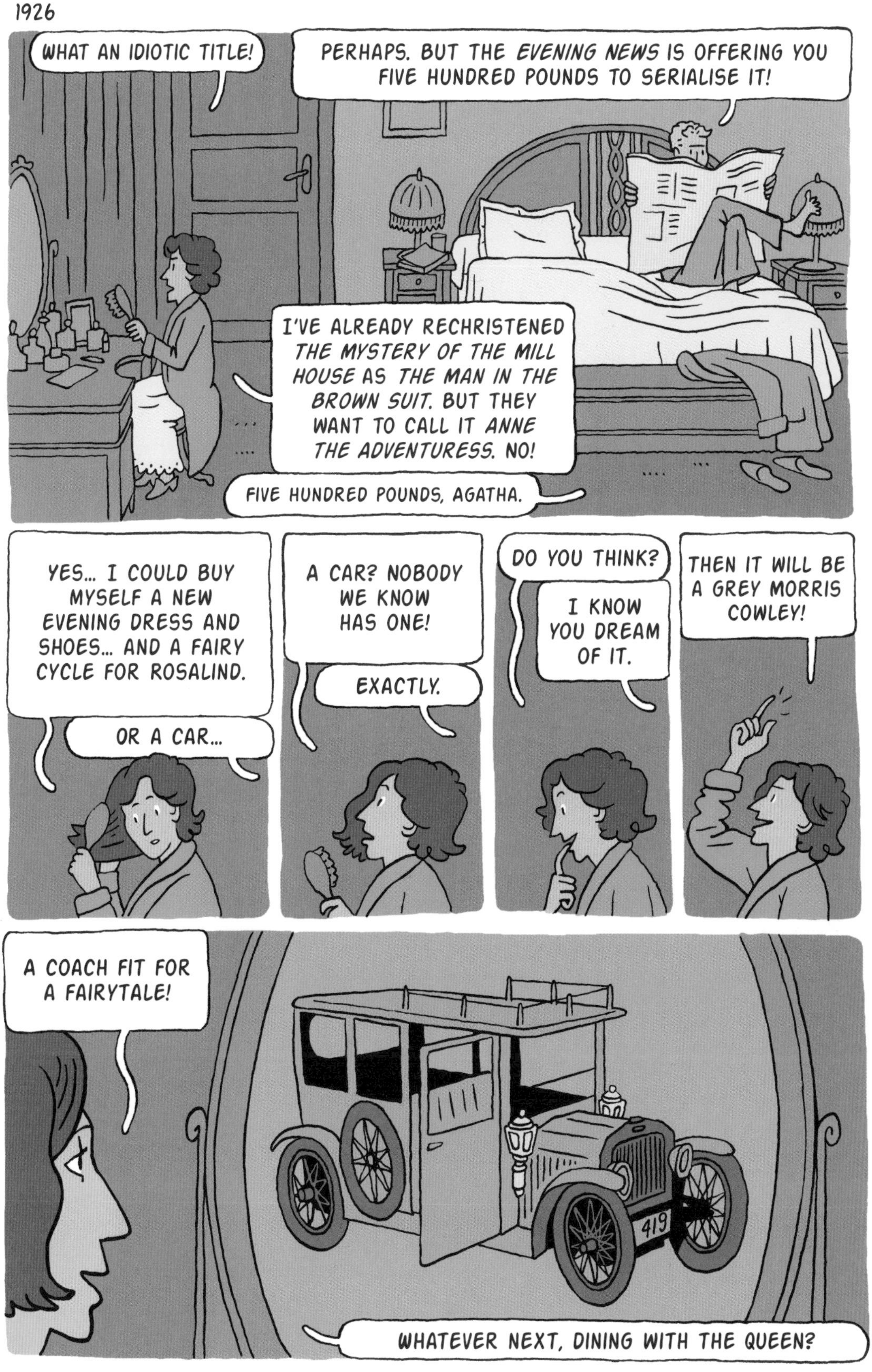
1926
WHAT AN IDIOTIC TITLE!
PERHAPS. BUT THE *EVENING NEWS* IS OFFERING YOU FIVE HUNDRED POUNDS TO SERIALISE IT!
I'VE ALREADY RECHRISTENED *THE MYSTERY OF THE MILL HOUSE* AS *THE MAN IN THE BROWN SUIT*. BUT THEY WANT TO CALL IT *ANNE THE ADVENTURESS*. NO!
FIVE HUNDRED POUNDS, AGATHA.
YES... I COULD BUY MYSELF A NEW EVENING DRESS AND SHOES... AND A FAIRY CYCLE FOR ROSALIND.
OR A CAR...
A CAR? NOBODY WE KNOW HAS ONE!
EXACTLY.
DO YOU THINK?
I KNOW YOU DREAM OF IT.
THEN IT WILL BE A GREY MORRIS COWLEY!
A COACH FIT FOR A FAIRYTALE!
419
WHATEVER NEXT, DINING WITH THE QUEEN?

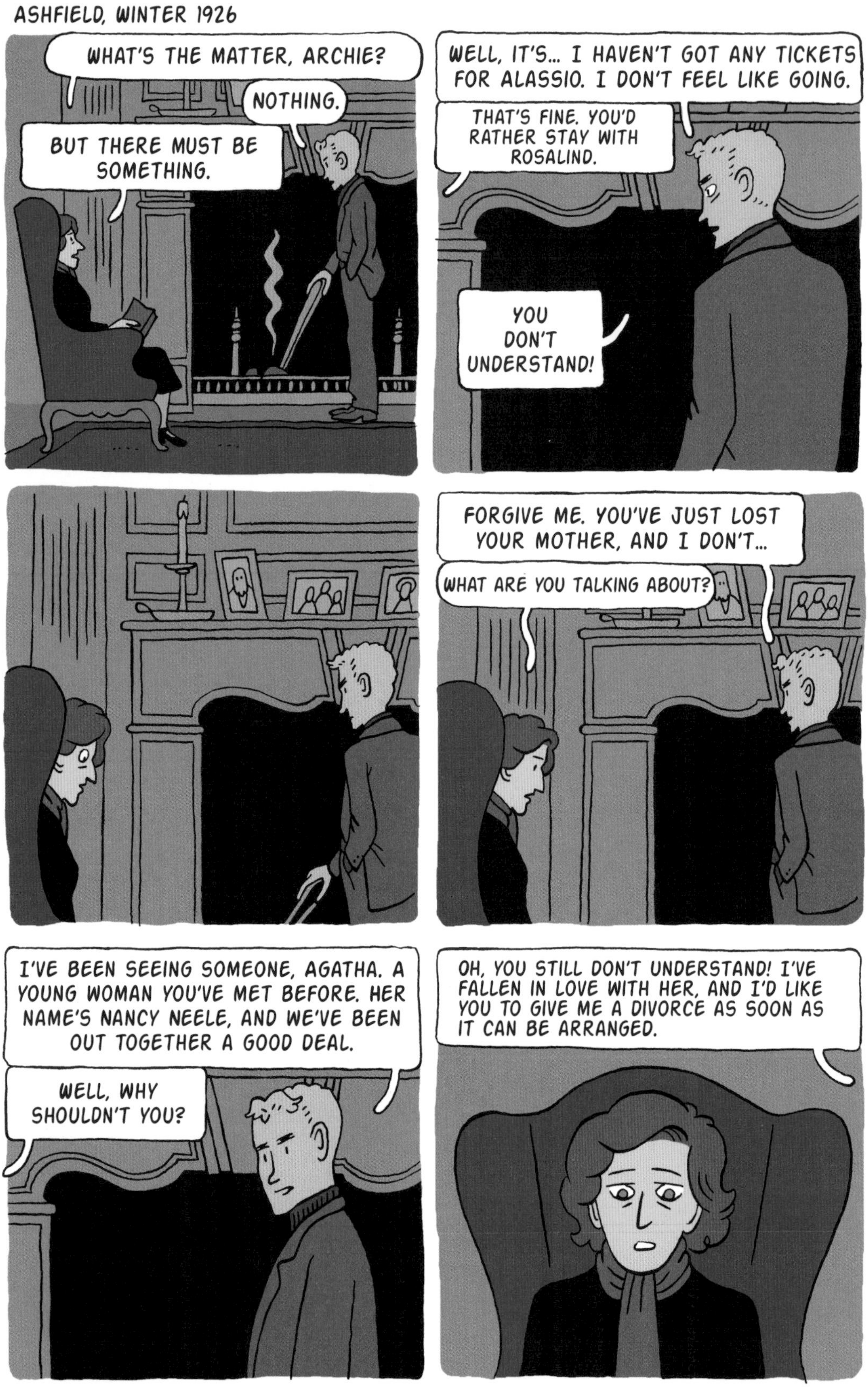
ASHFIELD, WINTER 1926
WHAT'S THE MATTER, ARCHIE?
NOTHING.
BUT THERE MUST BE SOMETHING.
WELL, IT'S... I HAVEN'T GOT ANY TICKETS FOR ALASSIO. I DON'T FEEL LIKE GOING.
THAT'S FINE. YOU'D RATHER STAY WITH ROSALIND.
YOU DON'T UNDERSTAND!
FORGIVE ME. YOU'VE JUST LOST YOUR MOTHER, AND I DON'T...
WHAT ARE YOU TALKING ABOUT?
I'VE BEEN SEEING SOMEONE, AGATHA. A YOUNG WOMAN YOU'VE MET BEFORE. HER NAME'S NANCY NEELE, AND WE'VE BEEN OUT TOGETHER A GOOD DEAL.
WELL, WHY SHOULDN'T YOU?
OH, YOU STILL DON'T UNDERSTAND! I'VE FALLEN IN LOVE WITH HER, AND I'D LIKE YOU TO GIVE ME A DIVORCE AS SOON AS IT CAN BE ARRANGED.

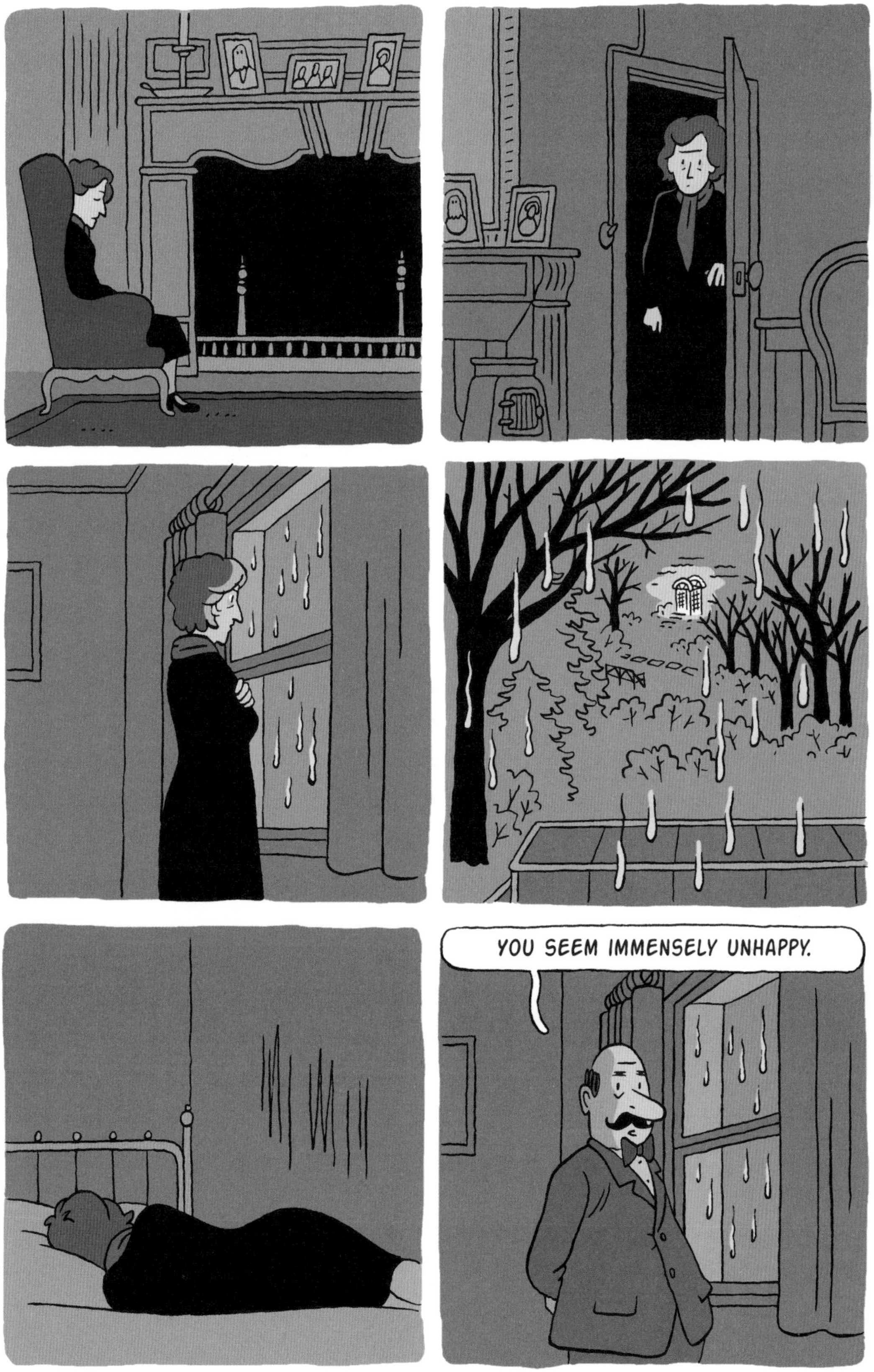
YOU SEEM IMMENSELY UNHAPPY.

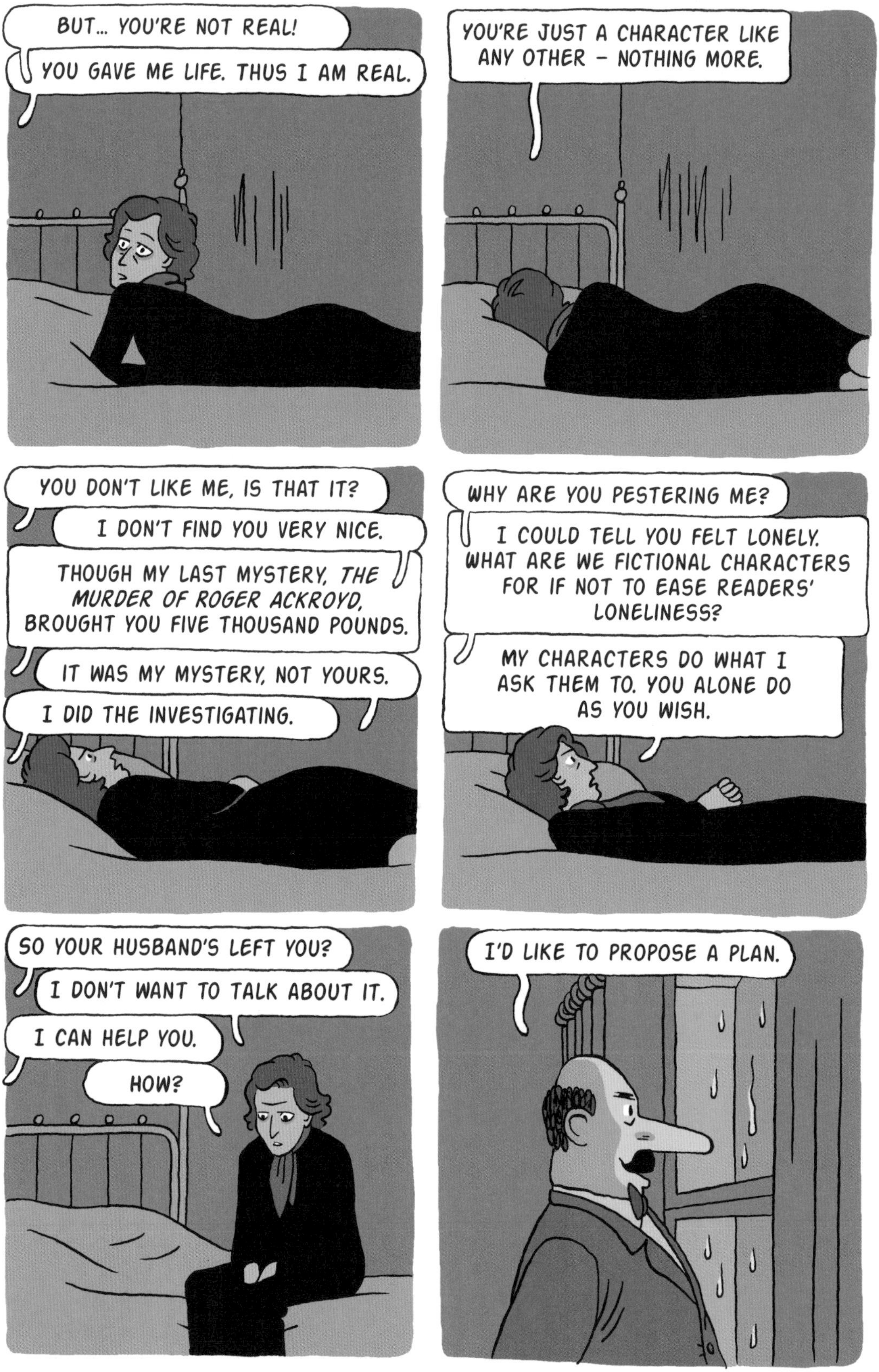
BUT... YOU'RE NOT REAL!
YOU GAVE ME LIFE. THUS I AM REAL.
YOU'RE JUST A CHARACTER LIKE ANY OTHER – NOTHING MORE.
YOU DON'T LIKE ME, IS THAT IT?
I DON'T FIND YOU VERY NICE.
THOUGH MY LAST MYSTERY, *THE MURDER OF ROGER ACKROYD*, BROUGHT YOU FIVE THOUSAND POUNDS.
IT WAS MY MYSTERY, NOT YOURS.
I DID THE INVESTIGATING.
WHY ARE YOU PESTERING ME?
I COULD TELL YOU FELT LONELY. WHAT ARE WE FICTIONAL CHARACTERS FOR IF NOT TO EASE READERS' LONELINESS?
MY CHARACTERS DO WHAT I ASK THEM TO. YOU ALONE DO AS YOU WISH.
SO YOUR HUSBAND'S LEFT YOU?
I DON'T WANT TO TALK ABOUT IT.
I CAN HELP YOU.
HOW?
I'D LIKE TO PROPOSE A PLAN.

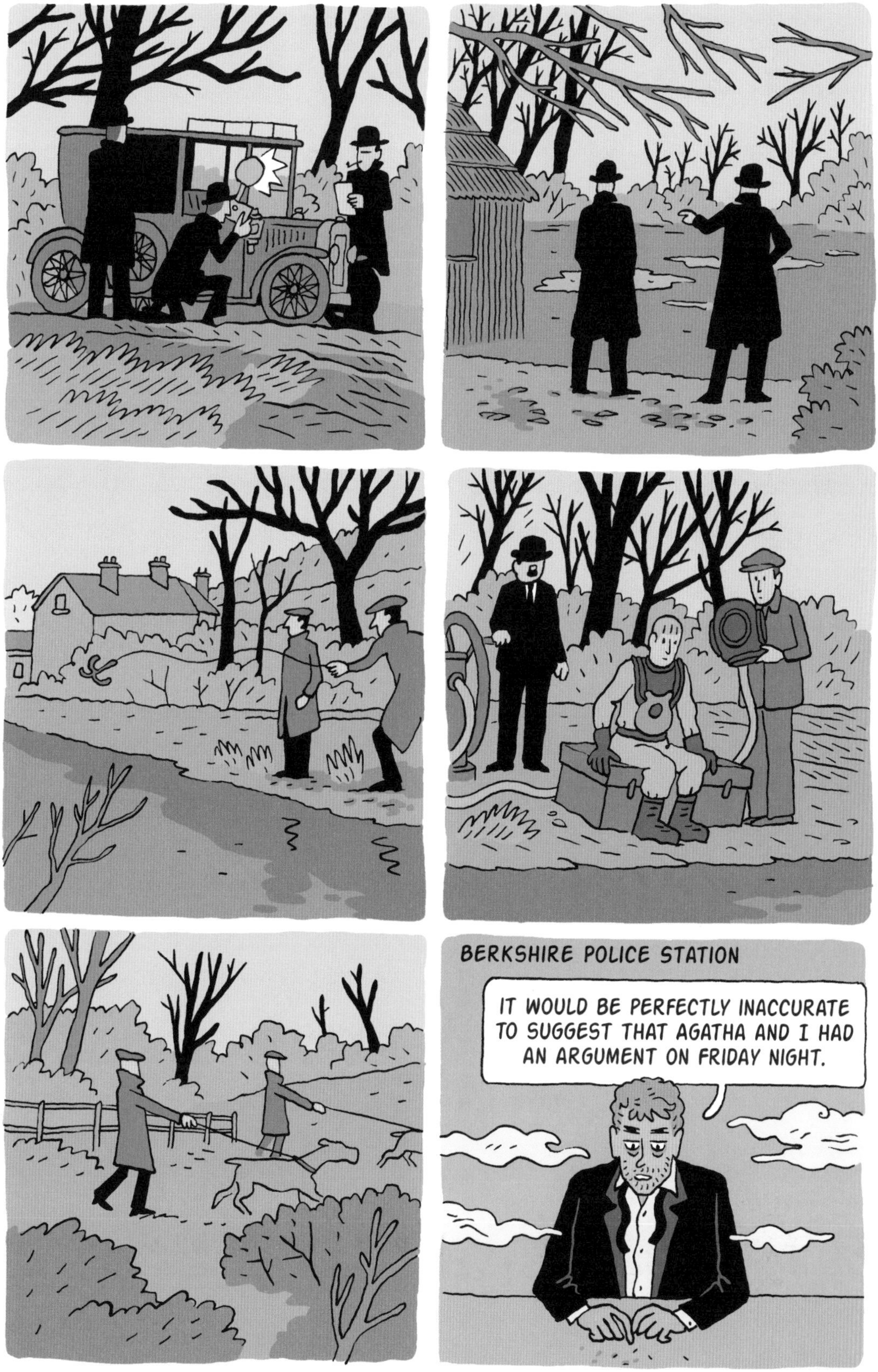
BERKSHIRE POLICE STATION
IT WOULD BE PERFECTLY INACCURATE TO SUGGEST THAT AGATHA AND I HAD AN ARGUMENT ON FRIDAY NIGHT.

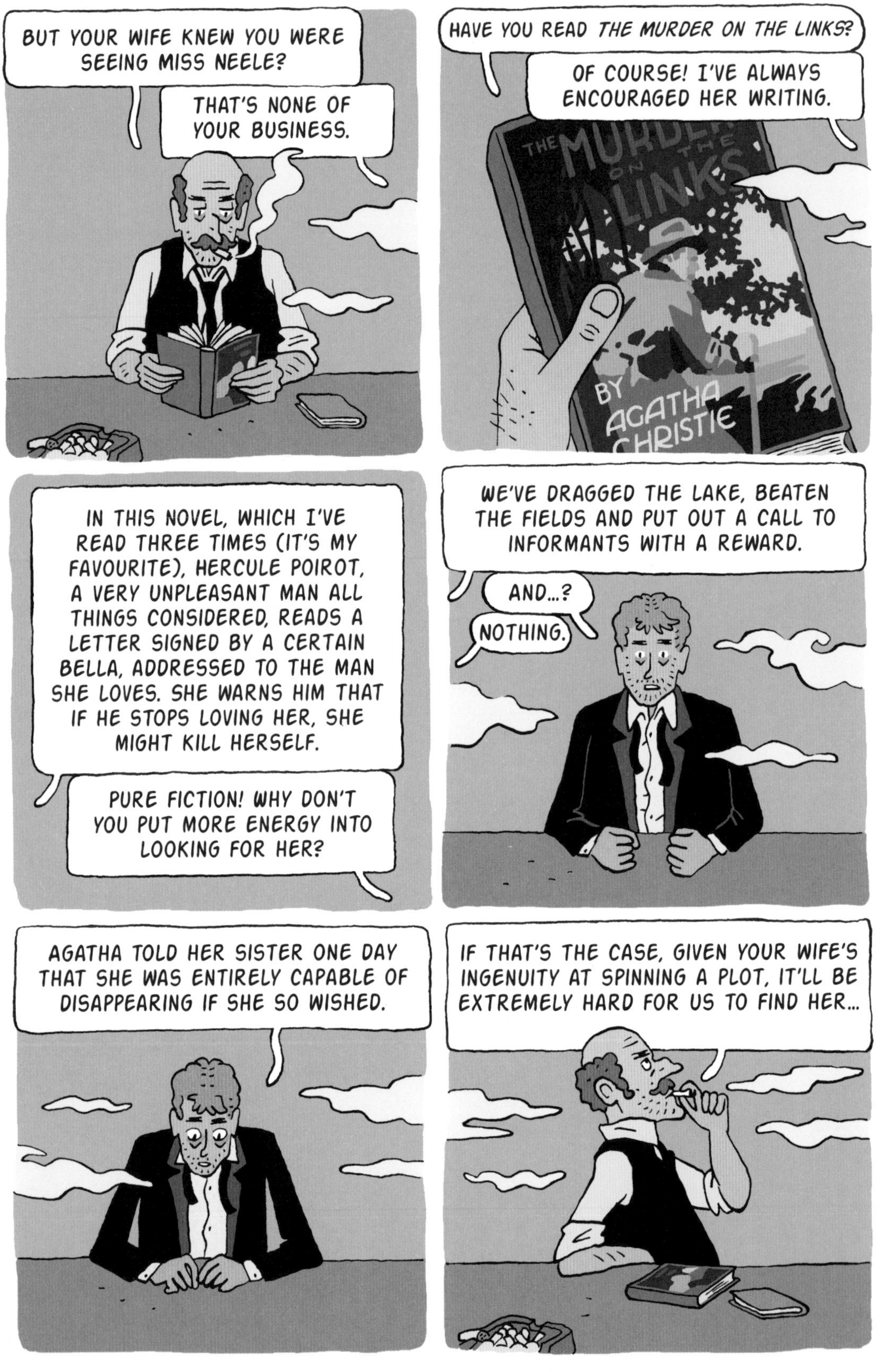
BUT YOUR WIFE KNEW YOU WERE SEEING MISS NEELE?
THAT'S NONE OF YOUR BUSINESS.
HAVE YOU READ *THE MURDER ON THE LINKS*?
OF COURSE! I'VE ALWAYS ENCOURAGED HER WRITING.
THE MURDER ON THE LINKS
BY AGATHA CHRISTIE
IN THIS NOVEL, WHICH I'VE READ THREE TIMES (IT'S MY FAVOURITE), HERCULE POIROT, A VERY UNPLEASANT MAN ALL THINGS CONSIDERED, READS A LETTER SIGNED BY A CERTAIN BELLA, ADDRESSED TO THE MAN SHE LOVES. SHE WARNS HIM THAT IF HE STOPS LOVING HER, SHE MIGHT KILL HERSELF.
PURE FICTION! WHY DON'T YOU PUT MORE ENERGY INTO LOOKING FOR HER?
WE'VE DRAGGED THE LAKE, BEATEN THE FIELDS AND PUT OUT A CALL TO INFORMANTS WITH A REWARD.
AND...?
NOTHING.
AGATHA TOLD HER SISTER ONE DAY THAT SHE WAS ENTIRELY CAPABLE OF DISAPPEARING IF SHE SO WISHED.
IF THAT'S THE CASE, GIVEN YOUR WIFE'S INGENUITY AT SPINNING A PLOT, IT'LL BE EXTREMELY HARD FOR US TO FIND HER...

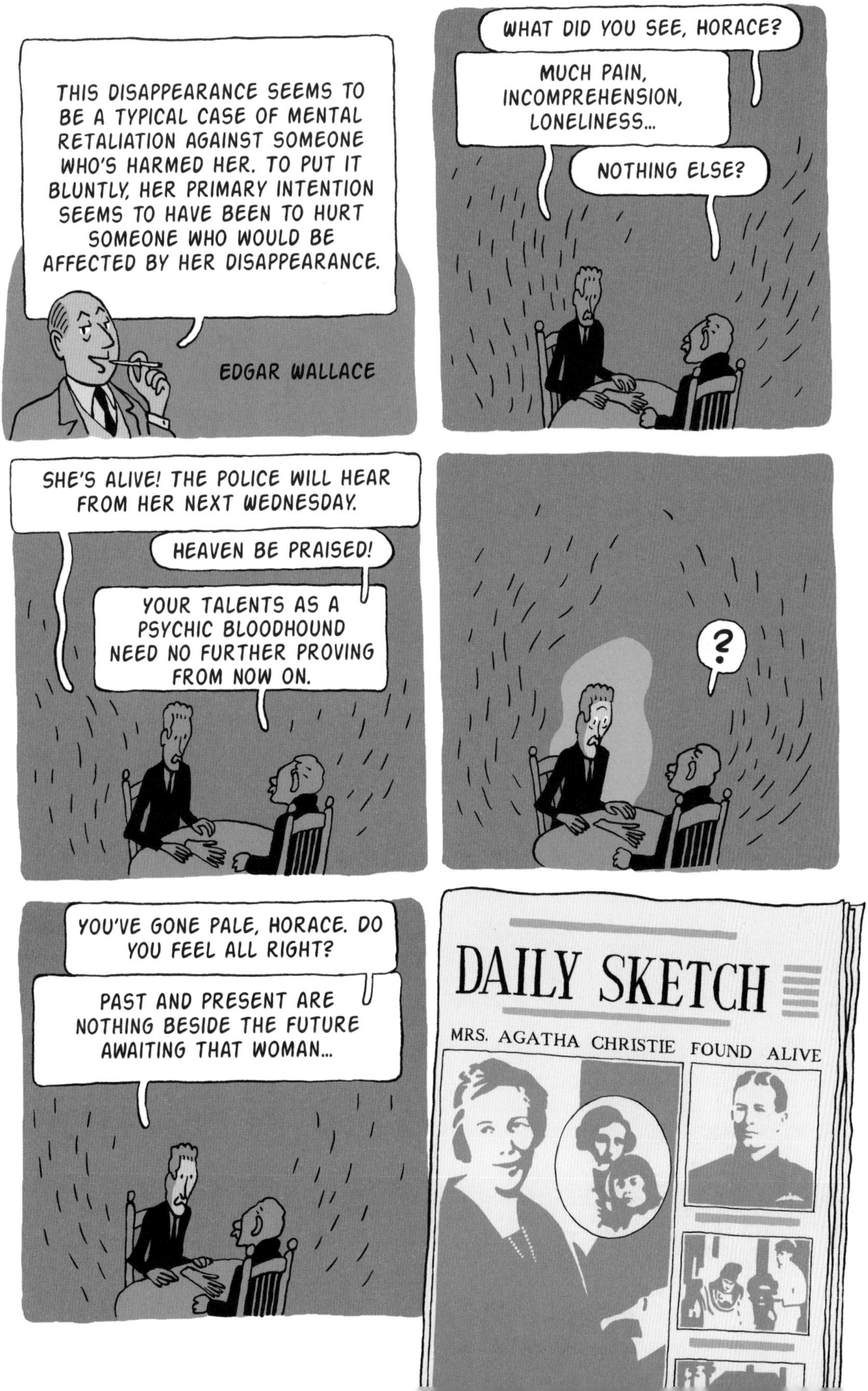
THIS DISAPPEARANCE SEEMS TO BE A TYPICAL CASE OF MENTAL RETALIATION AGAINST SOMEONE WHO'S HARMED HER. TO PUT IT BLUNTLY, HER PRIMARY INTENTION SEEMS TO HAVE BEEN TO HURT SOMEONE WHO WOULD BE AFFECTED BY HER DISAPPEARANCE.
EDGAR WALLACE
WHAT DID YOU SEE, HORACE?
MUCH PAIN, INCOMPREHENSION, LONELINESS...
NOTHING ELSE?
SHE'S ALIVE! THE POLICE WILL HEAR FROM HER NEXT WEDNESDAY.
HEAVEN BE PRAISED!
YOUR TALENTS AS A PSYCHIC BLOODHOUND NEED NO FURTHER PROVING FROM NOW ON.
?
YOU'VE GONE PALE, HORACE. DO YOU FEEL ALL RIGHT?
PAST AND PRESENT ARE NOTHING BESIDE THE FUTURE AWAITING THAT WOMAN...
DAILY SKETCH
MRS. AGATHA CHRISTIE FOUND ALIVE

LONDON, AUTUMN 1928

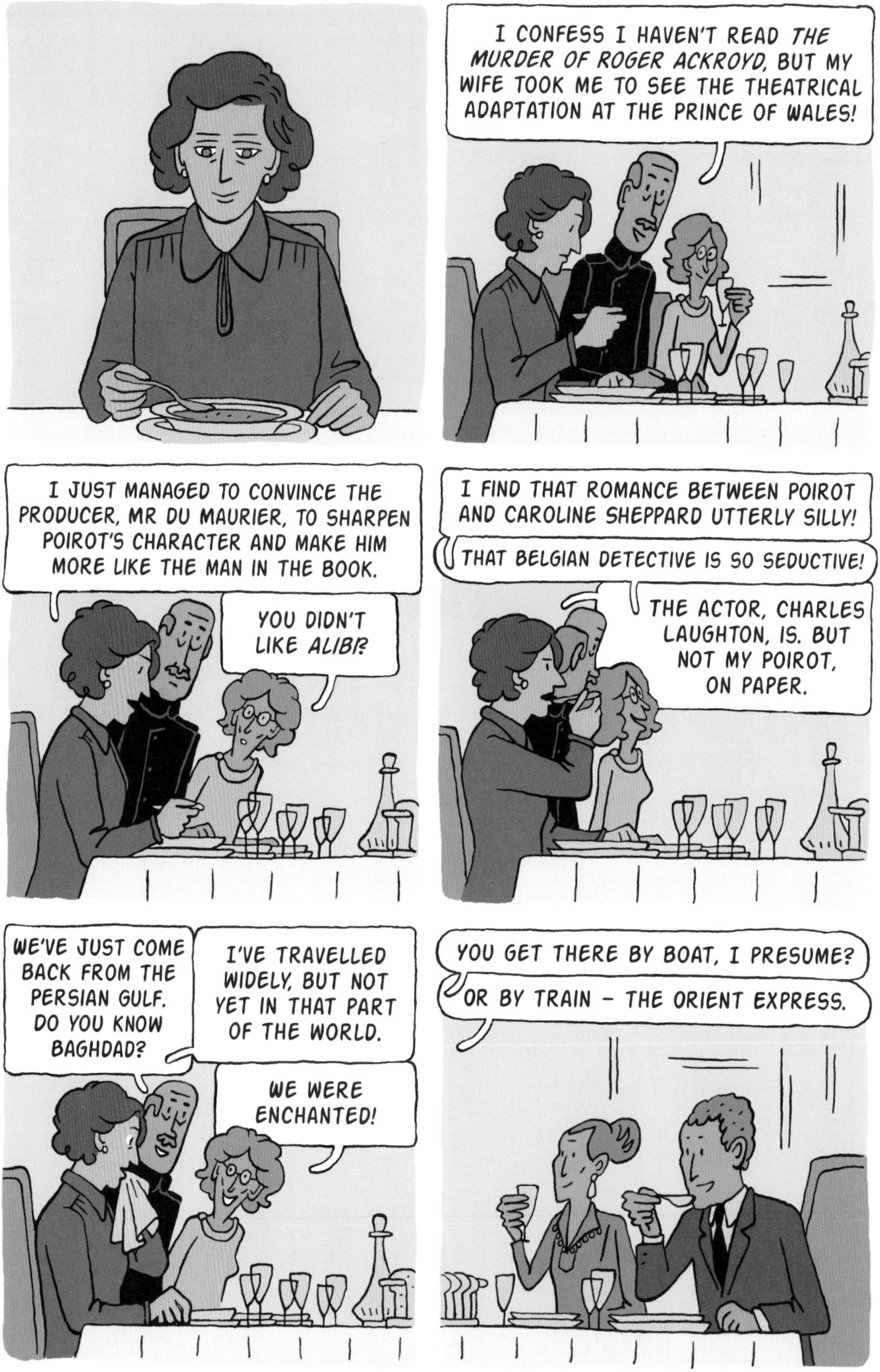
I CONFESS I HAVEN'T READ *THE MURDER OF ROGER ACKROYD*, BUT MY WIFE TOOK ME TO SEE THE THEATRICAL ADAPTATION AT THE PRINCE OF WALES!
I JUST MANAGED TO CONVINCE THE PRODUCER, MR DU MAURIER, TO SHARPEN POIROT'S CHARACTER AND MAKE HIM MORE LIKE THE MAN IN THE BOOK.
YOU DIDN'T LIKE *ALIBI*?
I FIND THAT ROMANCE BETWEEN POIROT AND CAROLINE SHEPPARD UTTERLY SILLY!
THAT BELGIAN DETECTIVE IS SO SEDUCTIVE!
THE ACTOR, CHARLES LAUGHTON, IS. BUT NOT MY POIROT, ON PAPER.
WE'VE JUST COME BACK FROM THE PERSIAN GULF. DO YOU KNOW BAGHDAD?
I'VE TRAVELLED WIDELY, BUT NOT YET IN THAT PART OF THE WORLD.
WE WERE ENCHANTED!
YOU GET THERE BY BOAT, I PRESUME?
OR BY TRAIN – THE ORIENT EXPRESS.

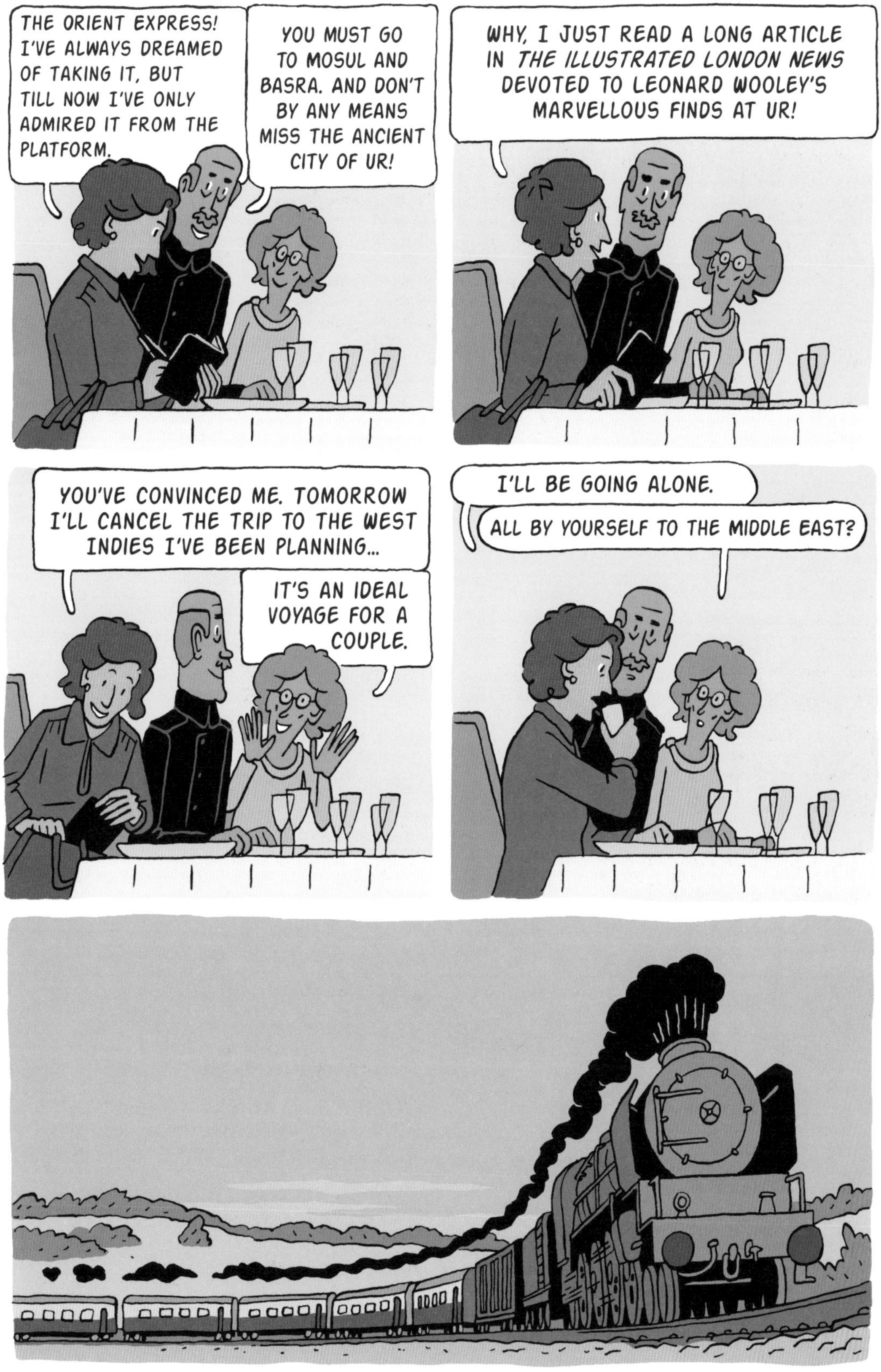
THE ORIENT EXPRESS! I'VE ALWAYS DREAMED OF TAKING IT, BUT TILL NOW I'VE ONLY ADMIRED IT FROM THE PLATFORM.
YOU MUST GO TO MOSUL AND BASRA. AND DON'T BY ANY MEANS MISS THE ANCIENT CITY OF UR!
WHY, I JUST READ A LONG ARTICLE IN *THE ILLUSTRATED LONDON NEWS* DEVOTED TO LEONARD WOOLEY'S MARVELLOUS FINDS AT UR!
YOU'VE CONVINCED ME. TOMORROW I'LL CANCEL THE TRIP TO THE WEST INDIES I'VE BEEN PLANNING...
IT'S AN IDEAL VOYAGE FOR A COUPLE.
I'LL BE GOING ALONE.
ALL BY YOURSELF TO THE MIDDLE EAST?

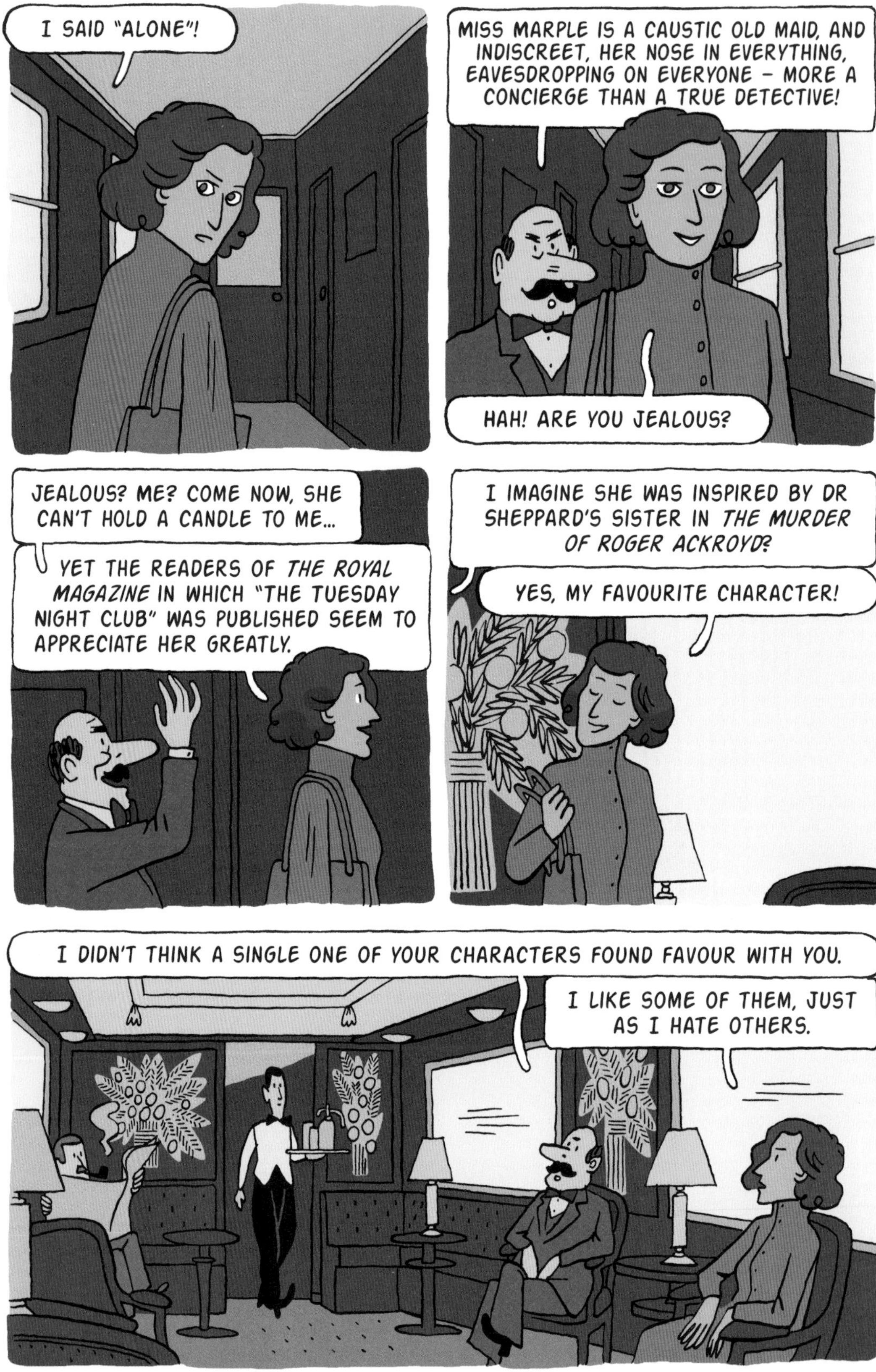

I SAID "ALONE"!
MISS MARPLE IS A CAUSTIC OLD MAID, AND INDISCREET, HER NOSE IN EVERYTHING, EAVESDROPPING ON EVERYONE – MORE A CONCIERGE THAN A TRUE DETECTIVE!
HAH! ARE YOU JEALOUS?
JEALOUS? ME? COME NOW, SHE CAN'T HOLD A CANDLE TO ME...
YET THE READERS OF *THE ROYAL MAGAZINE* IN WHICH "THE TUESDAY NIGHT CLUB" WAS PUBLISHED SEEM TO APPRECIATE HER GREATLY.
I IMAGINE SHE WAS INSPIRED BY DR SHEPPARD'S SISTER IN *THE MURDER OF ROGER ACKROYD*?
YES, MY FAVOURITE CHARACTER!
I DIDN'T THINK A SINGLE ONE OF YOUR CHARACTERS FOUND FAVOUR WITH YOU.
I LIKE SOME OF THEM, JUST AS I HATE OTHERS.

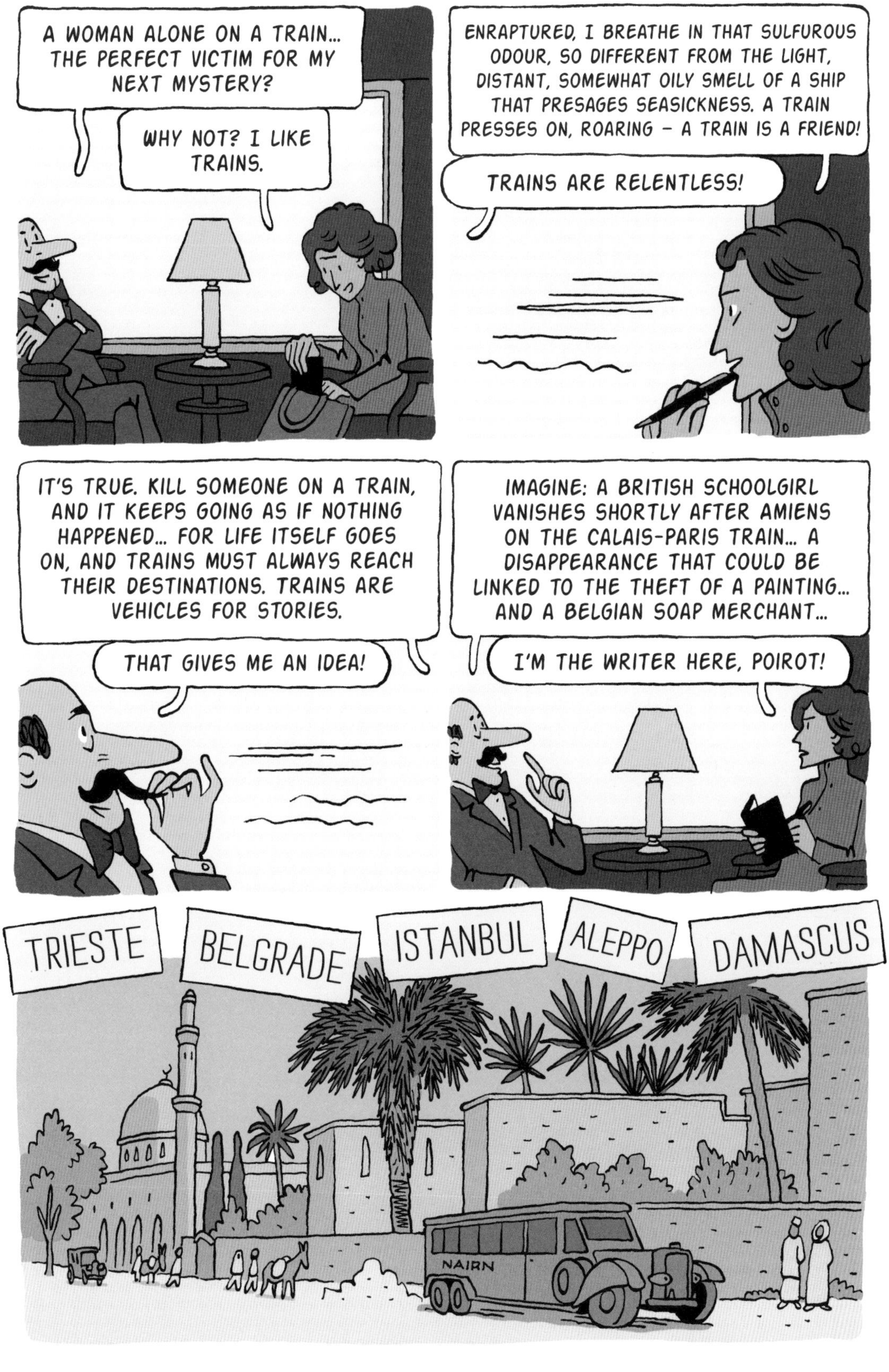
A WOMAN ALONE ON A TRAIN... THE PERFECT VICTIM FOR MY NEXT MYSTERY?
WHY NOT? I LIKE TRAINS.
ENRAPTURED, I BREATHE IN THAT SULFUROUS ODOUR, SO DIFFERENT FROM THE LIGHT, DISTANT, SOMEWHAT OILY SMELL OF A SHIP THAT PRESAGES SEASICKNESS. A TRAIN PRESSES ON, ROARING – A TRAIN IS A FRIEND!
TRAINS ARE RELENTLESS!
IT'S TRUE. KILL SOMEONE ON A TRAIN, AND IT KEEPS GOING AS IF NOTHING HAPPENED... FOR LIFE ITSELF GOES ON, AND TRAINS MUST ALWAYS REACH THEIR DESTINATIONS. TRAINS ARE VEHICLES FOR STORIES.
THAT GIVES ME AN IDEA!
IMAGINE: A BRITISH SCHOOLGIRL VANISHES SHORTLY AFTER AMIENS ON THE CALAIS-PARIS TRAIN... A DISAPPEARANCE THAT COULD BE LINKED TO THE THEFT OF A PAINTING... AND A BELGIAN SOAP MERCHANT...
I'M THE WRITER HERE, POIROT!
TRIESTE
BELGRADE
ISTANBUL
ALEPPO
DAMASCUS
NAIRN

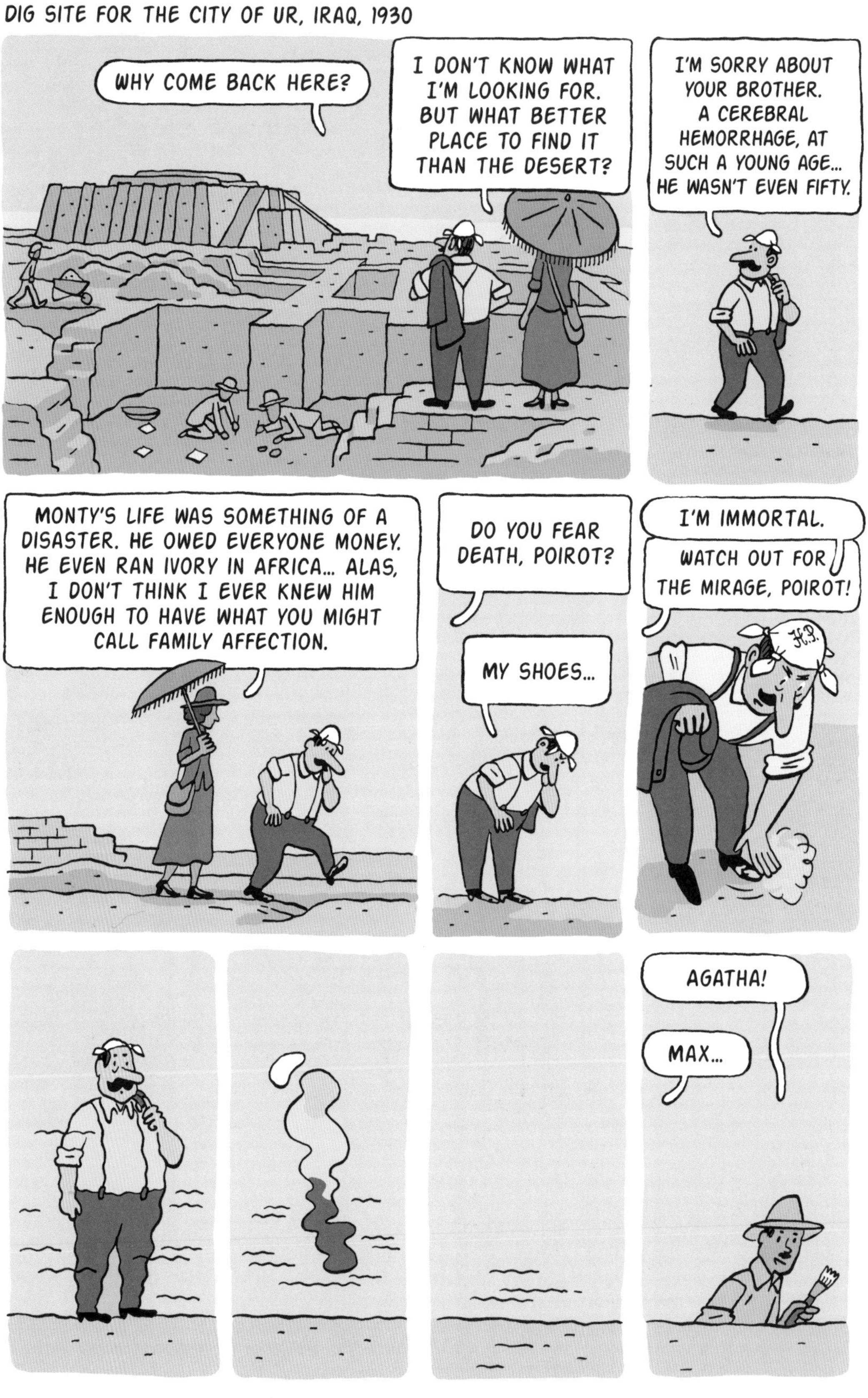
DIG SITE FOR THE CITY OF UR, IRAQ, 1930
WHY COME BACK HERE?
I DON'T KNOW WHAT I'M LOOKING FOR. BUT WHAT BETTER PLACE TO FIND IT THAN THE DESERT?
I'M SORRY ABOUT YOUR BROTHER. A CEREBRAL HEMORRHAGE, AT SUCH A YOUNG AGE... HE WASN'T EVEN FIFTY.
MONTY'S LIFE WAS SOMETHING OF A DISASTER. HE OWED EVERYONE MONEY. HE EVEN RAN IVORY IN AFRICA... ALAS, I DON'T THINK I EVER KNEW HIM ENOUGH TO HAVE WHAT YOU MIGHT CALL FAMILY AFFECTION.
DO YOU FEAR DEATH, POIROT?
MY SHOES...
I'M IMMORTAL.
WATCH OUT FOR THE MIRAGE, POIROT!
H.P.
AGATHA!
MAX...

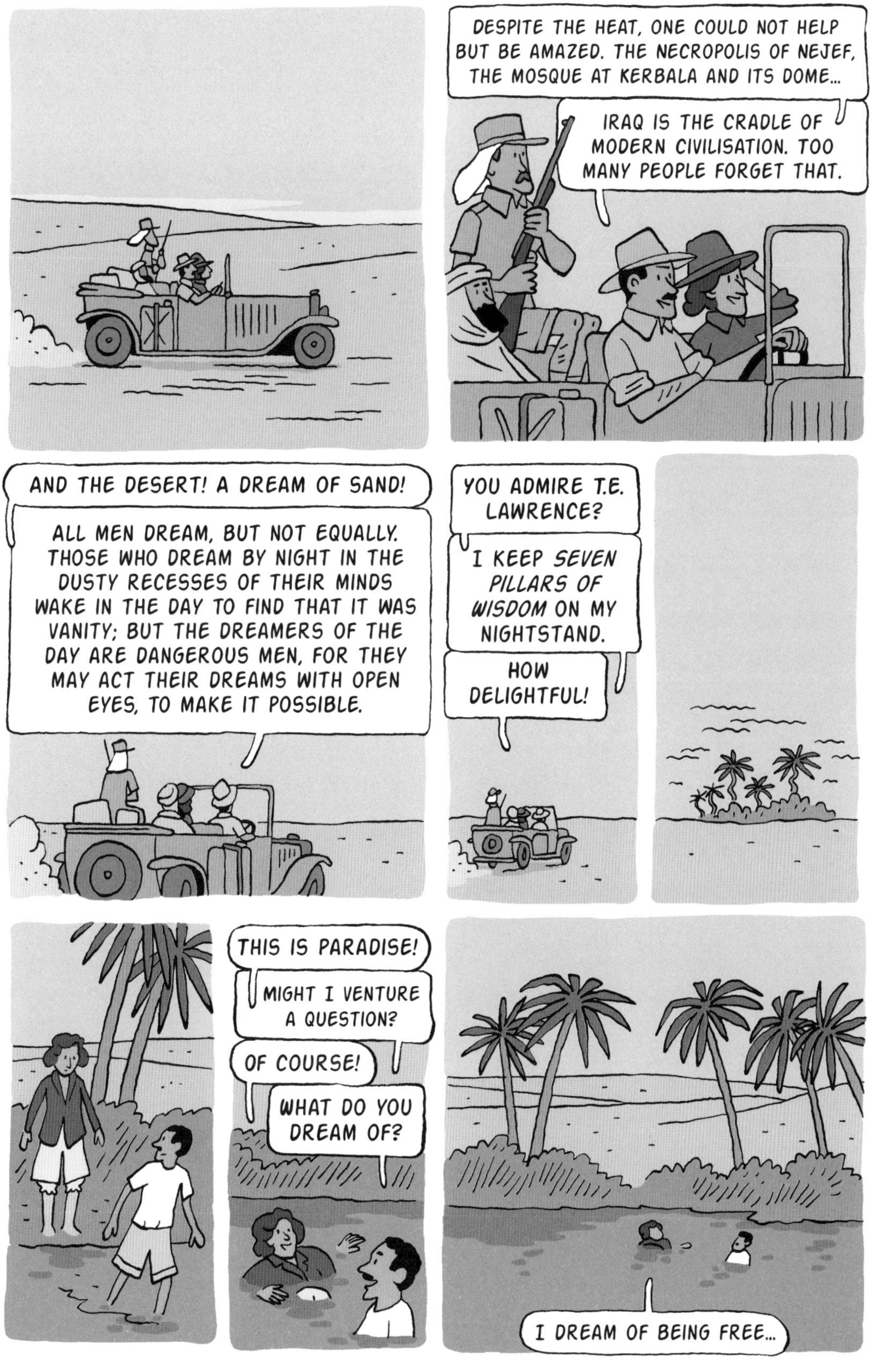
DESPITE THE HEAT, ONE COULD NOT HELP BUT BE AMAZED. THE NECROPOLIS OF NEJEF, THE MOSQUE AT KERBALA AND ITS DOME...
IRAQ IS THE CRADLE OF MODERN CIVILISATION. TOO MANY PEOPLE FORGET THAT.
AND THE DESERT! A DREAM OF SAND!
ALL MEN DREAM, BUT NOT EQUALLY. THOSE WHO DREAM BY NIGHT IN THE DUSTY RECESSES OF THEIR MINDS WAKE IN THE DAY TO FIND THAT IT WAS VANITY; BUT THE DREAMERS OF THE DAY ARE DANGEROUS MEN, FOR THEY MAY ACT THEIR DREAMS WITH OPEN EYES, TO MAKE IT POSSIBLE.
YOU ADMIRE T.E. LAWRENCE?
I KEEP *SEVEN PILLARS OF WISDOM* ON MY NIGHTSTAND.
HOW DELIGHTFUL!
THIS IS PARADISE!
MIGHT I VENTURE A QUESTION?
OF COURSE!
WHAT DO YOU DREAM OF?
I DREAM OF BEING FREE...

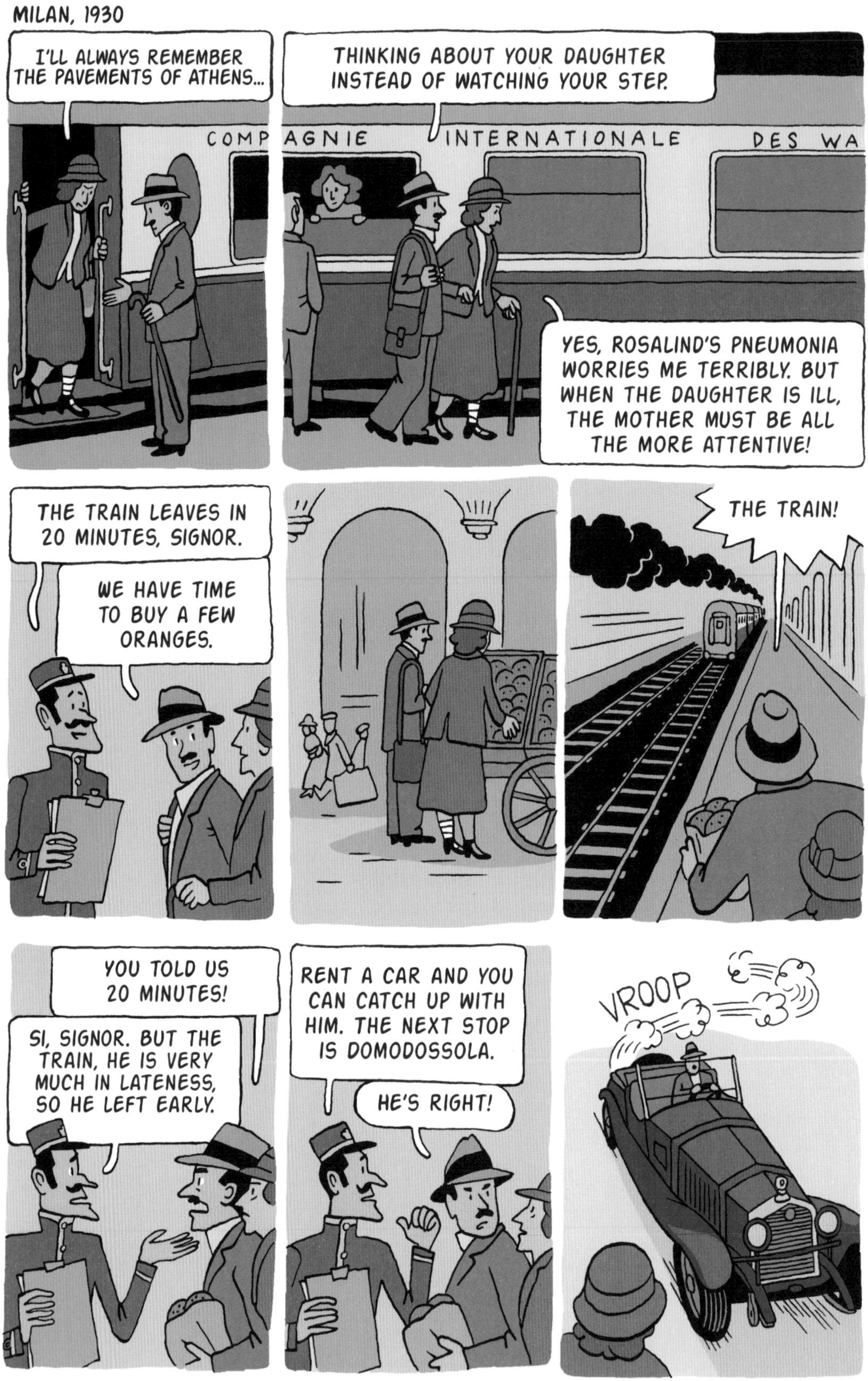
MILAN, 1930
I'LL ALWAYS REMEMBER THE PAVEMENTS OF ATHENS...
THINKING ABOUT YOUR DAUGHTER INSTEAD OF WATCHING YOUR STEP.
COMPAGNIE INTERNATIONALE DES WA
YES, ROSALIND'S PNEUMONIA WORRIES ME TERRIBLY. BUT WHEN THE DAUGHTER IS ILL, THE MOTHER MUST BE ALL THE MORE ATTENTIVE!
THE TRAIN LEAVES IN 20 MINUTES, SIGNOR.
WE HAVE TIME TO BUY A FEW ORANGES.
THE TRAIN!
YOU TOLD US 20 MINUTES!
SI, SIGNOR. BUT THE TRAIN, HE IS VERY MUCH IN LATENESS, SO HE LEFT EARLY.
RENT A CAR AND YOU CAN CATCH UP WITH HIM. THE NEXT STOP IS DOMODOSSOLA.
HE'S RIGHT!
VROOP

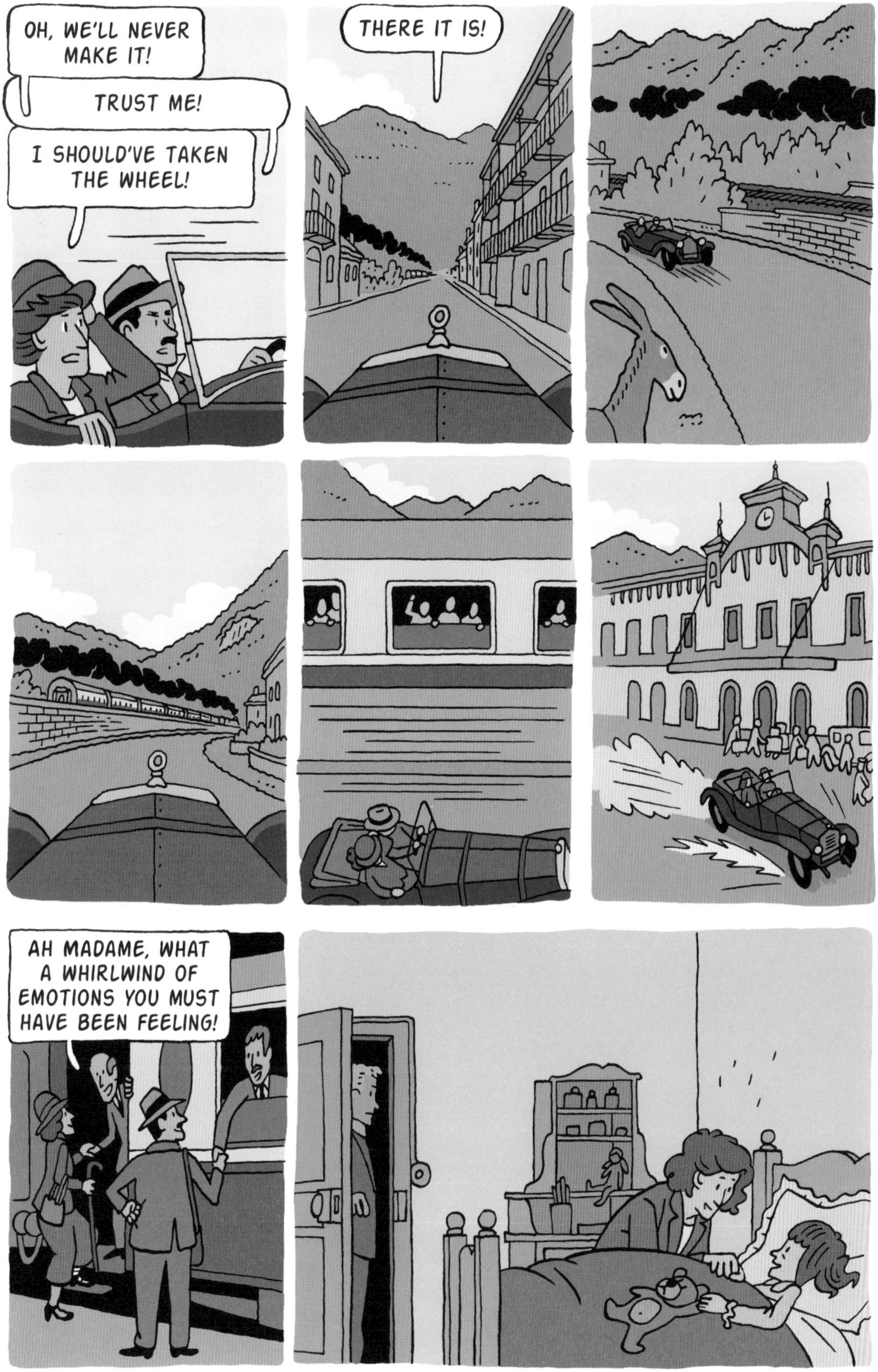
OH, WE'LL NEVER MAKE IT!
TRUST ME!
I SHOULD'VE TAKEN THE WHEEL!
THERE IT IS!
AH MADAME, WHAT A WHIRLWIND OF EMOTIONS YOU MUST HAVE BEEN FEELING!

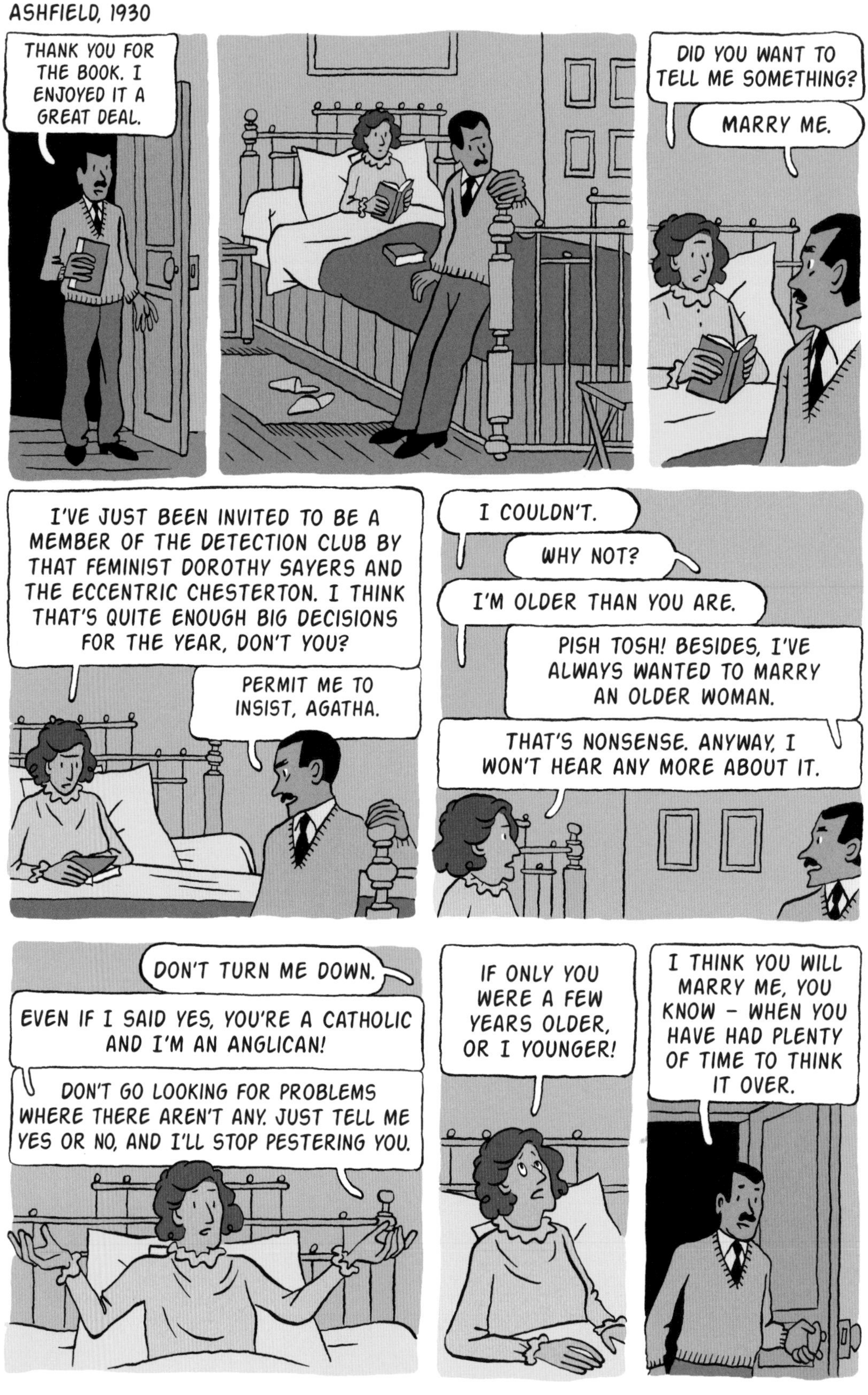
ASHFIELD, 1930
THANK YOU FOR THE BOOK. I ENJOYED IT A GREAT DEAL.
DID YOU WANT TO TELL ME SOMETHING?
MARRY ME.
I'VE JUST BEEN INVITED TO BE A MEMBER OF THE DETECTION CLUB BY THAT FEMINIST DOROTHY SAYERS AND THE ECCENTRIC CHESTERTON. I THINK THAT'S QUITE ENOUGH BIG DECISIONS FOR THE YEAR, DON'T YOU?
PERMIT ME TO INSIST, AGATHA.
I COULDN'T.
WHY NOT?
I'M OLDER THAN YOU ARE.
PISH TOSH! BESIDES, I'VE ALWAYS WANTED TO MARRY AN OLDER WOMAN.
THAT'S NONSENSE. ANYWAY, I WON'T HEAR ANY MORE ABOUT IT.
DON'T TURN ME DOWN.
EVEN IF I SAID YES, YOU'RE A CATHOLIC AND I'M AN ANGLICAN!
DON'T GO LOOKING FOR PROBLEMS WHERE THERE AREN'T ANY. JUST TELL ME YES OR NO, AND I'LL STOP PESTERING YOU.
IF ONLY YOU WERE A FEW YEARS OLDER, OR I YOUNGER!
I THINK YOU WILL MARRY ME, YOU KNOW – WHEN YOU HAVE HAD PLENTY OF TIME TO THINK IT OVER.

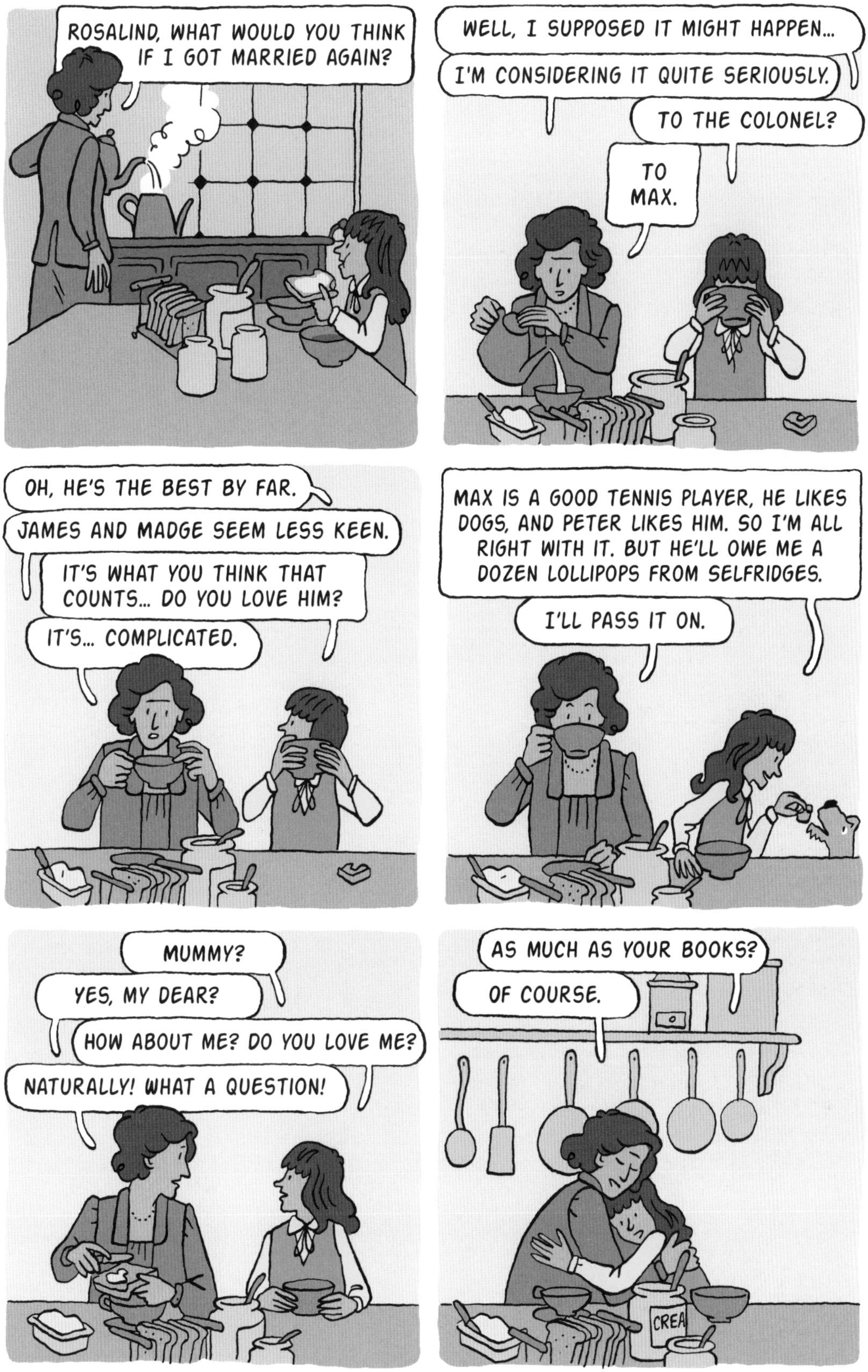
ROSALIND, WHAT WOULD YOU THINK IF I GOT MARRIED AGAIN?
WELL, I SUPPOSED IT MIGHT HAPPEN...
I'M CONSIDERING IT QUITE SERIOUSLY.
TO THE COLONEL?
TO MAX.
OH, HE'S THE BEST BY FAR.
JAMES AND MADGE SEEM LESS KEEN.
IT'S WHAT YOU THINK THAT COUNTS... DO YOU LOVE HIM?
IT'S... COMPLICATED.
MAX IS A GOOD TENNIS PLAYER, HE LIKES DOGS, AND PETER LIKES HIM. SO I'M ALL RIGHT WITH IT. BUT HE'LL OWE ME A DOZEN LOLLIPOPS FROM SELFRIDGES.
I'LL PASS IT ON.
MUMMY?
YES, MY DEAR?
HOW ABOUT ME? DO YOU LOVE ME?
NATURALLY! WHAT A QUESTION!
AS MUCH AS YOUR BOOKS?
OF COURSE.
CREA

UR, SPRING 1931

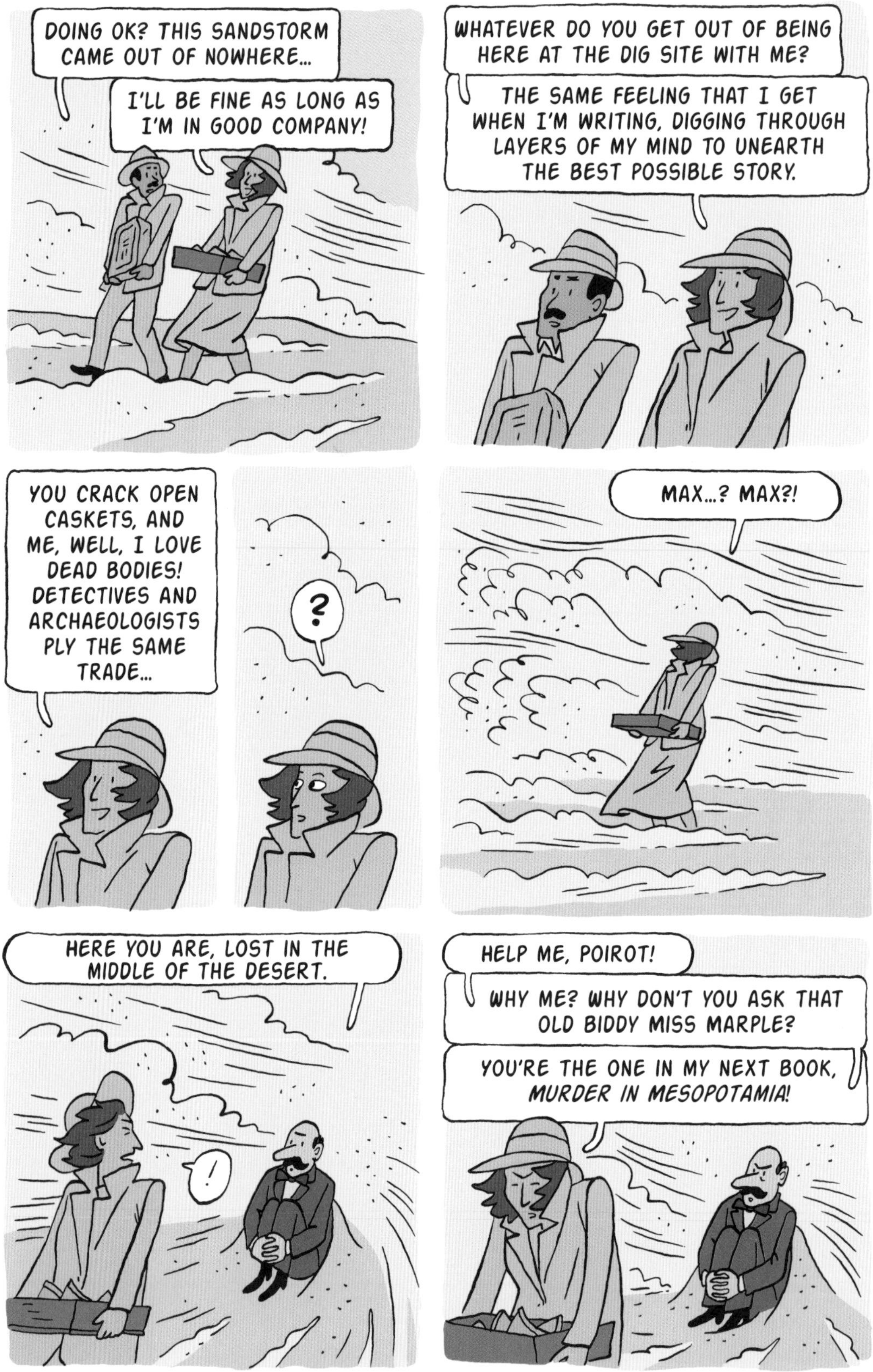
DOING OK? THIS SANDSTORM CAME OUT OF NOWHERE...
I'LL BE FINE AS LONG AS I'M IN GOOD COMPANY!
WHATEVER DO YOU GET OUT OF BEING HERE AT THE DIG SITE WITH ME?
THE SAME FEELING THAT I GET WHEN I'M WRITING, DIGGING THROUGH LAYERS OF MY MIND TO UNEARTH THE BEST POSSIBLE STORY.
YOU CRACK OPEN CASKETS, AND ME, WELL, I LOVE DEAD BODIES! DETECTIVES AND ARCHAEOLOGISTS PLY THE SAME TRADE...
?
MAX...? MAX?!
HERE YOU ARE, LOST IN THE MIDDLE OF THE DESERT.
!
HELP ME, POIROT!
WHY ME? WHY DON'T YOU ASK THAT OLD BIDDY MISS MARPLE?
YOU'RE THE ONE IN MY NEXT BOOK, *MURDER IN MESOPOTAMIA*!

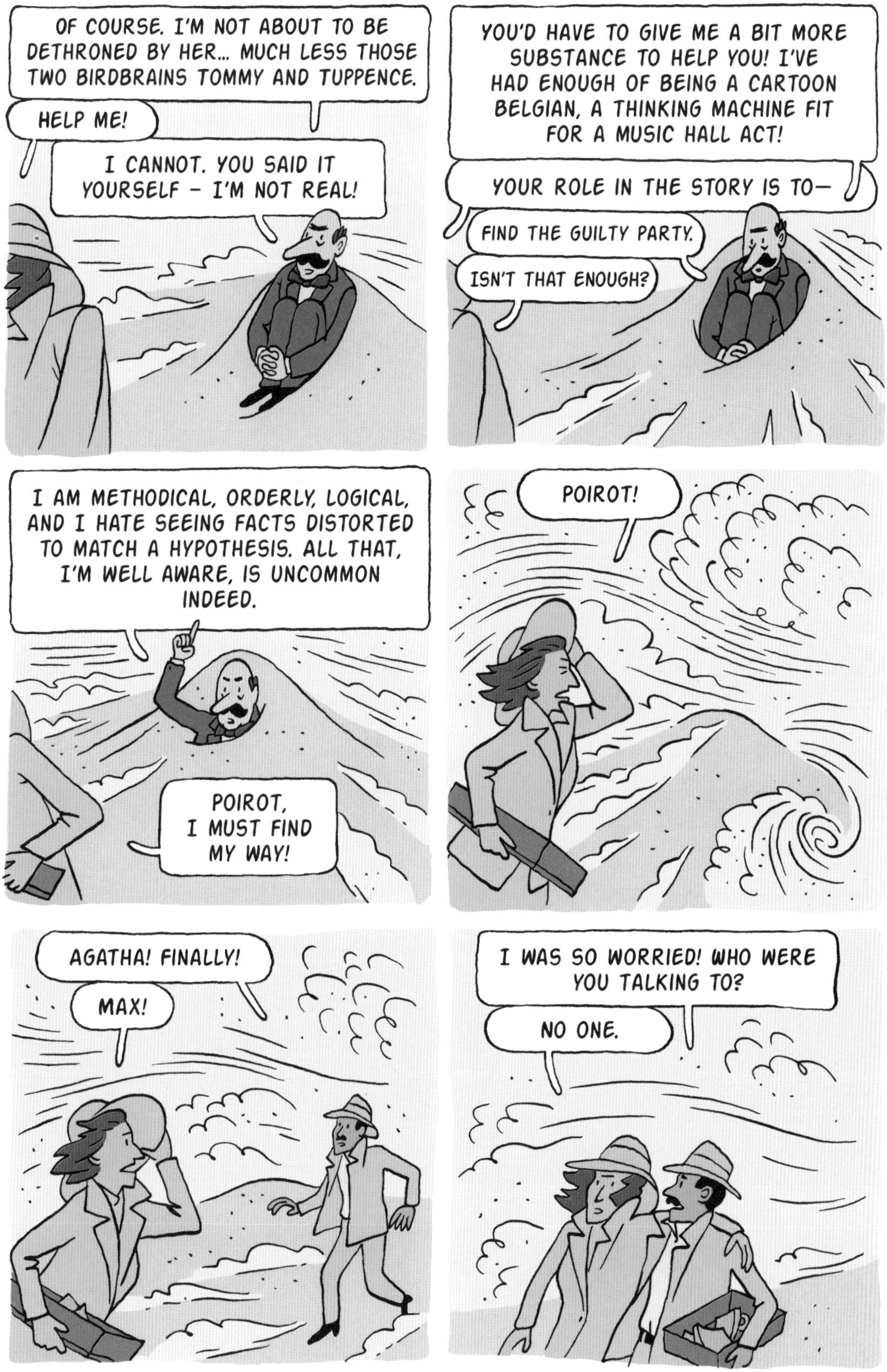
OF COURSE. I'M NOT ABOUT TO BE DETHRONED BY HER... MUCH LESS THOSE TWO BIRDBRAINS TOMMY AND TUPPENCE.
HELP ME!
I CANNOT. YOU SAID IT YOURSELF – I'M NOT REAL!
YOU'D HAVE TO GIVE ME A BIT MORE SUBSTANCE TO HELP YOU! I'VE HAD ENOUGH OF BEING A CARTOON BELGIAN, A THINKING MACHINE FIT FOR A MUSIC HALL ACT!
YOUR ROLE IN THE STORY IS TO—
FIND THE GUILTY PARTY.
ISN'T THAT ENOUGH?
I AM METHODICAL, ORDERLY, LOGICAL, AND I HATE SEEING FACTS DISTORTED TO MATCH A HYPOTHESIS. ALL THAT, I'M WELL AWARE, IS UNCOMMON INDEED.
POIROT, I MUST FIND MY WAY!
POIROT!
AGATHA! FINALLY!
MAX!
I WAS SO WORRIED! WHO WERE YOU TALKING TO?
NO ONE.

DECEMBER 1931

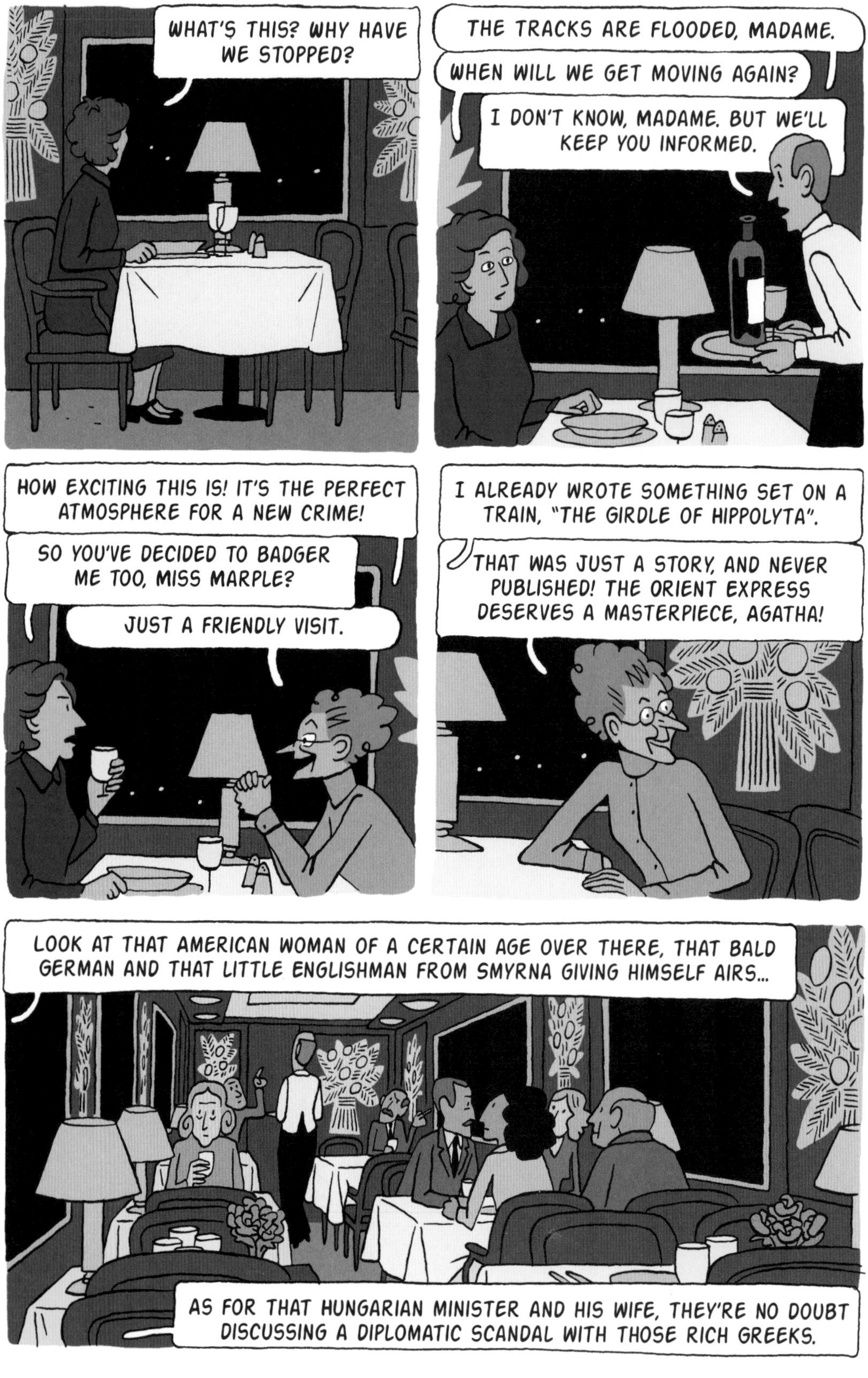
WHAT'S THIS? WHY HAVE WE STOPPED?
THE TRACKS ARE FLOODED, MADAME.
WHEN WILL WE GET MOVING AGAIN?
I DON'T KNOW, MADAME. BUT WE'LL KEEP YOU INFORMED.
HOW EXCITING THIS IS! IT'S THE PERFECT ATMOSPHERE FOR A NEW CRIME!
SO YOU'VE DECIDED TO BADGER ME TOO, MISS MARPLE?
JUST A FRIENDLY VISIT.
I ALREADY WROTE SOMETHING SET ON A TRAIN, "THE GIRDLE OF HIPPOLYTA".
THAT WAS JUST A STORY, AND NEVER PUBLISHED! THE ORIENT EXPRESS DESERVES A MASTERPIECE, AGATHA!
LOOK AT THAT AMERICAN WOMAN OF A CERTAIN AGE OVER THERE, THAT BALD GERMAN AND THAT LITTLE ENGLISHMAN FROM SMYRNA GIVING HIMSELF AIRS...
AS FOR THAT HUNGARIAN MINISTER AND HIS WIFE, THEY'RE NO DOUBT DISCUSSING A DIPLOMATIC SCANDAL WITH THOSE RICH GREEKS.

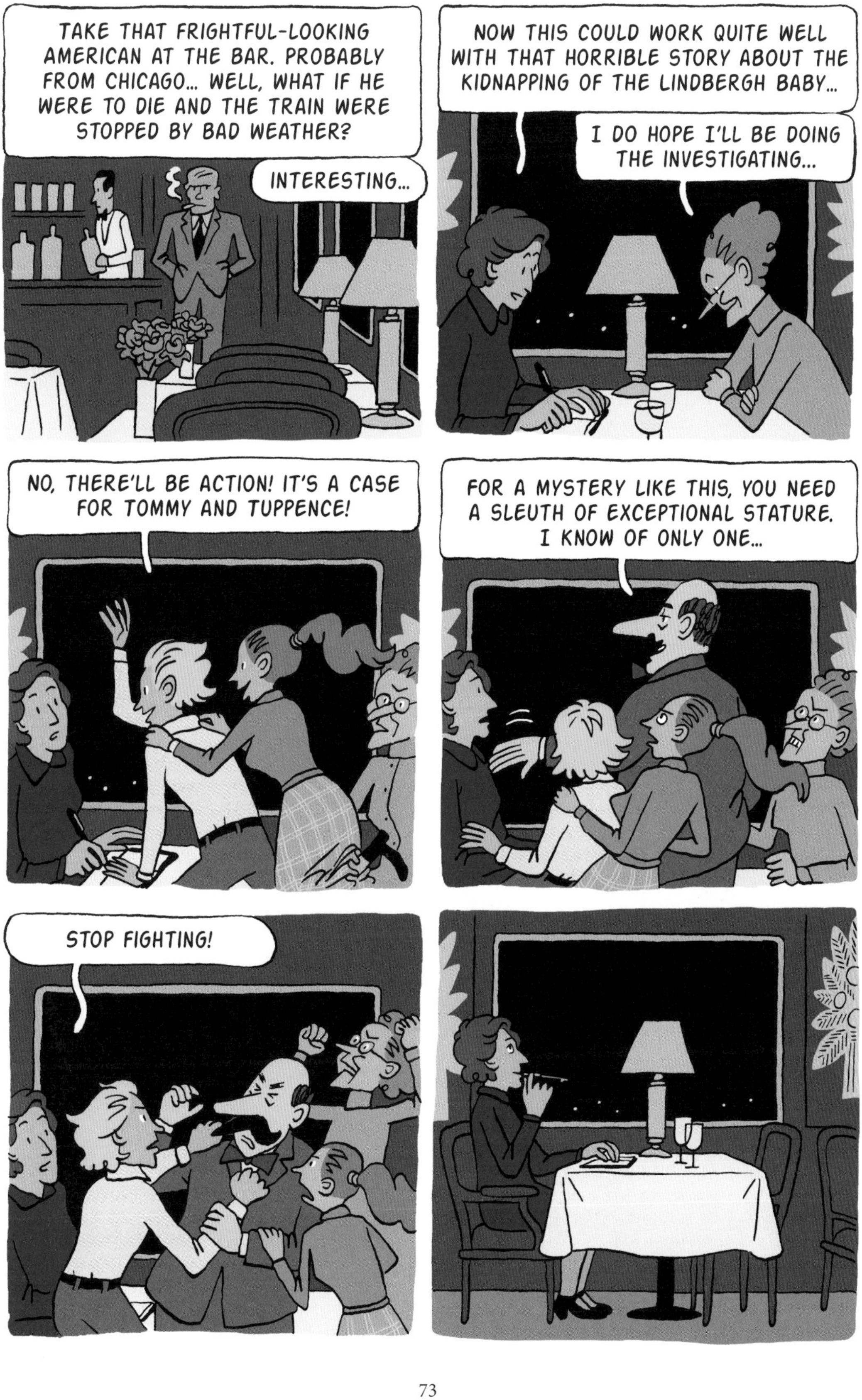
TAKE THAT FRIGHTFUL-LOOKING AMERICAN AT THE BAR. PROBABLY FROM CHICAGO... WELL, WHAT IF HE WERE TO DIE AND THE TRAIN WERE STOPPED BY BAD WEATHER?
INTERESTING...
NOW THIS COULD WORK QUITE WELL WITH THAT HORRIBLE STORY ABOUT THE KIDNAPPING OF THE LINDBERGH BABY...
I DO HOPE I'LL BE DOING THE INVESTIGATING...
NO, THERE'LL BE ACTION! IT'S A CASE FOR TOMMY AND TUPPENCE!
FOR A MYSTERY LIKE THIS, YOU NEED A SLEUTH OF EXCEPTIONAL STATURE. I KNOW OF ONLY ONE...
STOP FIGHTING!

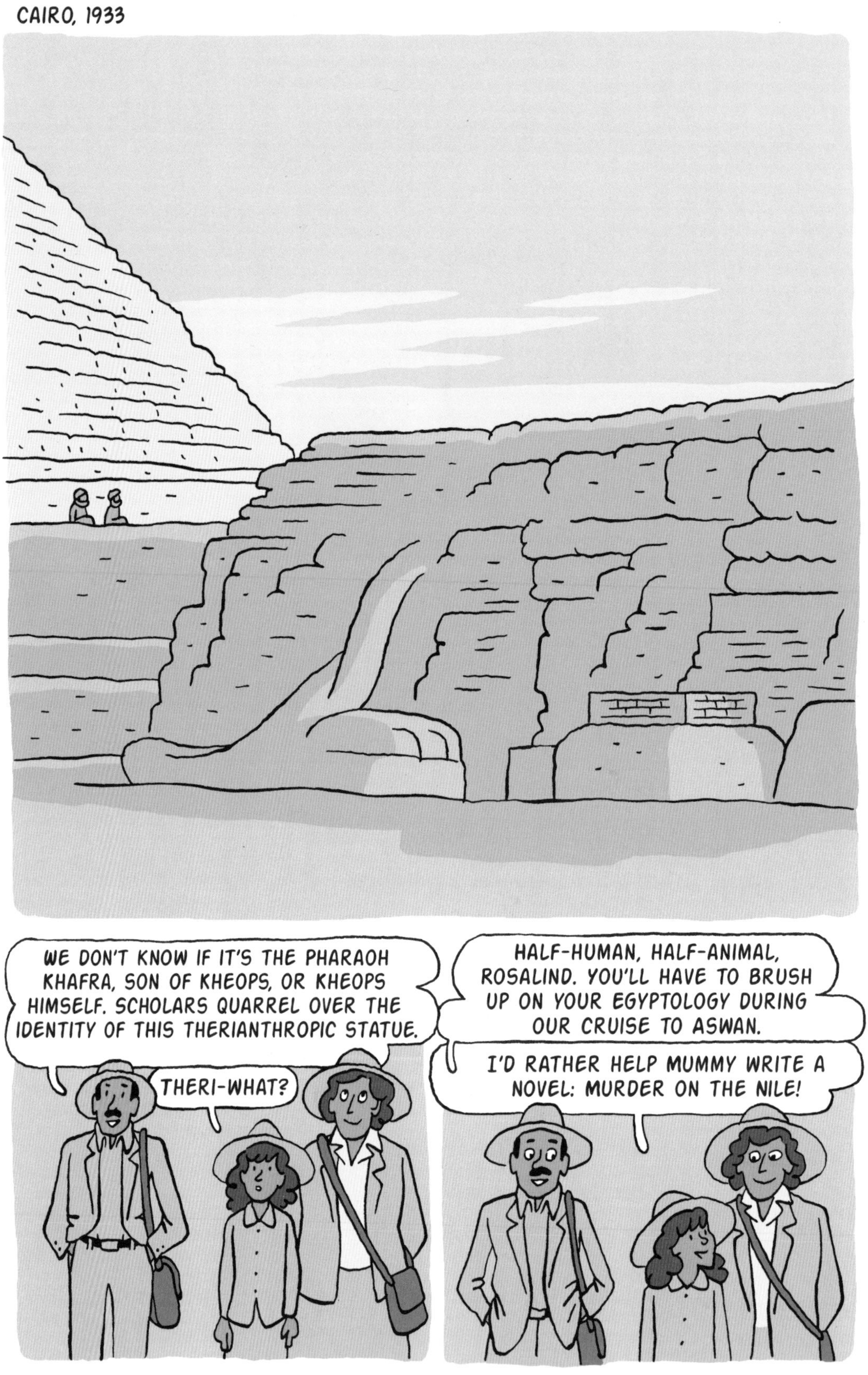
CAIRO, 1933
WE DON'T KNOW IF IT'S THE PHARAOH KHAFRA, SON OF KHEOPS, OR KHEOPS HIMSELF. SCHOLARS QUARREL OVER THE IDENTITY OF THIS THERIANTHROPIC STATUE.
THERI-WHAT?
HALF-HUMAN, HALF-ANIMAL, ROSALIND. YOU'LL HAVE TO BRUSH UP ON YOUR EGYPTOLOGY DURING OUR CRUISE TO ASWAN.
I'D RATHER HELP MUMMY WRITE A NOVEL: MURDER ON THE NILE!

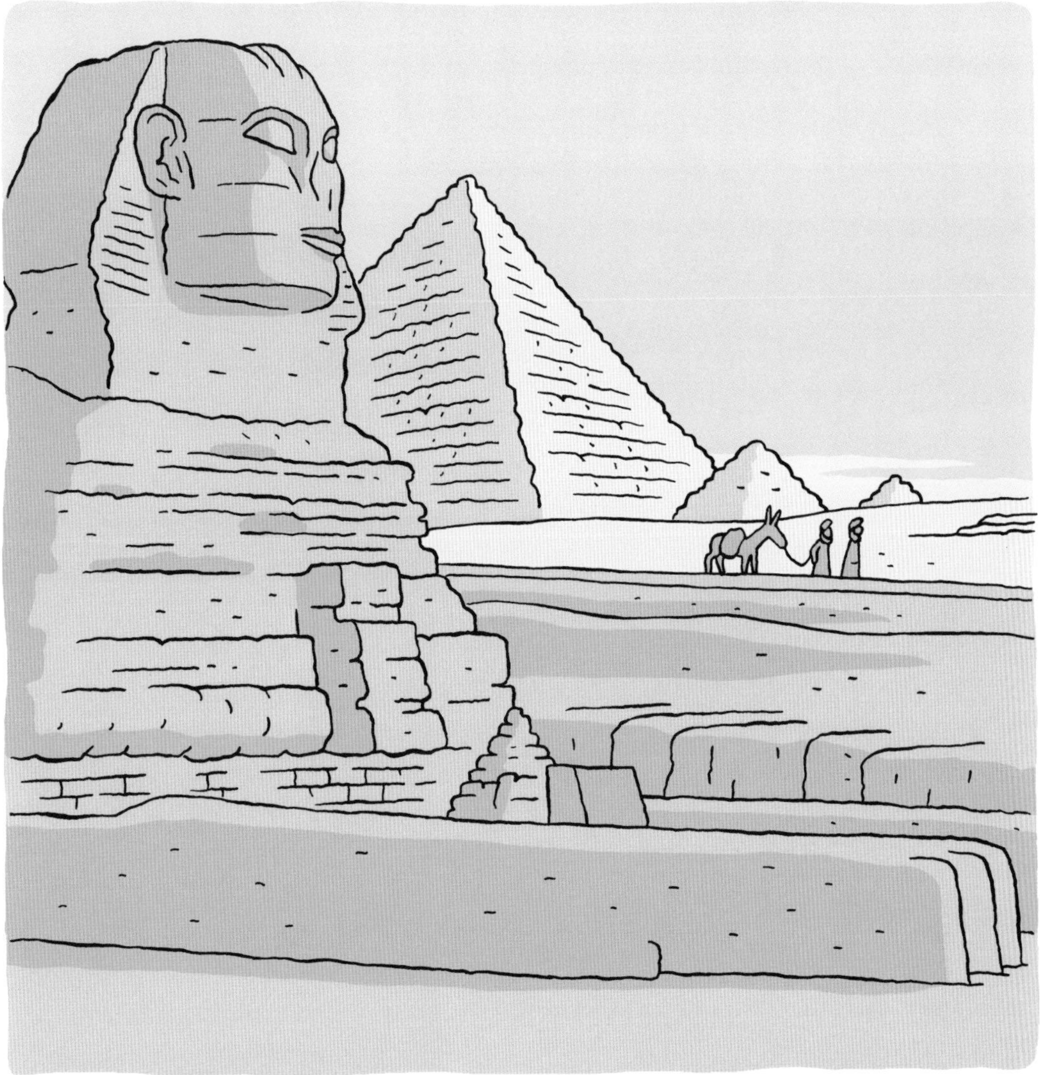

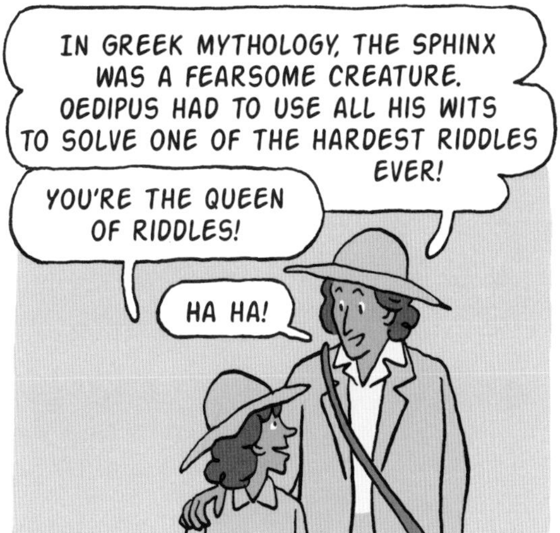
IN GREEK MYTHOLOGY, THE SPHINX WAS A FEARSOME CREATURE. OEDIPUS HAD TO USE ALL HIS WITS TO SOLVE ONE OF THE HARDEST RIDDLES EVER!
YOU'RE THE QUEEN OF RIDDLES!
HA HA!

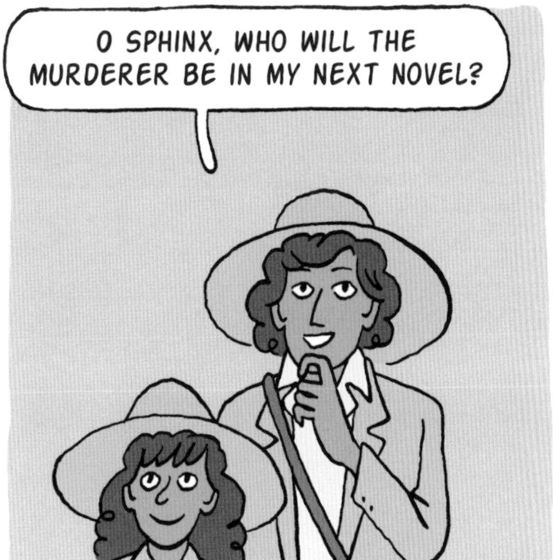
O SPHINX, WHO WILL THE MURDERER BE IN MY NEXT NOVEL?

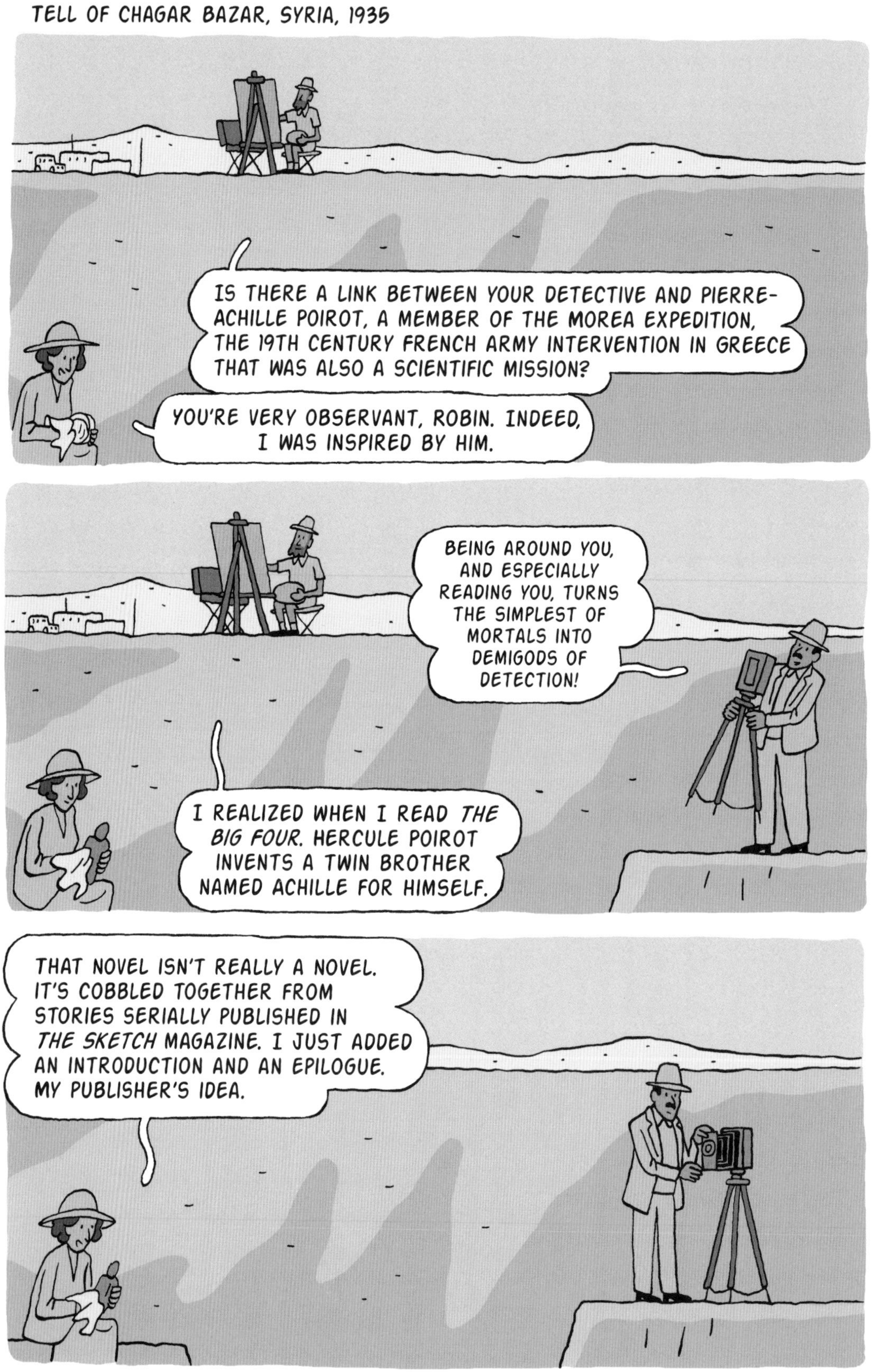
TELL OF CHAGAR BAZAR, SYRIA, 1935
IS THERE A LINK BETWEEN YOUR DETECTIVE AND PIERRE-ACHILLE POIROT, A MEMBER OF THE MOREA EXPEDITION, THE 19TH CENTURY FRENCH ARMY INTERVENTION IN GREECE THAT WAS ALSO A SCIENTIFIC MISSION?
YOU'RE VERY OBSERVANT, ROBIN. INDEED, I WAS INSPIRED BY HIM.
BEING AROUND YOU, AND ESPECIALLY READING YOU, TURNS THE SIMPLEST OF MORTALS INTO DEMIGODS OF DETECTION!
I REALIZED WHEN I READ *THE BIG FOUR*. HERCULE POIROT INVENTS A TWIN BROTHER NAMED ACHILLE FOR HIMSELF.
THAT NOVEL ISN'T REALLY A NOVEL. IT'S COBBLED TOGETHER FROM STORIES SERIALLY PUBLISHED IN *THE SKETCH* MAGAZINE. I JUST ADDED AN INTRODUCTION AND AN EPILOGUE. MY PUBLISHER'S IDEA.

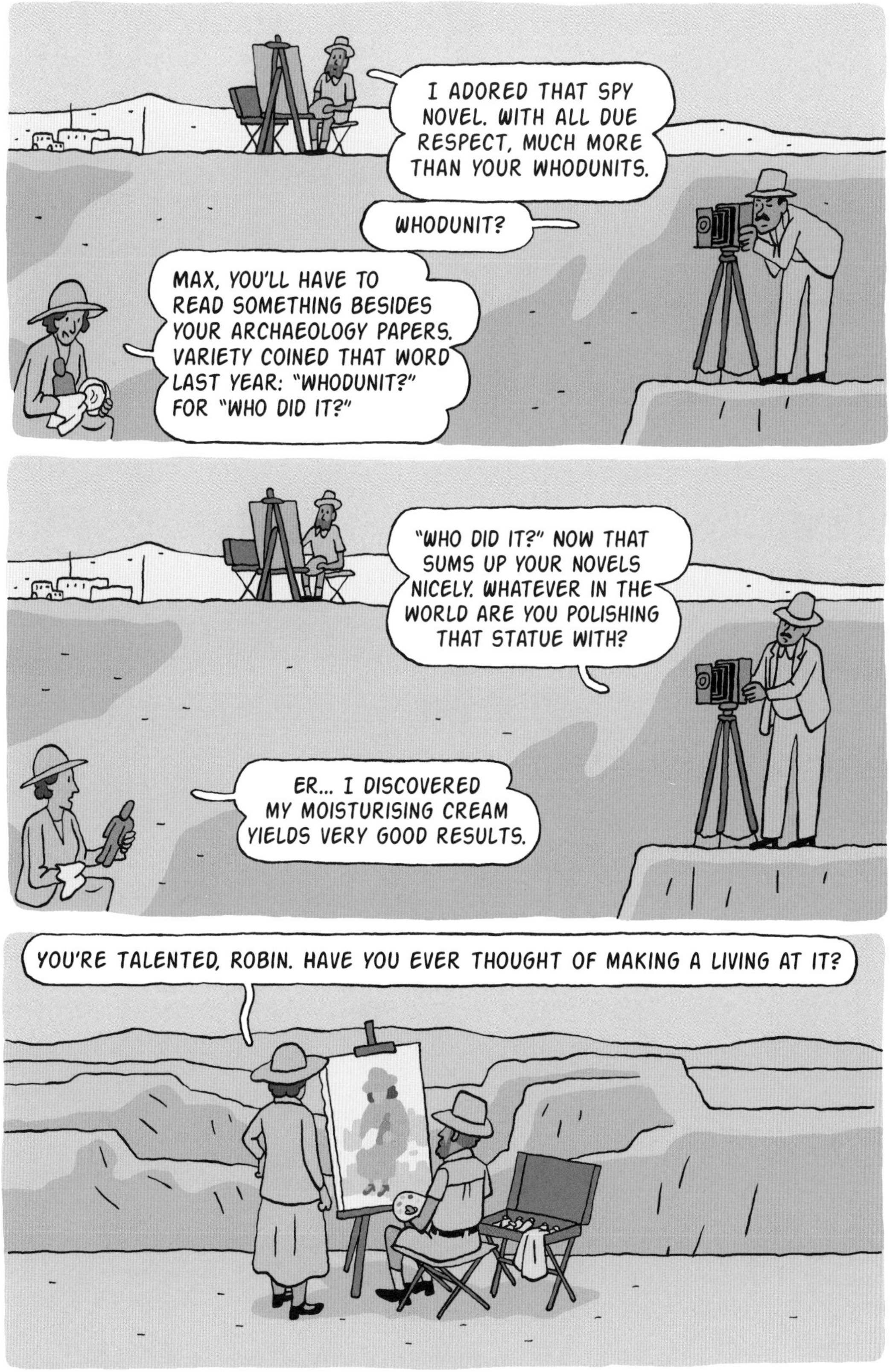
I ADORED THAT SPY NOVEL. WITH ALL DUE RESPECT, MUCH MORE THAN YOUR WHODUNITS.
WHODUNIT?
MAX, YOU'LL HAVE TO READ SOMETHING BESIDES YOUR ARCHAEOLOGY PAPERS. VARIETY COINED THAT WORD LAST YEAR: "WHODUNIT?" FOR "WHO DID IT?"
"WHO DID IT?" NOW THAT SUMS UP YOUR NOVELS NICELY. WHATEVER IN THE WORLD ARE YOU POLISHING THAT STATUE WITH?
ER... I DISCOVERED MY MOISTURISING CREAM YIELDS VERY GOOD RESULTS.
YOU'RE TALENTED, ROBIN. HAVE YOU EVER THOUGHT OF MAKING A LIVING AT IT?

BURGH ISLAND, SUMMER 1938

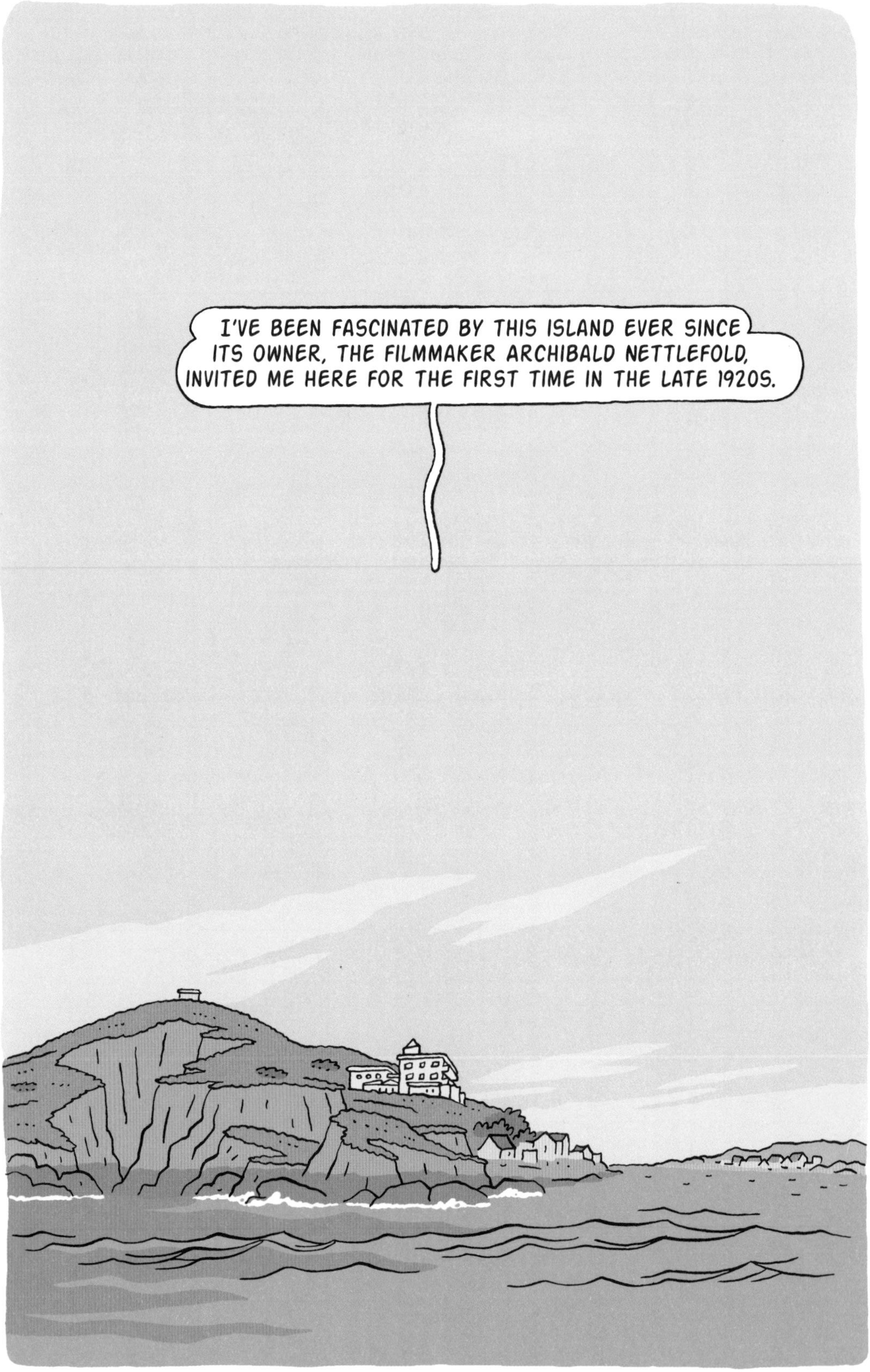
I'VE BEEN FASCINATED BY THIS ISLAND EVER SINCE ITS OWNER, THE FILMMAKER ARCHIBALD NETTLEFOLD, INVITED ME HERE FOR THE FIRST TIME IN THE LATE 1920S.

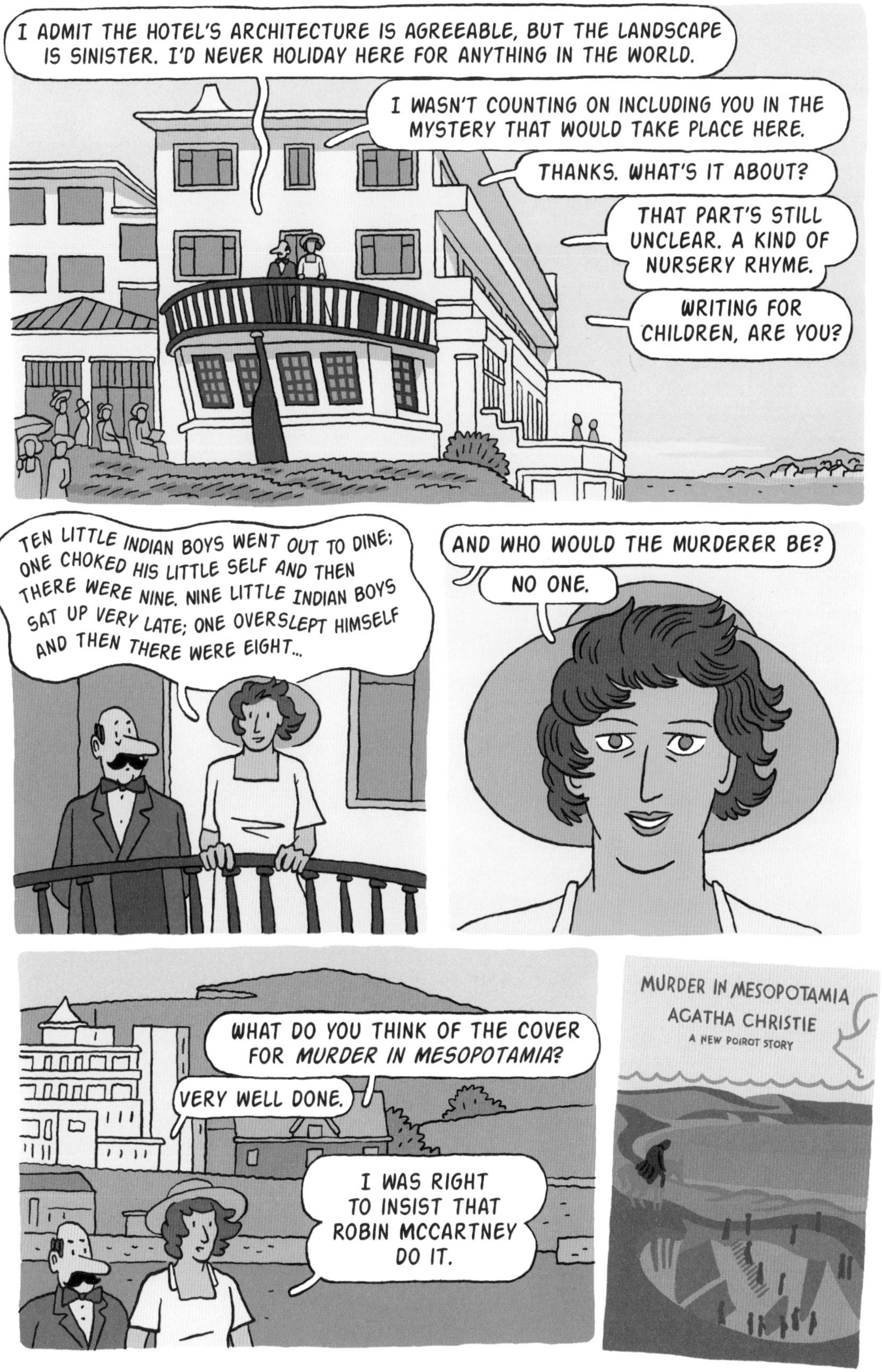

I ADMIT THE HOTEL'S ARCHITECTURE IS AGREEABLE, BUT THE LANDSCAPE IS SINISTER. I'D NEVER HOLIDAY HERE FOR ANYTHING IN THE WORLD.
I WASN'T COUNTING ON INCLUDING YOU IN THE MYSTERY THAT WOULD TAKE PLACE HERE.
THANKS. WHAT'S IT ABOUT?
THAT PART'S STILL UNCLEAR. A KIND OF NURSERY RHYME.
WRITING FOR CHILDREN, ARE YOU?
TEN LITTLE INDIAN BOYS WENT OUT TO DINE; ONE CHOKED HIS LITTLE SELF AND THEN THERE WERE NINE. NINE LITTLE INDIAN BOYS SAT UP VERY LATE; ONE OVERSLEPT HIMSELF AND THEN THERE WERE EIGHT...
AND WHO WOULD THE MURDERER BE?
NO ONE.
WHAT DO YOU THINK OF THE COVER FOR *MURDER IN MESOPOTAMIA*?
VERY WELL DONE.
I WAS RIGHT TO INSIST THAT ROBIN MCCARTNEY DO IT.
MURDER IN MESOPOTAMIA
AGATHA CHRISTIE
A NEW POIROT STORY

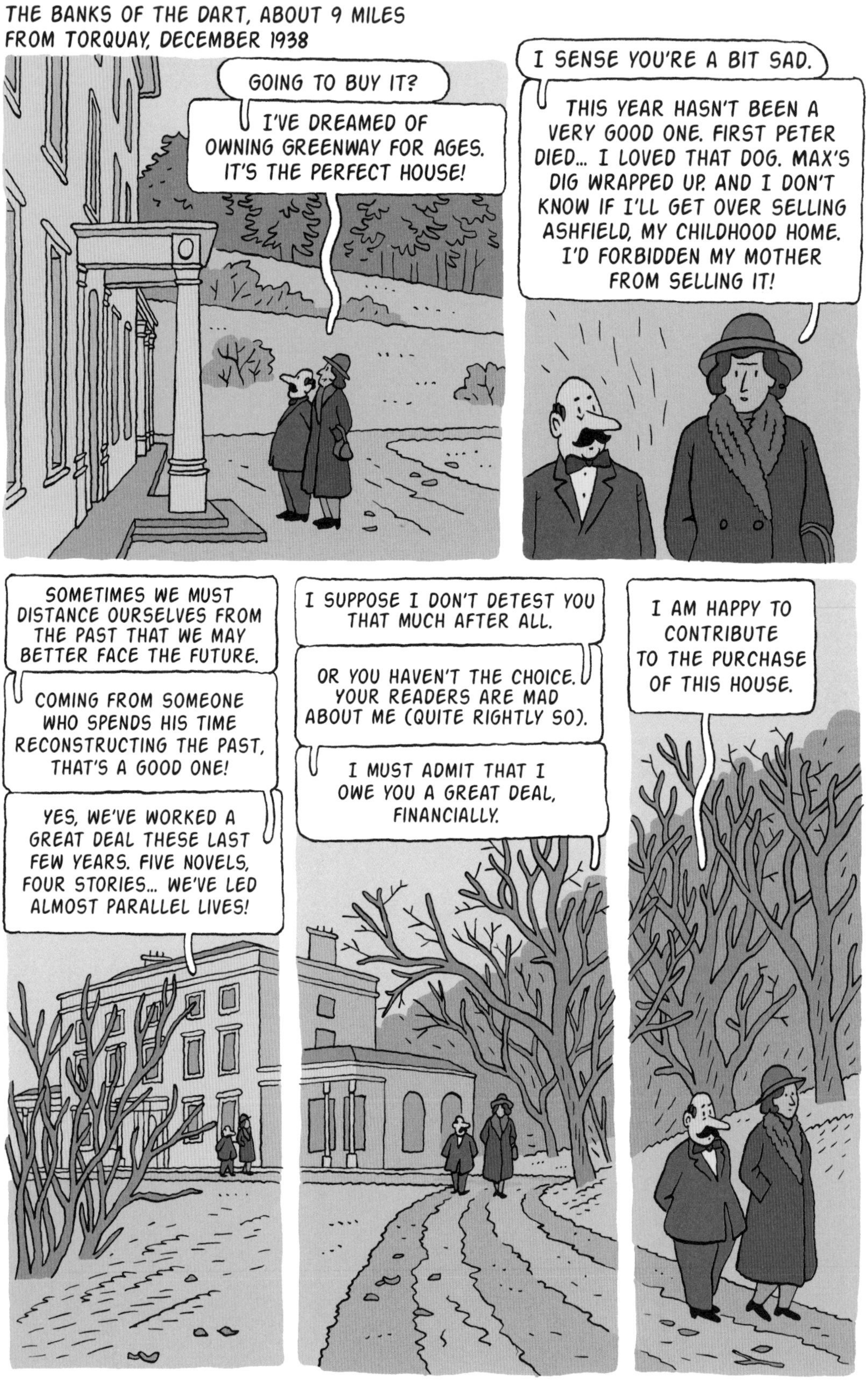
THE BANKS OF THE DART, ABOUT 9 MILES FROM TORQUAY, DECEMBER 1938
GOING TO BUY IT?
I'VE DREAMED OF OWNING GREENWAY FOR AGES. IT'S THE PERFECT HOUSE!
I SENSE YOU'RE A BIT SAD.
THIS YEAR HASN'T BEEN A VERY GOOD ONE. FIRST PETER DIED... I LOVED THAT DOG. MAX'S DIG WRAPPED UP. AND I DON'T KNOW IF I'LL GET OVER SELLING ASHFIELD, MY CHILDHOOD HOME. I'D FORBIDDEN MY MOTHER FROM SELLING IT!
SOMETIMES WE MUST DISTANCE OURSELVES FROM THE PAST THAT WE MAY BETTER FACE THE FUTURE.
COMING FROM SOMEONE WHO SPENDS HIS TIME RECONSTRUCTING THE PAST, THAT'S A GOOD ONE!
YES, WE'VE WORKED A GREAT DEAL THESE LAST FEW YEARS. FIVE NOVELS, FOUR STORIES... WE'VE LED ALMOST PARALLEL LIVES!
I SUPPOSE I DON'T DETEST YOU THAT MUCH AFTER ALL.
OR YOU HAVEN'T THE CHOICE. YOUR READERS ARE MAD ABOUT ME (QUITE RIGHTLY SO).
I MUST ADMIT THAT I OWE YOU A GREAT DEAL, FINANCIALLY.
I AM HAPPY TO CONTRIBUTE TO THE PURCHASE OF THIS HOUSE.

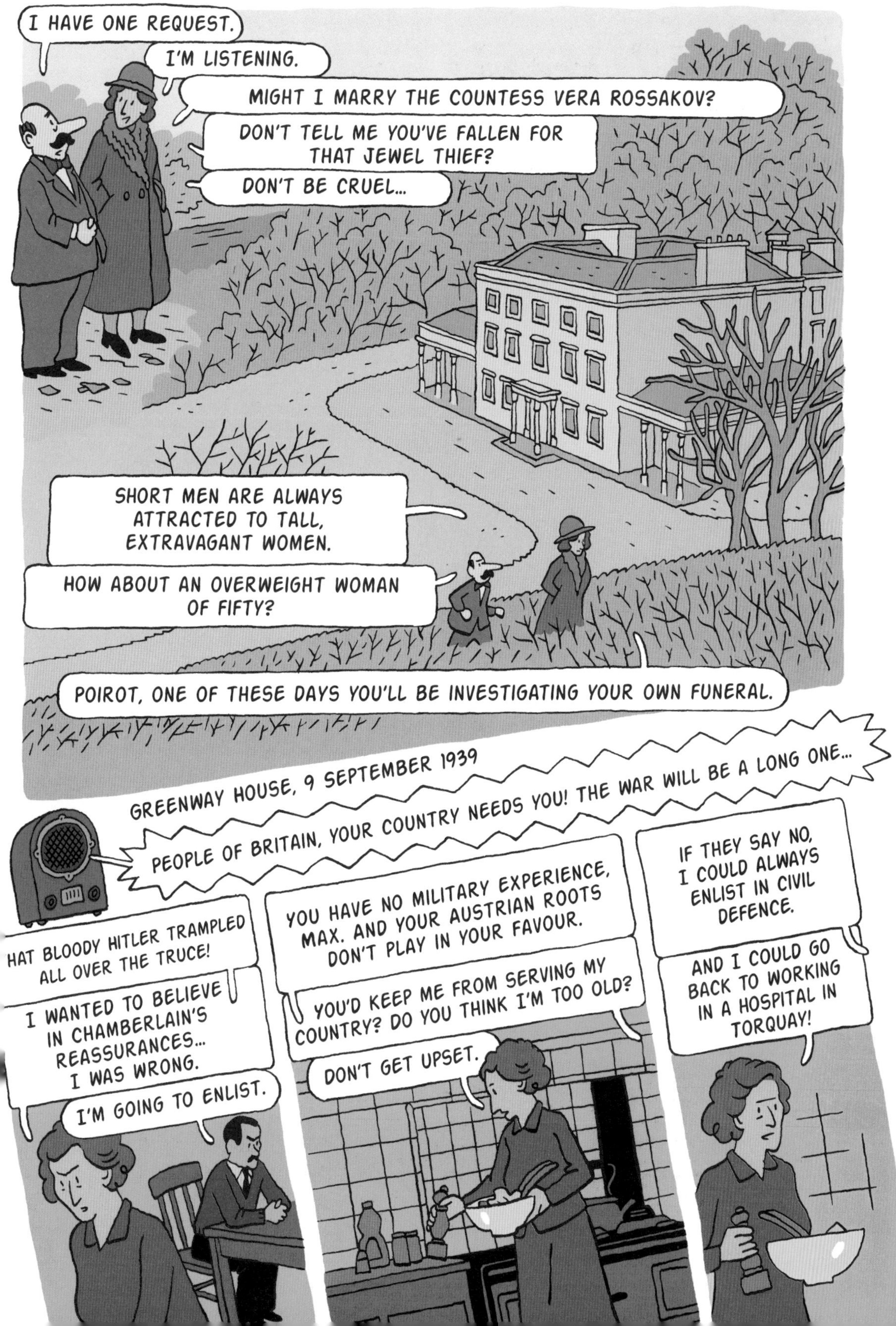
I HAVE ONE REQUEST.
I'M LISTENING.
MIGHT I MARRY THE COUNTESS VERA ROSSAKOV?
DON'T TELL ME YOU'VE FALLEN FOR THAT JEWEL THIEF?
DON'T BE CRUEL...
SHORT MEN ARE ALWAYS ATTRACTED TO TALL, EXTRAVAGANT WOMEN.
HOW ABOUT AN OVERWEIGHT WOMAN OF FIFTY?
POIROT, ONE OF THESE DAYS YOU'LL BE INVESTIGATING YOUR OWN FUNERAL.
GREENWAY HOUSE, 9 SEPTEMBER 1939
PEOPLE OF BRITAIN, YOUR COUNTRY NEEDS YOU! THE WAR WILL BE A LONG ONE...
HAT BLOODY HITLER TRAMPLED ALL OVER THE TRUCE!
I WANTED TO BELIEVE IN CHAMBERLAIN'S REASSURANCES... I WAS WRONG.
I'M GOING TO ENLIST.
YOU HAVE NO MILITARY EXPERIENCE, MAX. AND YOUR AUSTRIAN ROOTS DON'T PLAY IN YOUR FAVOUR.
YOU'D KEEP ME FROM SERVING MY COUNTRY? DO YOU THINK I'M TOO OLD?
DON'T GET UPSET.
IF THEY SAY NO, I COULD ALWAYS ENLIST IN CIVIL DEFENCE.
AND I COULD GO BACK TO WORKING IN A HOSPITAL IN TORQUAY!

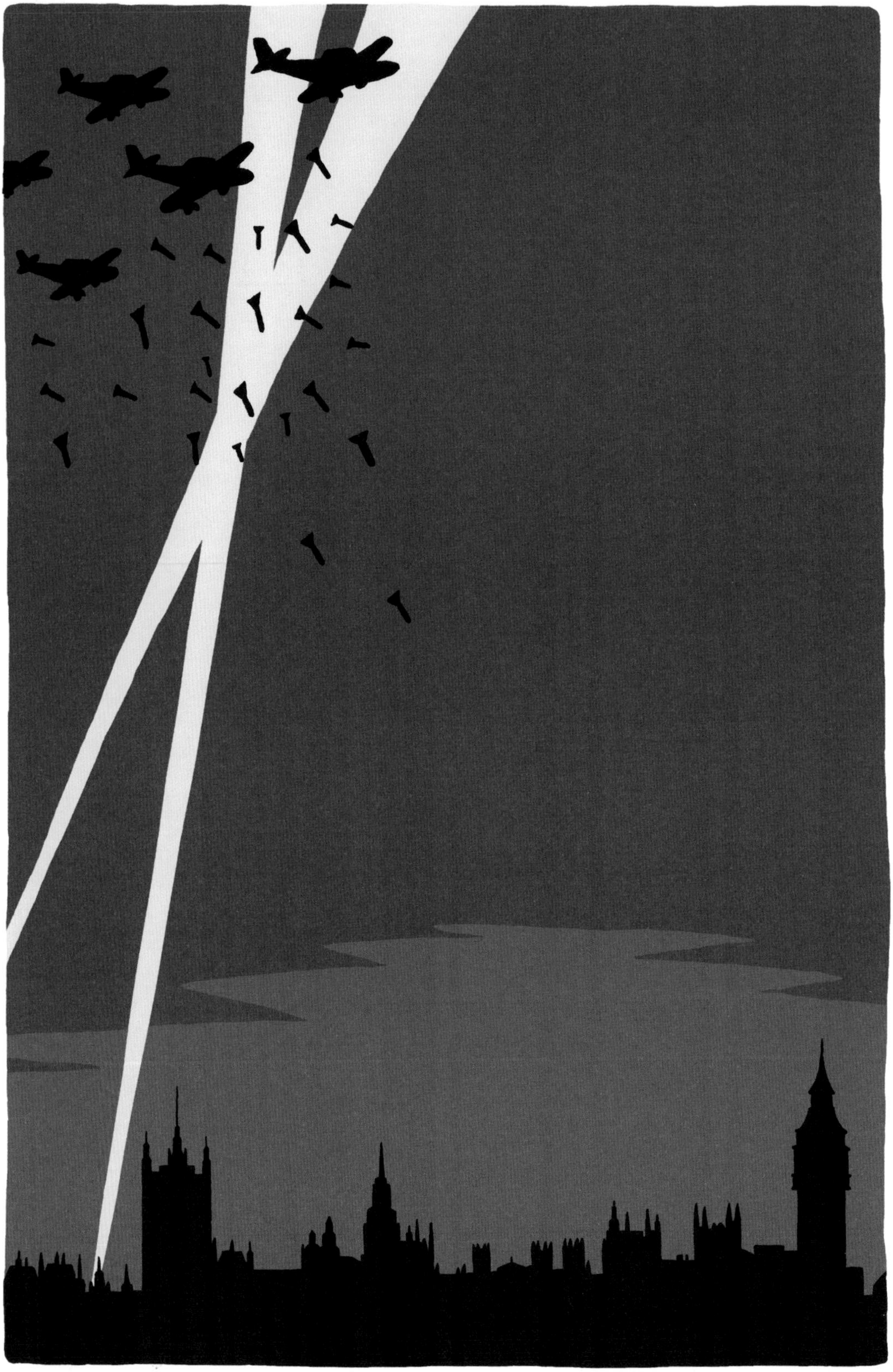

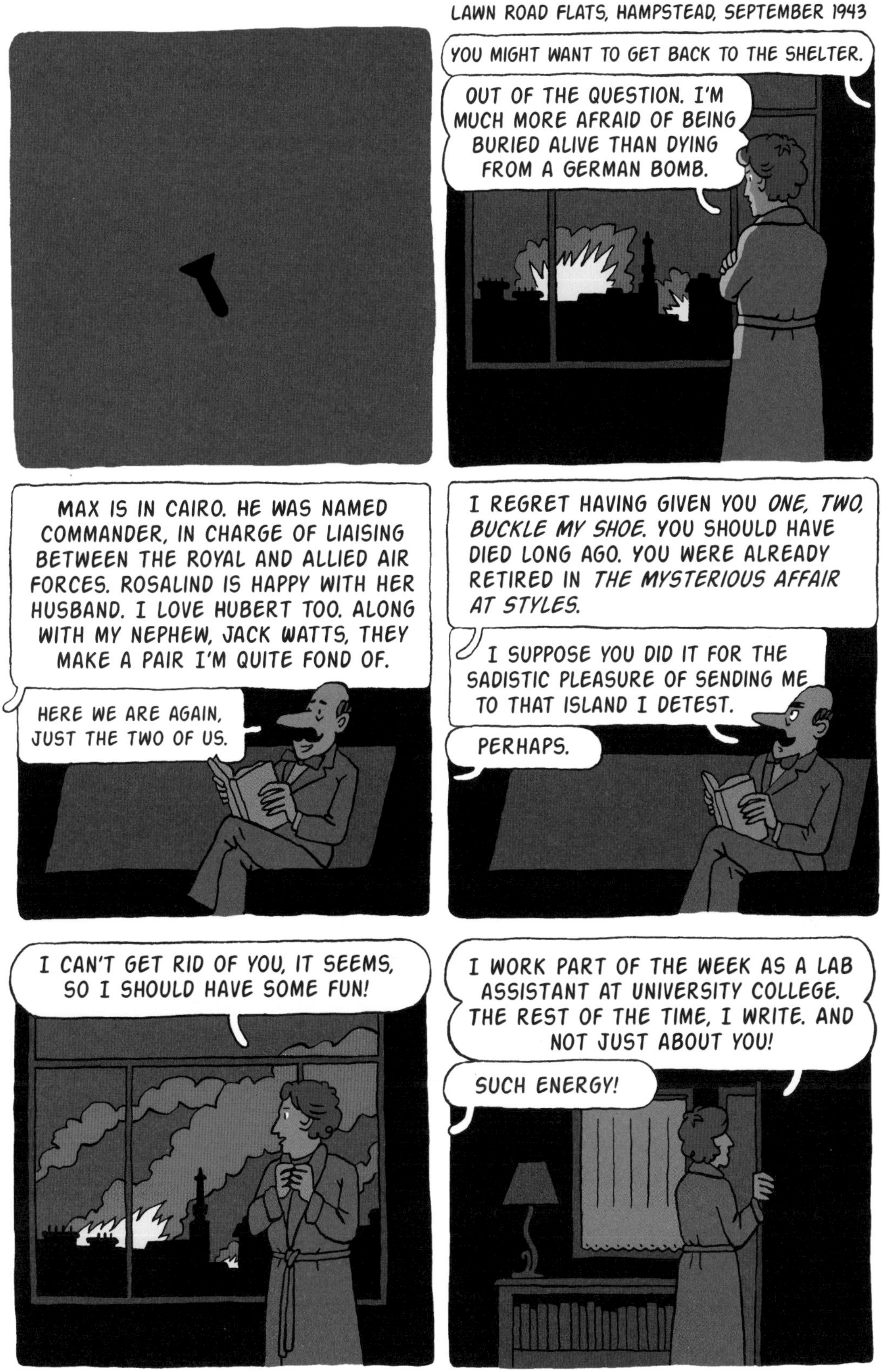
LAWN ROAD FLATS, HAMPSTEAD, SEPTEMBER 1943
YOU MIGHT WANT TO GET BACK TO THE SHELTER.
OUT OF THE QUESTION. I'M MUCH MORE AFRAID OF BEING BURIED ALIVE THAN DYING FROM A GERMAN BOMB.
MAX IS IN CAIRO. HE WAS NAMED COMMANDER, IN CHARGE OF LIAISING BETWEEN THE ROYAL AND ALLIED AIR FORCES. ROSALIND IS HAPPY WITH HER HUSBAND. I LOVE HUBERT TOO. ALONG WITH MY NEPHEW, JACK WATTS, THEY MAKE A PAIR I'M QUITE FOND OF.
HERE WE ARE AGAIN, JUST THE TWO OF US.
I REGRET HAVING GIVEN YOU *ONE, TWO, BUCKLE MY SHOE*. YOU SHOULD HAVE DIED LONG AGO. YOU WERE ALREADY RETIRED IN *THE MYSTERIOUS AFFAIR AT STYLES*.
I SUPPOSE YOU DID IT FOR THE SADISTIC PLEASURE OF SENDING ME TO THAT ISLAND I DETEST.
PERHAPS.
I CAN'T GET RID OF YOU, IT SEEMS, SO I SHOULD HAVE SOME FUN!
I WORK PART OF THE WEEK AS A LAB ASSISTANT AT UNIVERSITY COLLEGE. THE REST OF THE TIME, I WRITE. AND NOT JUST ABOUT YOU!
SUCH ENERGY!

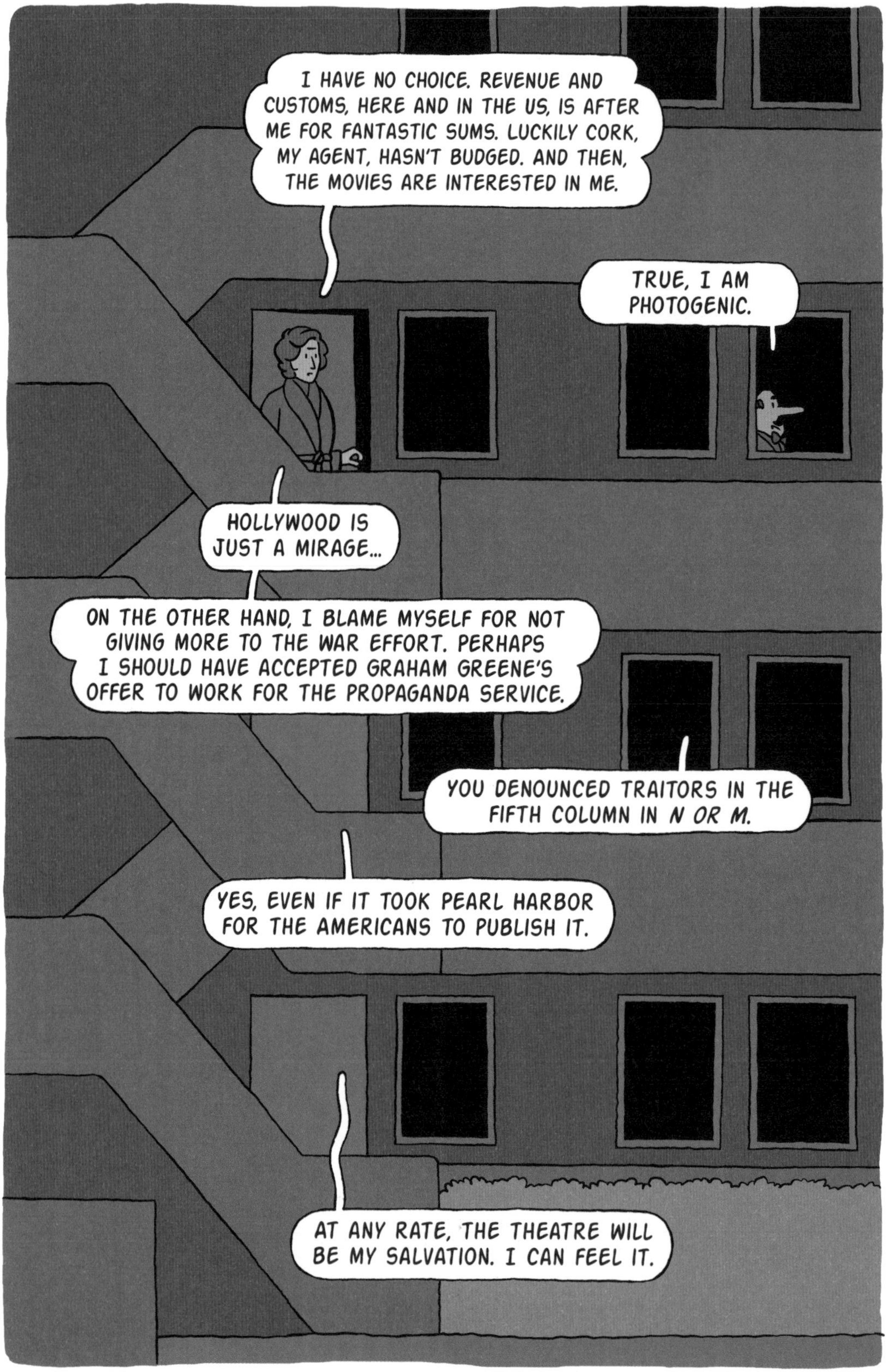
I HAVE NO CHOICE. REVENUE AND CUSTOMS, HERE AND IN THE US, IS AFTER ME FOR FANTASTIC SUMS. LUCKILY CORK, MY AGENT, HASN'T BUDGED. AND THEN, THE MOVIES ARE INTERESTED IN ME.
TRUE, I AM PHOTOGENIC.
HOLLYWOOD IS JUST A MIRAGE...
ON THE OTHER HAND, I BLAME MYSELF FOR NOT GIVING MORE TO THE WAR EFFORT. PERHAPS I SHOULD HAVE ACCEPTED GRAHAM GREENE'S OFFER TO WORK FOR THE PROPAGANDA SERVICE.
YOU DENOUNCED TRAITORS IN THE FIFTH COLUMN IN *N OR M*.
YES, EVEN IF IT TOOK PEARL HARBOR FOR THE AMERICANS TO PUBLISH IT.
AT ANY RATE, THE THEATRE WILL BE MY SALVATION. I CAN FEEL IT.

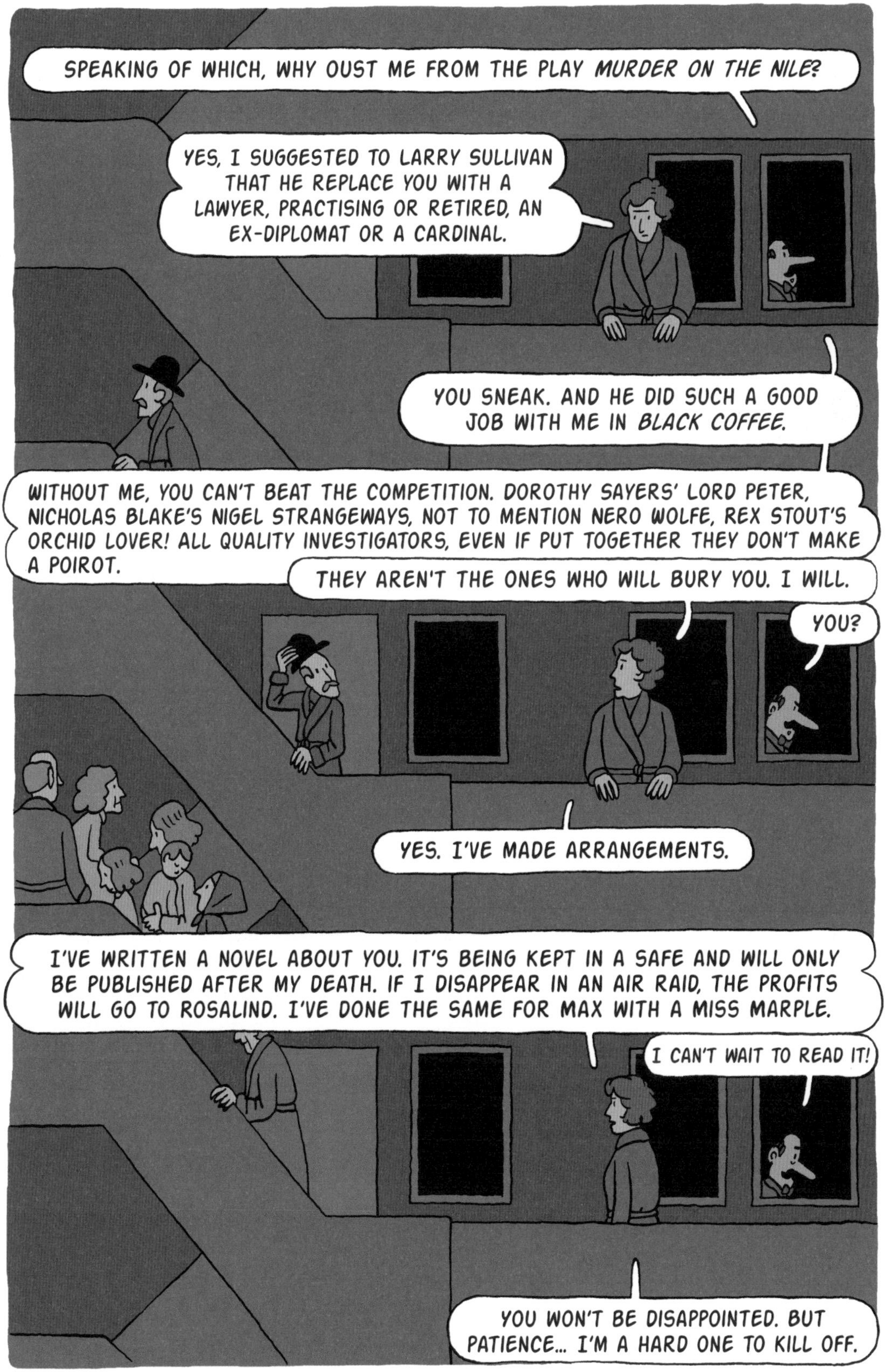
SPEAKING OF WHICH, WHY OUST ME FROM THE PLAY *MURDER ON THE NILE*?
YES, I SUGGESTED TO LARRY SULLIVAN THAT HE REPLACE YOU WITH A LAWYER, PRACTISING OR RETIRED, AN EX-DIPLOMAT OR A CARDINAL.
YOU SNEAK. AND HE DID SUCH A GOOD JOB WITH ME IN *BLACK COFFEE*.
WITHOUT ME, YOU CAN'T BEAT THE COMPETITION. DOROTHY SAYERS' LORD PETER, NICHOLAS BLAKE'S NIGEL STRANGEWAYS, NOT TO MENTION NERO WOLFE, REX STOUT'S ORCHID LOVER! ALL QUALITY INVESTIGATORS, EVEN IF PUT TOGETHER THEY DON'T MAKE A POIROT.
THEY AREN'T THE ONES WHO WILL BURY YOU. I WILL.
YOU?
YES. I'VE MADE ARRANGEMENTS.
I'VE WRITTEN A NOVEL ABOUT YOU. IT'S BEING KEPT IN A SAFE AND WILL ONLY BE PUBLISHED AFTER MY DEATH. IF I DISAPPEAR IN AN AIR RAID, THE PROFITS WILL GO TO ROSALIND. I'VE DONE THE SAME FOR MAX WITH A MISS MARPLE.
I CAN'T WAIT TO READ IT!
YOU WON'T BE DISAPPOINTED. BUT PATIENCE... I'M A HARD ONE TO KILL OFF.

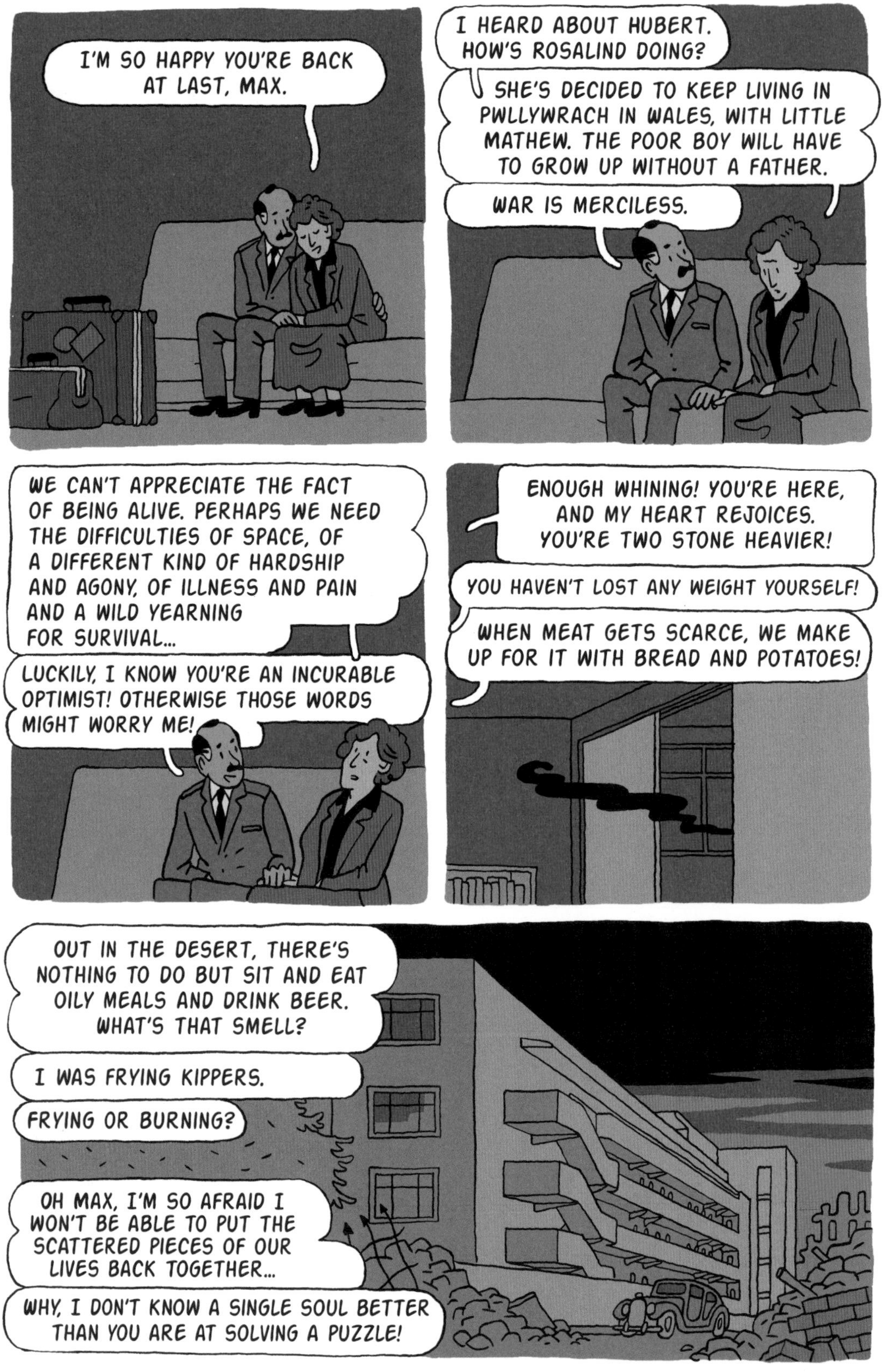
I'M SO HAPPY YOU'RE BACK AT LAST, MAX.
I HEARD ABOUT HUBERT. HOW'S ROSALIND DOING?
SHE'S DECIDED TO KEEP LIVING IN PWLLYWRACH IN WALES, WITH LITTLE MATHEW. THE POOR BOY WILL HAVE TO GROW UP WITHOUT A FATHER.
WAR IS MERCILESS.
WE CAN'T APPRECIATE THE FACT OF BEING ALIVE. PERHAPS WE NEED THE DIFFICULTIES OF SPACE, OF A DIFFERENT KIND OF HARDSHIP AND AGONY, OF ILLNESS AND PAIN AND A WILD YEARNING FOR SURVIVAL...
LUCKILY, I KNOW YOU'RE AN INCURABLE OPTIMIST! OTHERWISE THOSE WORDS MIGHT WORRY ME!
ENOUGH WHINING! YOU'RE HERE, AND MY HEART REJOICES. YOU'RE TWO STONE HEAVIER!
YOU HAVEN'T LOST ANY WEIGHT YOURSELF!
WHEN MEAT GETS SCARCE, WE MAKE UP FOR IT WITH BREAD AND POTATOES!
OUT IN THE DESERT, THERE'S NOTHING TO DO BUT SIT AND EAT OILY MEALS AND DRINK BEER. WHAT'S THAT SMELL?
I WAS FRYING KIPPERS.
FRYING OR BURNING?
OH MAX, I'M SO AFRAID I WON'T BE ABLE TO PUT THE SCATTERED PIECES OF OUR LIVES BACK TOGETHER...
WHY, I DON'T KNOW A SINGLE SOUL BETTER THAN YOU ARE AT SOLVING A PUZZLE!

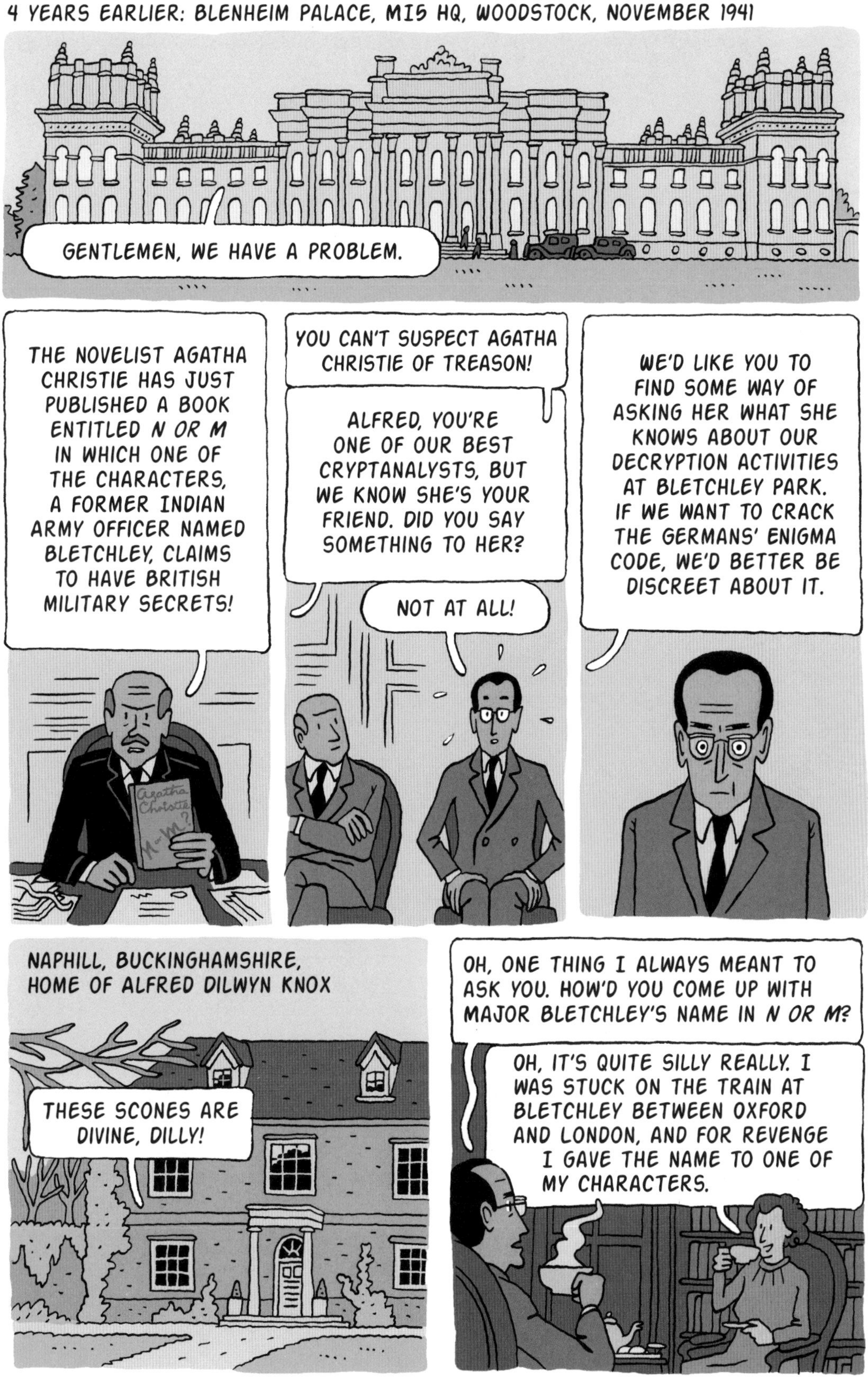
4 YEARS EARLIER: BLENHEIM PALACE, MI5 HQ, WOODSTOCK, NOVEMBER 1941
GENTLEMEN, WE HAVE A PROBLEM.
THE NOVELIST AGATHA CHRISTIE HAS JUST PUBLISHED A BOOK ENTITLED *N OR M* IN WHICH ONE OF THE CHARACTERS, A FORMER INDIAN ARMY OFFICER NAMED BLETCHLEY, CLAIMS TO HAVE BRITISH MILITARY SECRETS!
Agatha Christie N or M?
YOU CAN'T SUSPECT AGATHA CHRISTIE OF TREASON!
ALFRED, YOU'RE ONE OF OUR BEST CRYPTANALYSTS, BUT WE KNOW SHE'S YOUR FRIEND. DID YOU SAY SOMETHING TO HER?
NOT AT ALL!
WE'D LIKE YOU TO FIND SOME WAY OF ASKING HER WHAT SHE KNOWS ABOUT OUR DECRYPTION ACTIVITIES AT BLETCHLEY PARK. IF WE WANT TO CRACK THE GERMANS' ENIGMA CODE, WE'D BETTER BE DISCREET ABOUT IT.
NAPHILL, BUCKINGHAMSHIRE, HOME OF ALFRED DILWYN KNOX
THESE SCONES ARE DIVINE, DILLY!
OH, ONE THING I ALWAYS MEANT TO ASK YOU. HOW'D YOU COME UP WITH MAJOR BLETCHLEY'S NAME IN *N OR M*?
OH, IT'S QUITE SILLY REALLY. I WAS STUCK ON THE TRAIN AT BLETCHLEY BETWEEN OXFORD AND LONDON, AND FOR REVENGE I GAVE THE NAME TO ONE OF MY CHARACTERS.

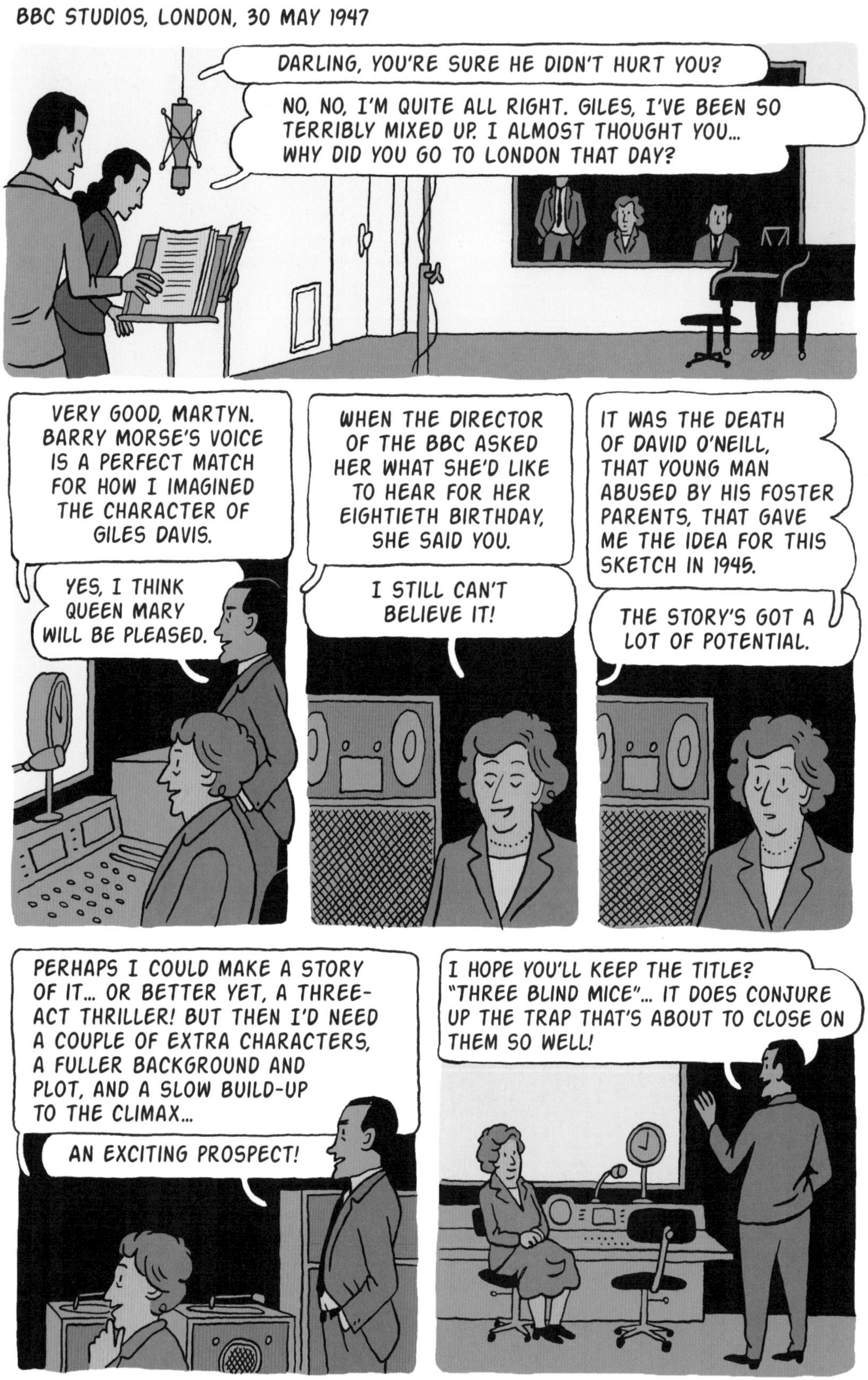
BBC STUDIOS, LONDON, 30 MAY 1947
DARLING, YOU'RE SURE HE DIDN'T HURT YOU?
NO, NO, I'M QUITE ALL RIGHT. GILES, I'VE BEEN SO TERRIBLY MIXED UP. I ALMOST THOUGHT YOU... WHY DID YOU GO TO LONDON THAT DAY?
VERY GOOD, MARTYN. BARRY MORSE'S VOICE IS A PERFECT MATCH FOR HOW I IMAGINED THE CHARACTER OF GILES DAVIS.
YES, I THINK QUEEN MARY WILL BE PLEASED.
WHEN THE DIRECTOR OF THE BBC ASKED HER WHAT SHE'D LIKE TO HEAR FOR HER EIGHTIETH BIRTHDAY, SHE SAID YOU.
I STILL CAN'T BELIEVE IT!
IT WAS THE DEATH OF DAVID O'NEILL, THAT YOUNG MAN ABUSED BY HIS FOSTER PARENTS, THAT GAVE ME THE IDEA FOR THIS SKETCH IN 1945.
THE STORY'S GOT A LOT OF POTENTIAL.
PERHAPS I COULD MAKE A STORY OF IT... OR BETTER YET, A THREE-ACT THRILLER! BUT THEN I'D NEED A COUPLE OF EXTRA CHARACTERS, A FULLER BACKGROUND AND PLOT, AND A SLOW BUILD-UP TO THE CLIMAX...
AN EXCITING PROSPECT!
I HOPE YOU'LL KEEP THE TITLE? "THREE BLIND MICE"... IT DOES CONJURE UP THE TRAP THAT'S ABOUT TO CLOSE ON THEM SO WELL!

GREENWAY HOUSE, AUGUST 1950

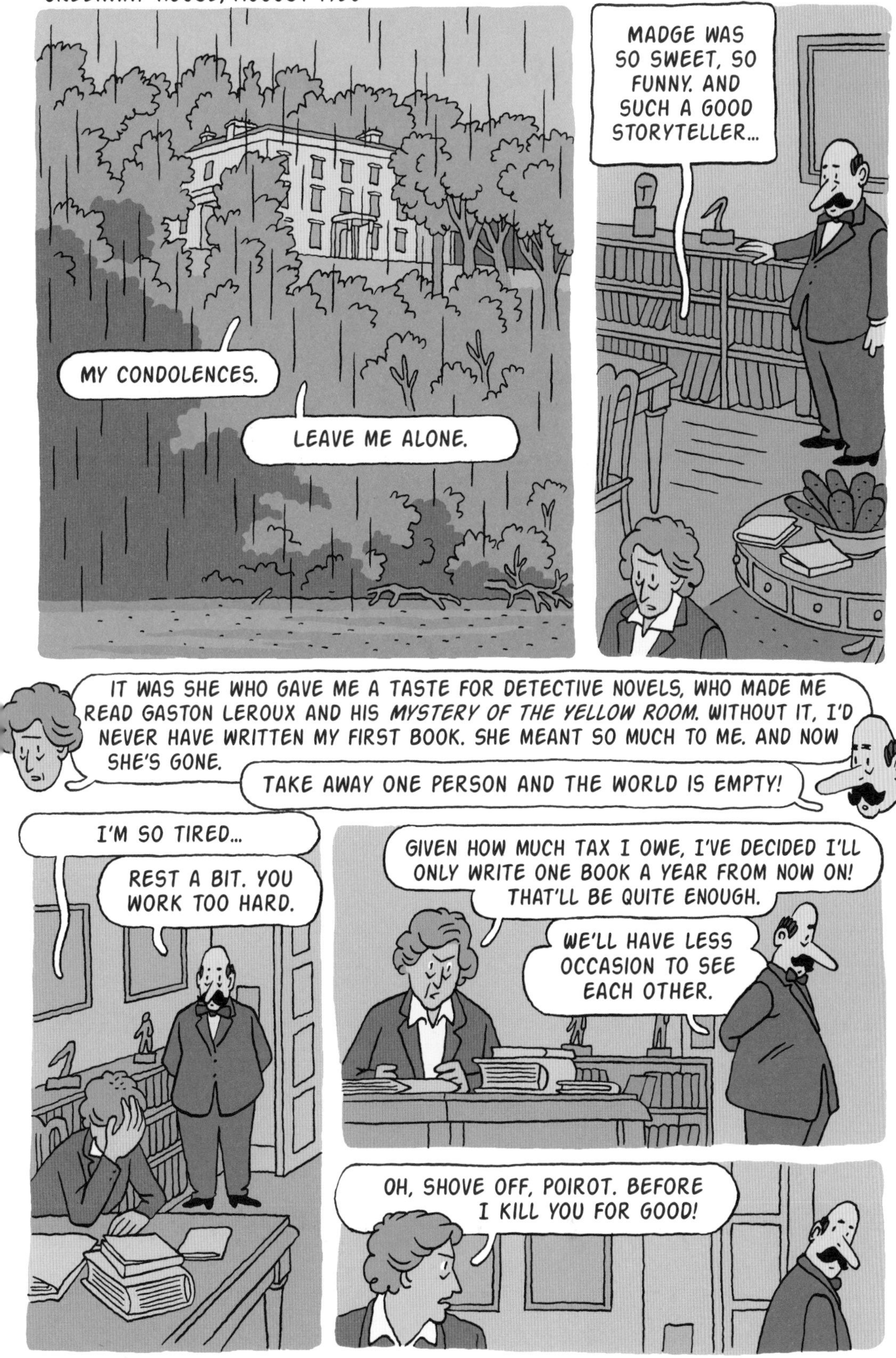
MY CONDOLENCES.
LEAVE ME ALONE.
MADGE WAS SO SWEET, SO FUNNY. AND SUCH A GOOD STORYTELLER...
IT WAS SHE WHO GAVE ME A TASTE FOR DETECTIVE NOVELS, WHO MADE ME READ GASTON LEROUX AND HIS *MYSTERY OF THE YELLOW ROOM*. WITHOUT IT, I'D NEVER HAVE WRITTEN MY FIRST BOOK. SHE MEANT SO MUCH TO ME. AND NOW SHE'S GONE.
TAKE AWAY ONE PERSON AND THE WORLD IS EMPTY!
I'M SO TIRED...
REST A BIT. YOU WORK TOO HARD.
GIVEN HOW MUCH TAX I OWE, I'VE DECIDED I'LL ONLY WRITE ONE BOOK A YEAR FROM NOW ON! THAT'LL BE QUITE ENOUGH.
WE'LL HAVE LESS OCCASION TO SEE EACH OTHER.
OH, SHOVE OFF, POIROT. BEFORE I KILL YOU FOR GOOD!

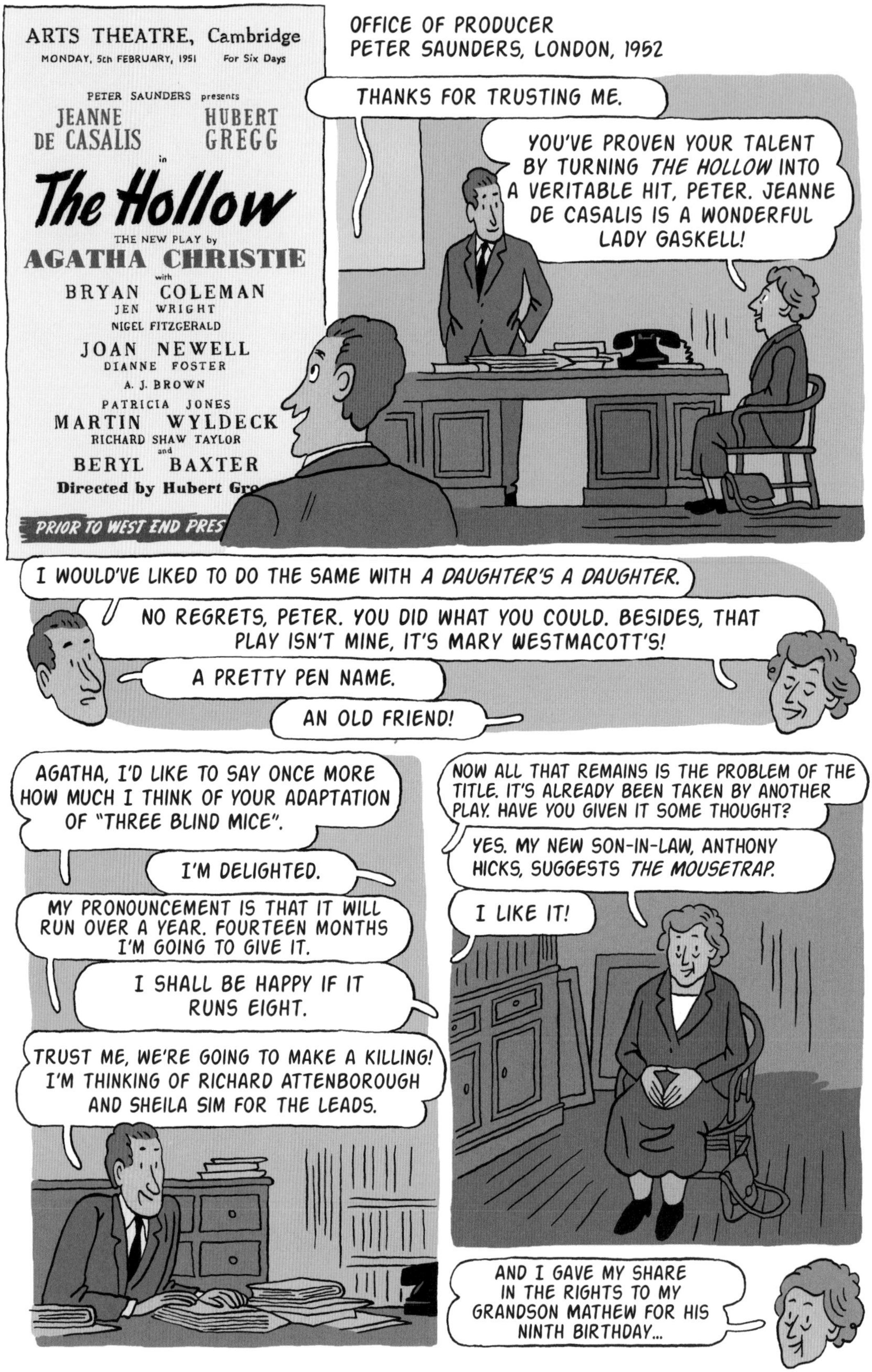
ARTS THEATRE, Cambridge
MONDAY, 5th FEBRUARY, 1951 For Six Days
PETER SAUNDERS presents
JEANNE DE CASALIS
HUBERT GREGG
in
The Hollow
THE NEW PLAY by
AGATHA CHRISTIE
with
BRYAN COLEMAN
JEN WRIGHT
NIGEL FITZGERALD
JOAN NEWELL
DIANNE FOSTER
A. J. BROWN
PATRICIA JONES
MARTIN WYLDECK
RICHARD SHAW TAYLOR
and
BERYL BAXTER
Directed by Hubert Gr
PRIOR TO WEST END PRES
OFFICE OF PRODUCER PETER SAUNDERS, LONDON, 1952
THANKS FOR TRUSTING ME.
YOU'VE PROVEN YOUR TALENT BY TURNING *THE HOLLOW* INTO A VERITABLE HIT, PETER. JEANNE DE CASALIS IS A WONDERFUL LADY GASKELL!
I WOULD'VE LIKED TO DO THE SAME WITH *A DAUGHTER'S A DAUGHTER*.
NO REGRETS, PETER. YOU DID WHAT YOU COULD. BESIDES, THAT PLAY ISN'T MINE, IT'S MARY WESTMACOTT'S!
A PRETTY PEN NAME.
AN OLD FRIEND!
AGATHA, I'D LIKE TO SAY ONCE MORE HOW MUCH I THINK OF YOUR ADAPTATION OF "THREE BLIND MICE".
I'M DELIGHTED.
MY PRONOUNCEMENT IS THAT IT WILL RUN OVER A YEAR. FOURTEEN MONTHS I'M GOING TO GIVE IT.
I SHALL BE HAPPY IF IT RUNS EIGHT.
TRUST ME, WE'RE GOING TO MAKE A KILLING! I'M THINKING OF RICHARD ATTENBOROUGH AND SHEILA SIM FOR THE LEADS.
NOW ALL THAT REMAINS IS THE PROBLEM OF THE TITLE. IT'S ALREADY BEEN TAKEN BY ANOTHER PLAY. HAVE YOU GIVEN IT SOME THOUGHT?
YES. MY NEW SON-IN-LAW, ANTHONY HICKS, SUGGESTS *THE MOUSETRAP*.
I LIKE IT!
AND I GAVE MY SHARE IN THE RIGHTS TO MY GRANDSON MATHEW FOR HIS NINTH BIRTHDAY...

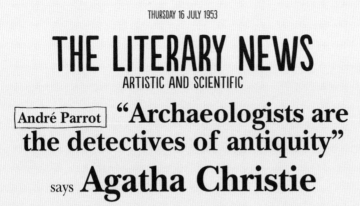

THE LITERARY NEWS

ARTISTIC AND SCIENTIFIC

André Parrot "Archaeologists are the detectives of antiquity"

says **Agatha Christie**

(…) Agatha Christie, archaeologist? Now there's an unexpected and hitherto unknown, but nevertheless utterly true, side to that woman, one of the world's most famous writers. (…) If we sometimes try to form a portrait of an author from their writings, I highly doubt we would suspect that great lady, with her silken hair, velvet eyes and extraordinarily fine lips – that lady whose magnificently mezzo voice is all too rarely heard, though from time to time it expresses itself in a brief remark often punctuated by a crystalline laugh – of being that enchantress who weaves the threads of her plots so well that we cannot untangle them except with her help, and only at the very end.

(…) Shortly after seeing Ur for the first time, Agatha Christie, who has since become Mrs Mallowan, made her debut as an archaeologist on the site at Nineveh. When I remarked that the experience must have changed her greatly, she immediately replied, "Not at all, archaeologists are the detectives of antiquity."

"But they're four thousand years too late. That must complicate the investigation."

"True, but the techniques are similar. In both cases, one must know how to look closely and take everything in. My husband was the one who taught me to walk while looking at my feet, since archaeologists always walk like that to gather shards."

"And that's how you see the traces a murderer leaves behind…"

F.L. Mallowan and his team

LA ROTISSERIE PÉRIGOURDINE, PARIS, NOVEMBER 1955

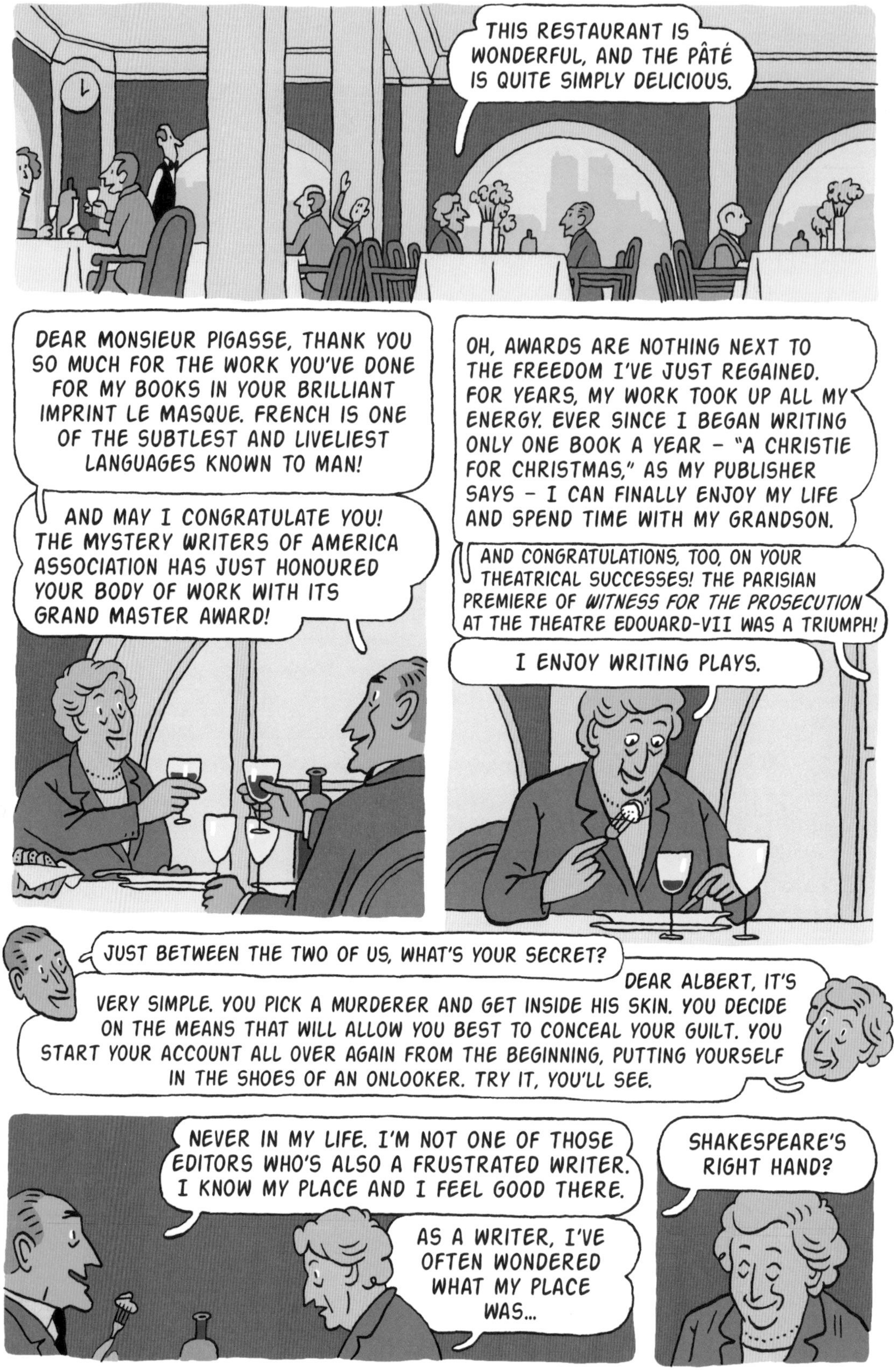
THIS RESTAURANT IS WONDERFUL, AND THE PÂTÉ IS QUITE SIMPLY DELICIOUS.
DEAR MONSIEUR PIGASSE, THANK YOU SO MUCH FOR THE WORK YOU'VE DONE FOR MY BOOKS IN YOUR BRILLIANT IMPRINT LE MASQUE. FRENCH IS ONE OF THE SUBTLEST AND LIVELIEST LANGUAGES KNOWN TO MAN!
AND MAY I CONGRATULATE YOU! THE MYSTERY WRITERS OF AMERICA ASSOCIATION HAS JUST HONOURED YOUR BODY OF WORK WITH ITS GRAND MASTER AWARD!
OH, AWARDS ARE NOTHING NEXT TO THE FREEDOM I'VE JUST REGAINED. FOR YEARS, MY WORK TOOK UP ALL MY ENERGY. EVER SINCE I BEGAN WRITING ONLY ONE BOOK A YEAR – "A CHRISTIE FOR CHRISTMAS," AS MY PUBLISHER SAYS – I CAN FINALLY ENJOY MY LIFE AND SPEND TIME WITH MY GRANDSON.
AND CONGRATULATIONS, TOO, ON YOUR THEATRICAL SUCCESSES! THE PARISIAN PREMIERE OF *WITNESS FOR THE PROSECUTION* AT THE THEATRE EDOUARD-VII WAS A TRIUMPH!
I ENJOY WRITING PLAYS.
JUST BETWEEN THE TWO OF US, WHAT'S YOUR SECRET?
DEAR ALBERT, IT'S VERY SIMPLE. YOU PICK A MURDERER AND GET INSIDE HIS SKIN. YOU DECIDE ON THE MEANS THAT WILL ALLOW YOU BEST TO CONCEAL YOUR GUILT. YOU START YOUR ACCOUNT ALL OVER AGAIN FROM THE BEGINNING, PUTTING YOURSELF IN THE SHOES OF AN ONLOOKER. TRY IT, YOU'LL SEE.
NEVER IN MY LIFE. I'M NOT ONE OF THOSE EDITORS WHO'S ALSO A FRUSTRATED WRITER. I KNOW MY PLACE AND I FEEL GOOD THERE.
AS A WRITER, I'VE OFTEN WONDERED WHAT MY PLACE WAS...
SHAKESPEARE'S RIGHT HAND?

COLORADO, USA, MAY 1956

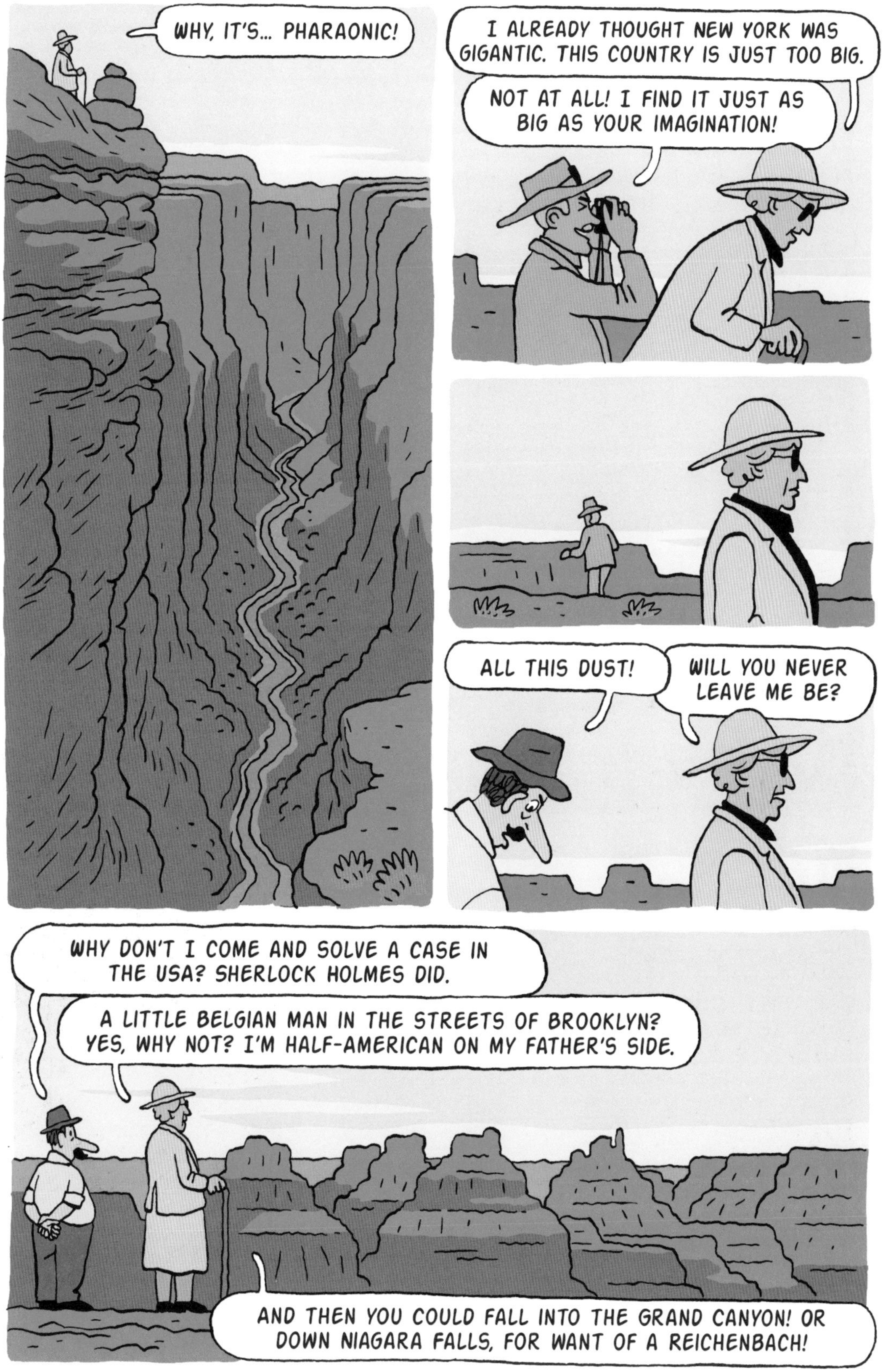
WHY, IT'S... PHARAONIC!
I ALREADY THOUGHT NEW YORK WAS GIGANTIC. THIS COUNTRY IS JUST TOO BIG.
NOT AT ALL! I FIND IT JUST AS BIG AS YOUR IMAGINATION!
ALL THIS DUST!
WILL YOU NEVER LEAVE ME BE?
WHY DON'T I COME AND SOLVE A CASE IN THE USA? SHERLOCK HOLMES DID.
A LITTLE BELGIAN MAN IN THE STREETS OF BROOKLYN? YES, WHY NOT? I'M HALF-AMERICAN ON MY FATHER'S SIDE.
AND THEN YOU COULD FALL INTO THE GRAND CANYON! OR DOWN NIAGARA FALLS, FOR WANT OF A REICHENBACH!

LOS ANGELES

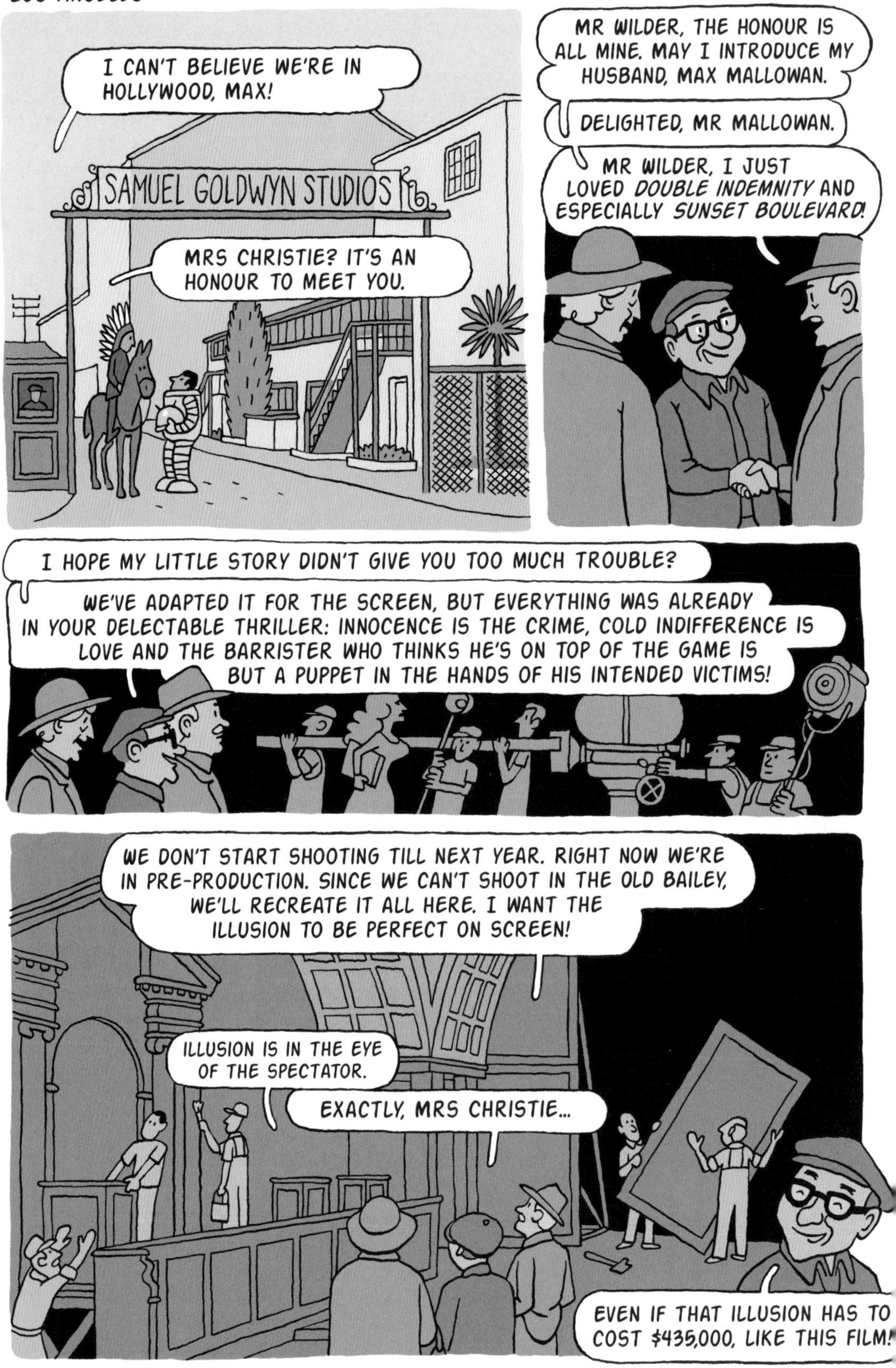
I CAN'T BELIEVE WE'RE IN HOLLYWOOD, MAX!
SAMUEL GOLDWYN STUDIOS
MRS CHRISTIE? IT'S AN HONOUR TO MEET YOU.
MR WILDER, THE HONOUR IS ALL MINE. MAY I INTRODUCE MY HUSBAND, MAX MALLOWAN.
DELIGHTED, MR MALLOWAN.
MR WILDER, I JUST LOVED *DOUBLE INDEMNITY* AND ESPECIALLY *SUNSET BOULEVARD*!
I HOPE MY LITTLE STORY DIDN'T GIVE YOU TOO MUCH TROUBLE?
WE'VE ADAPTED IT FOR THE SCREEN, BUT EVERYTHING WAS ALREADY IN YOUR DELECTABLE THRILLER: INNOCENCE IS THE CRIME, COLD INDIFFERENCE IS LOVE AND THE BARRISTER WHO THINKS HE'S ON TOP OF THE GAME IS BUT A PUPPET IN THE HANDS OF HIS INTENDED VICTIMS!
WE DON'T START SHOOTING TILL NEXT YEAR. RIGHT NOW WE'RE IN PRE-PRODUCTION. SINCE WE CAN'T SHOOT IN THE OLD BAILEY, WE'LL RECREATE IT ALL HERE. I WANT THE ILLUSION TO BE PERFECT ON SCREEN!
ILLUSION IS IN THE EYE OF THE SPECTATOR.
EXACTLY, MRS CHRISTIE...
EVEN IF THAT ILLUSION HAS TO COST $435,000, LIKE THIS FILM!

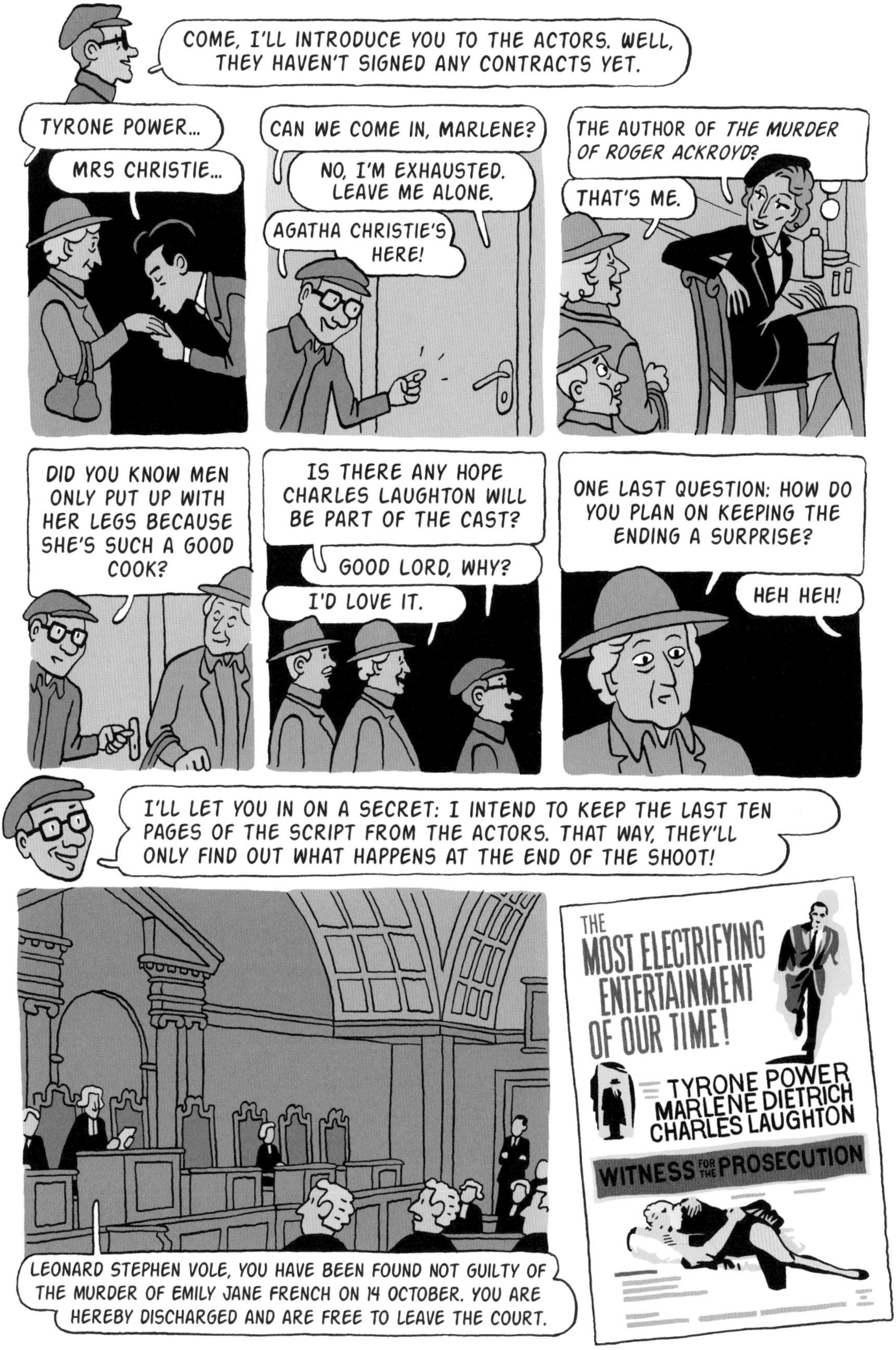
COME, I'LL INTRODUCE YOU TO THE ACTORS. WELL, THEY HAVEN'T SIGNED ANY CONTRACTS YET.
TYRONE POWER...
MRS CHRISTIE...
CAN WE COME IN, MARLENE?
NO, I'M EXHAUSTED. LEAVE ME ALONE.
AGATHA CHRISTIE'S HERE!
THE AUTHOR OF *THE MURDER OF ROGER ACKROYD*?
THAT'S ME.
DID YOU KNOW MEN ONLY PUT UP WITH HER LEGS BECAUSE SHE'S SUCH A GOOD COOK?
IS THERE ANY HOPE CHARLES LAUGHTON WILL BE PART OF THE CAST?
GOOD LORD, WHY?
I'D LOVE IT.
ONE LAST QUESTION: HOW DO YOU PLAN ON KEEPING THE ENDING A SURPRISE?
HEH HEH!
I'LL LET YOU IN ON A SECRET: I INTEND TO KEEP THE LAST TEN PAGES OF THE SCRIPT FROM THE ACTORS. THAT WAY, THEY'LL ONLY FIND OUT WHAT HAPPENS AT THE END OF THE SHOOT!
LEONARD STEPHEN VOLE, YOU HAVE BEEN FOUND NOT GUILTY OF THE MURDER OF EMILY JANE FRENCH ON 14 OCTOBER. YOU ARE HEREBY DISCHARGED AND ARE FREE TO LEAVE THE COURT.
THE MOST ELECTRIFYING ENTERTAINMENT OF OUR TIME!
TYRONE POWER
MARLENE DIETRICH
CHARLES LAUGHTON
WITNESS FOR THE PROSECUTION

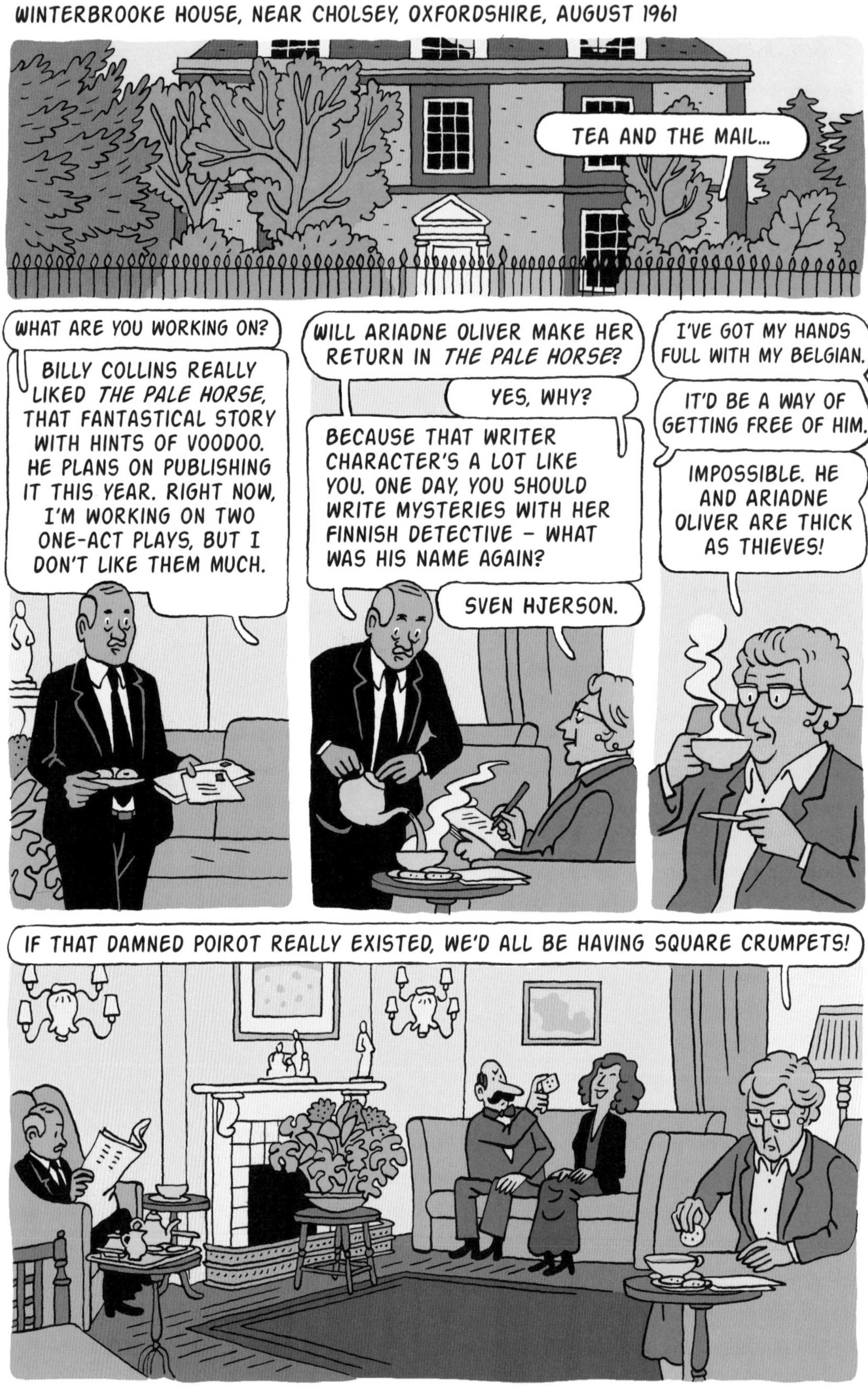
WINTERBROOKE HOUSE, NEAR CHOLSEY, OXFORDSHIRE, AUGUST 1961
TEA AND THE MAIL...
WHAT ARE YOU WORKING ON?
BILLY COLLINS REALLY LIKED *THE PALE HORSE*, THAT FANTASTICAL STORY WITH HINTS OF VOODOO. HE PLANS ON PUBLISHING IT THIS YEAR. RIGHT NOW, I'M WORKING ON TWO ONE-ACT PLAYS, BUT I DON'T LIKE THEM MUCH.
WILL ARIADNE OLIVER MAKE HER RETURN IN *THE PALE HORSE*?
YES, WHY?
BECAUSE THAT WRITER CHARACTER'S A LOT LIKE YOU. ONE DAY, YOU SHOULD WRITE MYSTERIES WITH HER FINNISH DETECTIVE – WHAT WAS HIS NAME AGAIN?
SVEN HJERSON.
I'VE GOT MY HANDS FULL WITH MY BELGIAN.
IT'D BE A WAY OF GETTING FREE OF HIM.
IMPOSSIBLE. HE AND ARIADNE OLIVER ARE THICK AS THIEVES!
IF THAT DAMNED POIROT REALLY EXISTED, WE'D ALL BE HAVING SQUARE CRUMPETS!

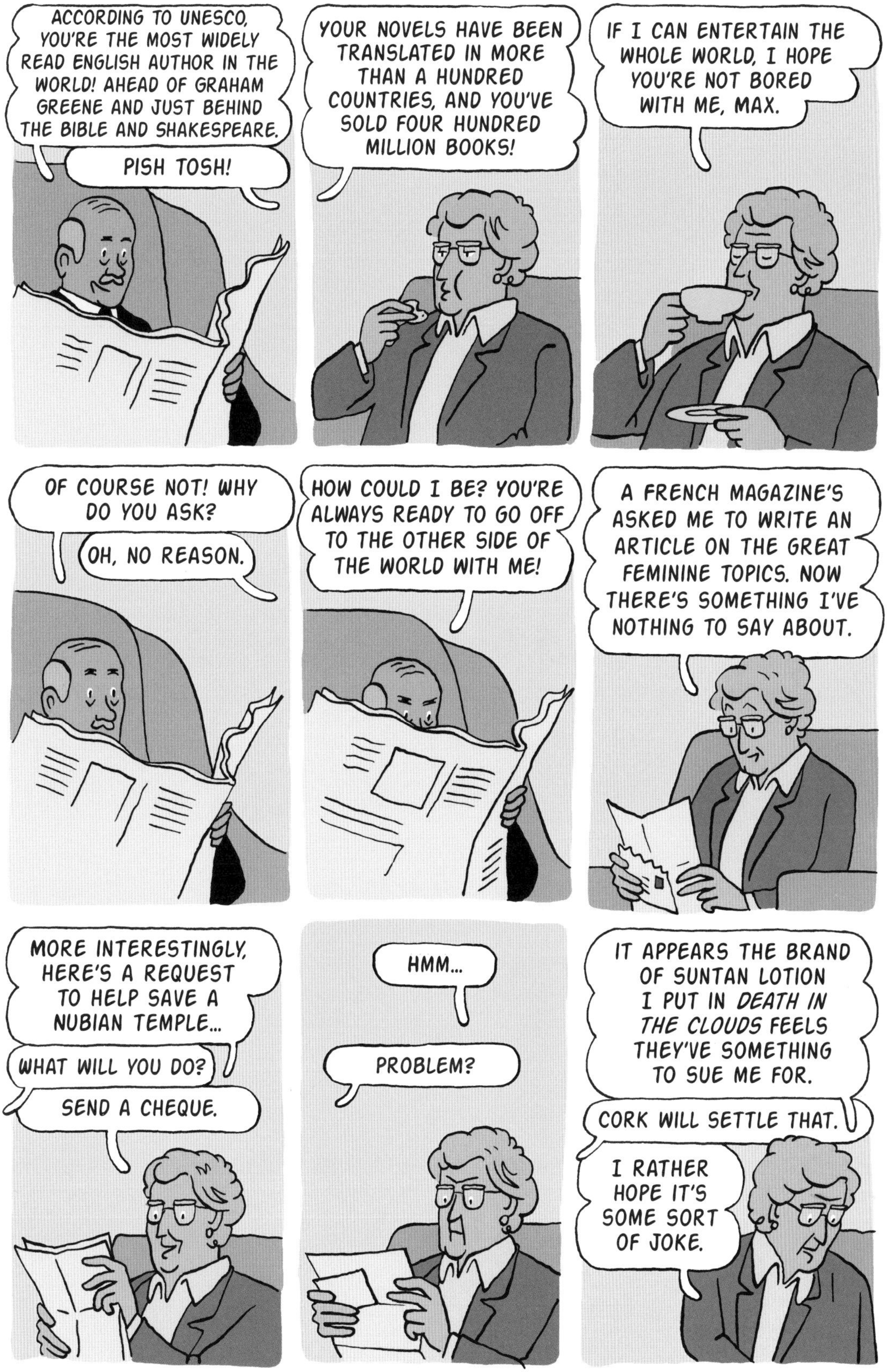
ACCORDING TO UNESCO, YOU'RE THE MOST WIDELY READ ENGLISH AUTHOR IN THE WORLD! AHEAD OF GRAHAM GREENE AND JUST BEHIND THE BIBLE AND SHAKESPEARE.
PISH TOSH!
YOUR NOVELS HAVE BEEN TRANSLATED IN MORE THAN A HUNDRED COUNTRIES, AND YOU'VE SOLD FOUR HUNDRED MILLION BOOKS!
IF I CAN ENTERTAIN THE WHOLE WORLD, I HOPE YOU'RE NOT BORED WITH ME, MAX.
OF COURSE NOT! WHY DO YOU ASK?
OH, NO REASON.
HOW COULD I BE? YOU'RE ALWAYS READY TO GO OFF TO THE OTHER SIDE OF THE WORLD WITH ME!
A FRENCH MAGAZINE'S ASKED ME TO WRITE AN ARTICLE ON THE GREAT FEMININE TOPICS. NOW THERE'S SOMETHING I'VE NOTHING TO SAY ABOUT.
MORE INTERESTINGLY, HERE'S A REQUEST TO HELP SAVE A NUBIAN TEMPLE...
WHAT WILL YOU DO?
SEND A CHEQUE.
HMM...
PROBLEM?
IT APPEARS THE BRAND OF SUNTAN LOTION I PUT IN *DEATH IN THE CLOUDS* FEELS THEY'VE SOMETHING TO SUE ME FOR.
CORK WILL SETTLE THAT.
I RATHER HOPE IT'S SOME SORT OF JOKE.

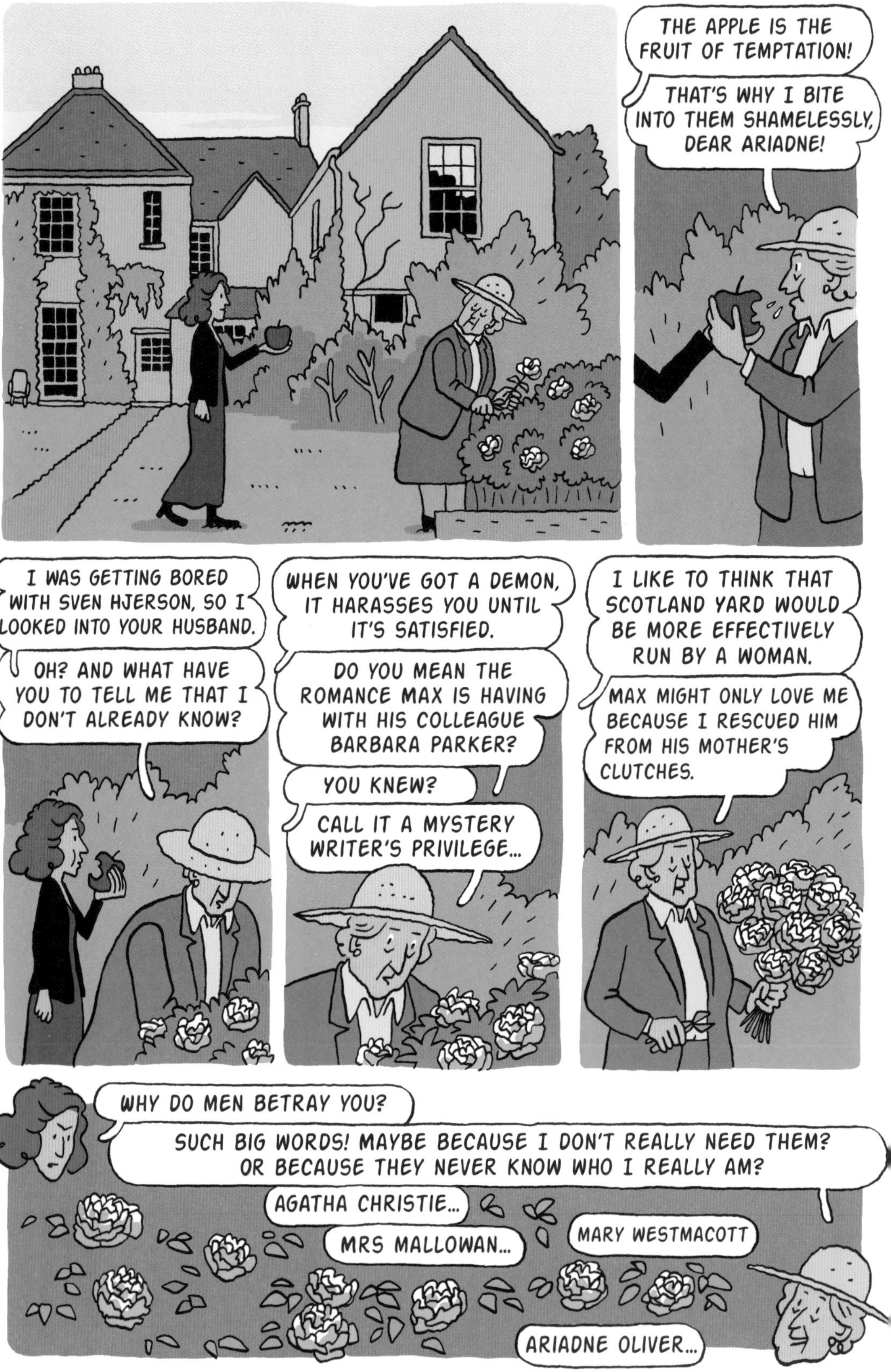
THE APPLE IS THE FRUIT OF TEMPTATION!
THAT'S WHY I BITE INTO THEM SHAMELESSLY, DEAR ARIADNE!
I WAS GETTING BORED WITH SVEN HJERSON, SO I LOOKED INTO YOUR HUSBAND.
OH? AND WHAT HAVE YOU TO TELL ME THAT I DON'T ALREADY KNOW?
WHEN YOU'VE GOT A DEMON, IT HARASSES YOU UNTIL IT'S SATISFIED.
DO YOU MEAN THE ROMANCE MAX IS HAVING WITH HIS COLLEAGUE BARBARA PARKER?
YOU KNEW?
CALL IT A MYSTERY WRITER'S PRIVILEGE...
I LIKE TO THINK THAT SCOTLAND YARD WOULD BE MORE EFFECTIVELY RUN BY A WOMAN.
MAX MIGHT ONLY LOVE ME BECAUSE I RESCUED HIM FROM HIS MOTHER'S CLUTCHES.
WHY DO MEN BETRAY YOU?
SUCH BIG WORDS! MAYBE BECAUSE I DON'T REALLY NEED THEM? OR BECAUSE THEY NEVER KNOW WHO I REALLY AM?
AGATHA CHRISTIE...
MRS MALLOWAN...
MARY WESTMACOTT
ARIADNE OLIVER...

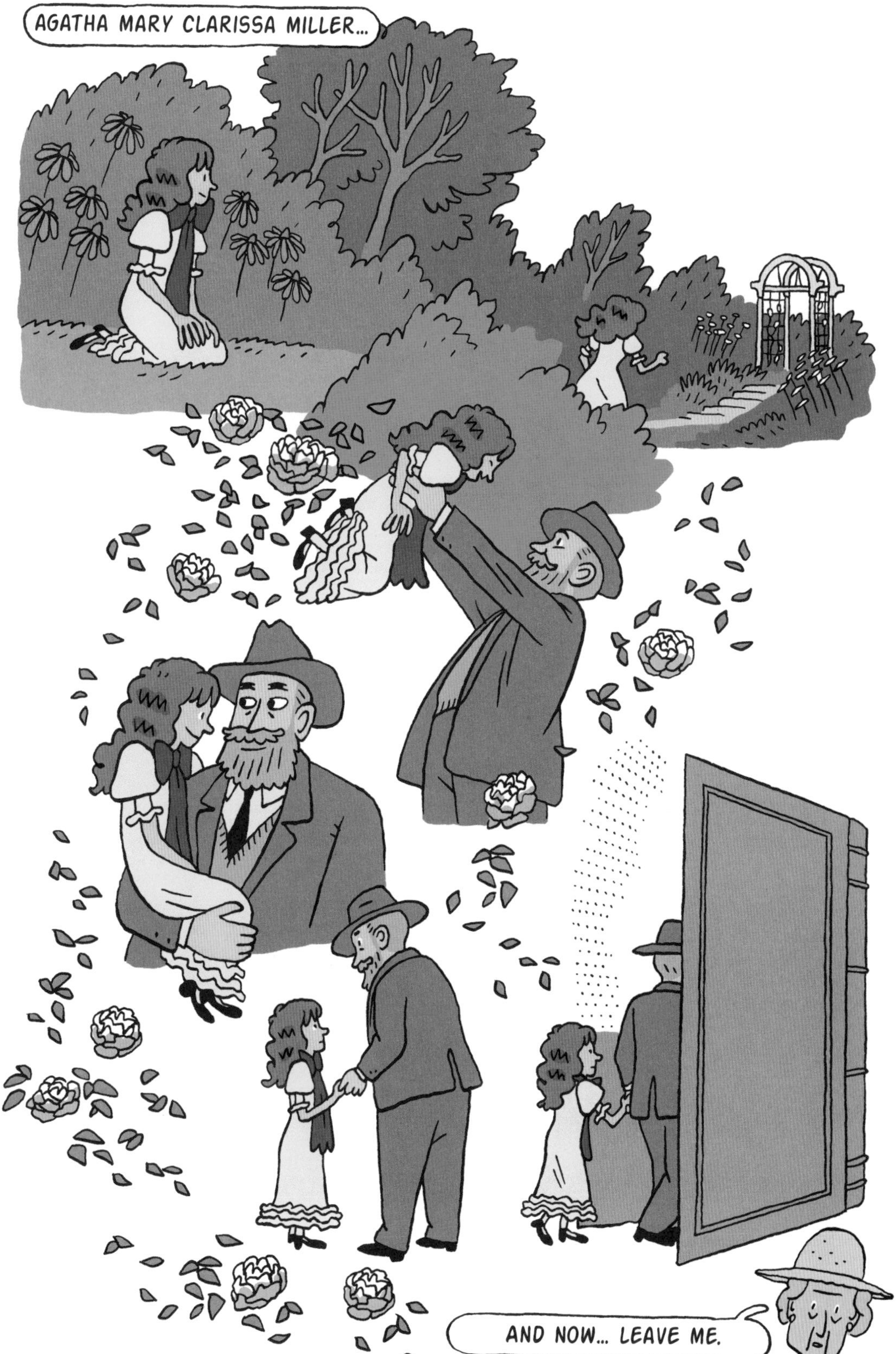
AGATHA MARY CLARISSA MILLER...
AND NOW... LEAVE ME.

WINTERBROOKE HOUSE, 11 OCTOBER 1965

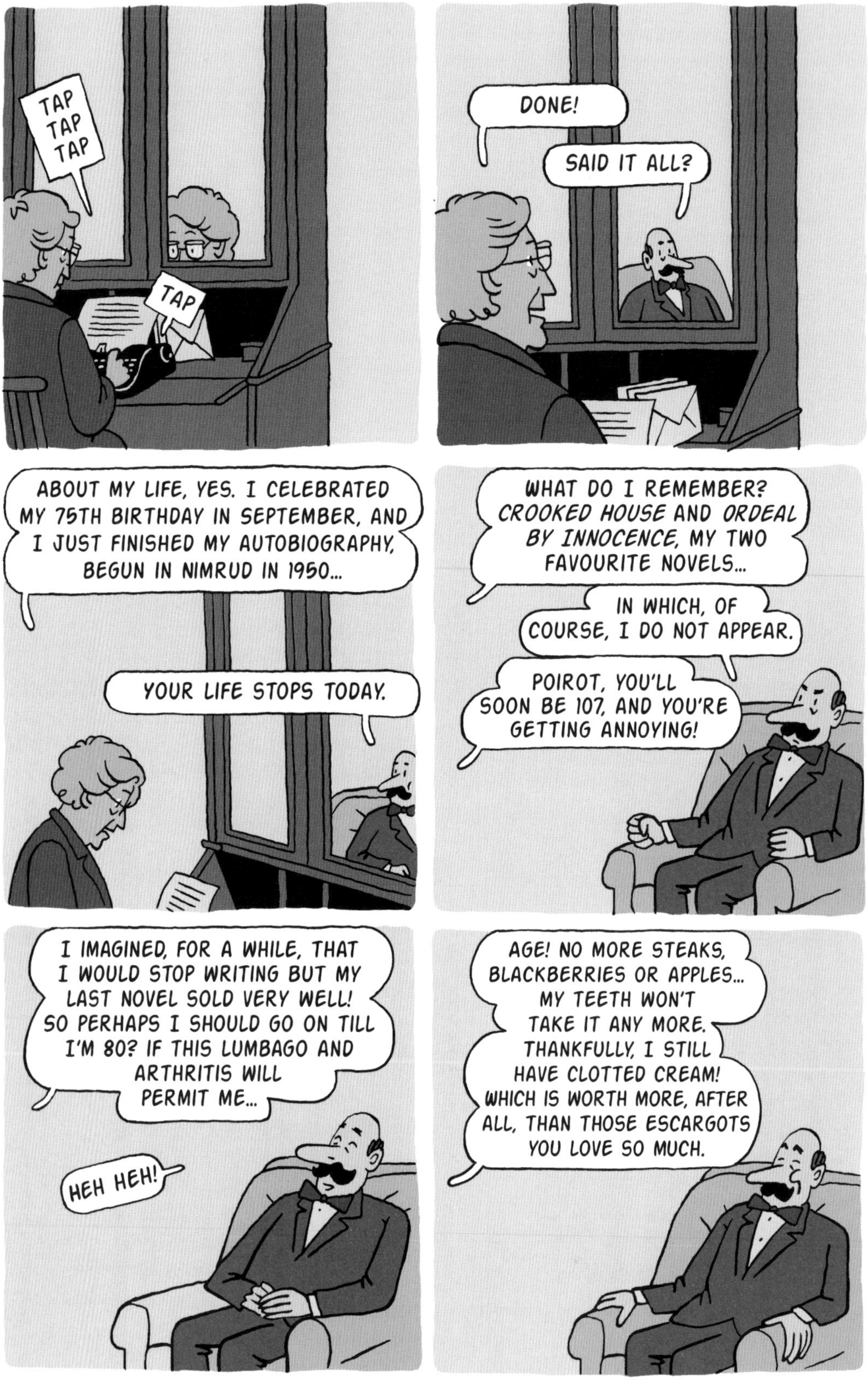
TAP TAP TAP
TAP
DONE!
SAID IT ALL?
ABOUT MY LIFE, YES. I CELEBRATED MY 75TH BIRTHDAY IN SEPTEMBER, AND I JUST FINISHED MY AUTOBIOGRAPHY, BEGUN IN NIMRUD IN 1950...
YOUR LIFE STOPS TODAY.
WHAT DO I REMEMBER? *CROOKED HOUSE* AND *ORDEAL BY INNOCENCE*, MY TWO FAVOURITE NOVELS...
IN WHICH, OF COURSE, I DO NOT APPEAR.
POIROT, YOU'LL SOON BE 107, AND YOU'RE GETTING ANNOYING!
I IMAGINED, FOR A WHILE, THAT I WOULD STOP WRITING BUT MY LAST NOVEL SOLD VERY WELL! SO PERHAPS I SHOULD GO ON TILL I'M 80? IF THIS LUMBAGO AND ARTHRITIS WILL PERMIT ME...
HEH HEH!
AGE! NO MORE STEAKS, BLACKBERRIES OR APPLES... MY TEETH WON'T TAKE IT ANY MORE. THANKFULLY, I STILL HAVE CLOTTED CREAM! WHICH IS WORTH MORE, AFTER ALL, THAN THOSE ESCARGOTS YOU LOVE SO MUCH.

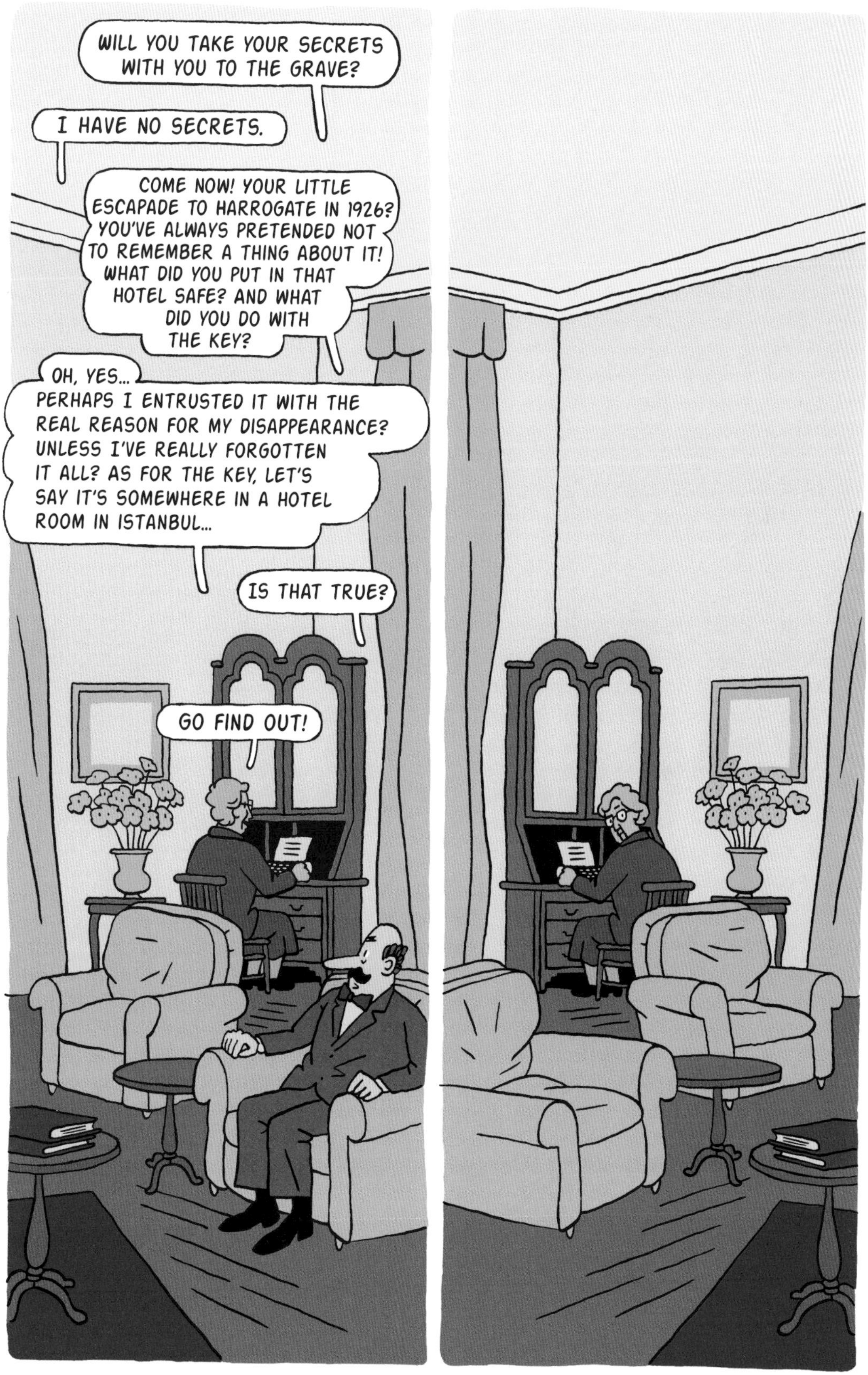

WILL YOU TAKE YOUR SECRETS WITH YOU TO THE GRAVE?
I HAVE NO SECRETS.
COME NOW! YOUR LITTLE ESCAPADE TO HARROGATE IN 1926? YOU'VE ALWAYS PRETENDED NOT TO REMEMBER A THING ABOUT IT! WHAT DID YOU PUT IN THAT HOTEL SAFE? AND WHAT DID YOU DO WITH THE KEY?
OH, YES...
PERHAPS I ENTRUSTED IT WITH THE REAL REASON FOR MY DISAPPEARANCE? UNLESS I'VE REALLY FORGOTTEN IT ALL? AS FOR THE KEY, LET'S SAY IT'S SOMEWHERE IN A HOTEL ROOM IN ISTANBUL...
IS THAT TRUE?
GO FIND OUT!

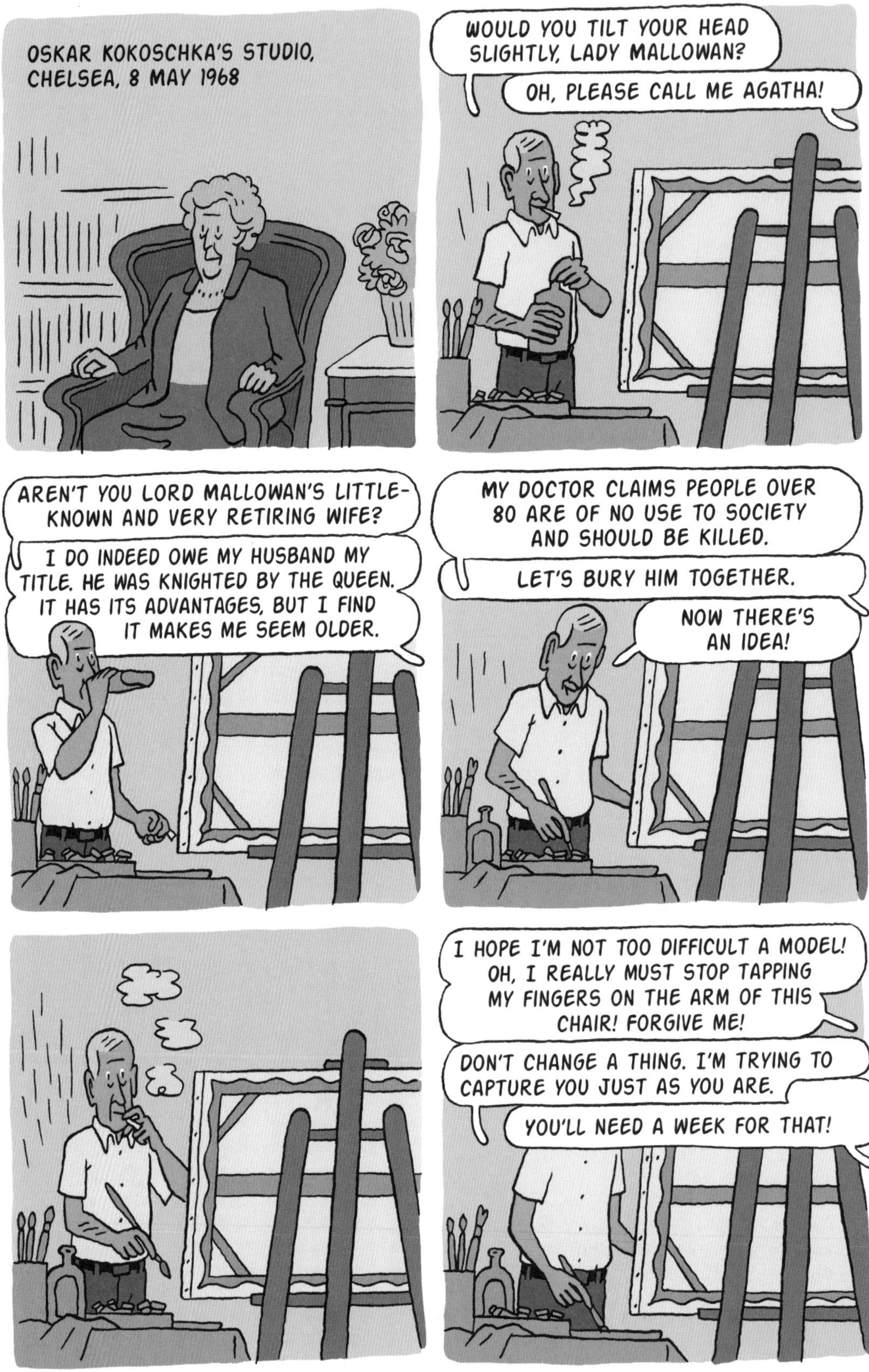
OSKAR KOKOSCHKA'S STUDIO, CHELSEA, 8 MAY 1968
WOULD YOU TILT YOUR HEAD SLIGHTLY, LADY MALLOWAN?
OH, PLEASE CALL ME AGATHA!
AREN'T YOU LORD MALLOWAN'S LITTLE-KNOWN AND VERY RETIRING WIFE?
I DO INDEED OWE MY HUSBAND MY TITLE. HE WAS KNIGHTED BY THE QUEEN. IT HAS ITS ADVANTAGES, BUT I FIND IT MAKES ME SEEM OLDER.
MY DOCTOR CLAIMS PEOPLE OVER 80 ARE OF NO USE TO SOCIETY AND SHOULD BE KILLED.
LET'S BURY HIM TOGETHER.
NOW THERE'S AN IDEA!
I HOPE I'M NOT TOO DIFFICULT A MODEL! OH, I REALLY MUST STOP TAPPING MY FINGERS ON THE ARM OF THIS CHAIR! FORGIVE ME!
DON'T CHANGE A THING. I'M TRYING TO CAPTURE YOU JUST AS YOU ARE.
YOU'LL NEED A WEEK FOR THAT!

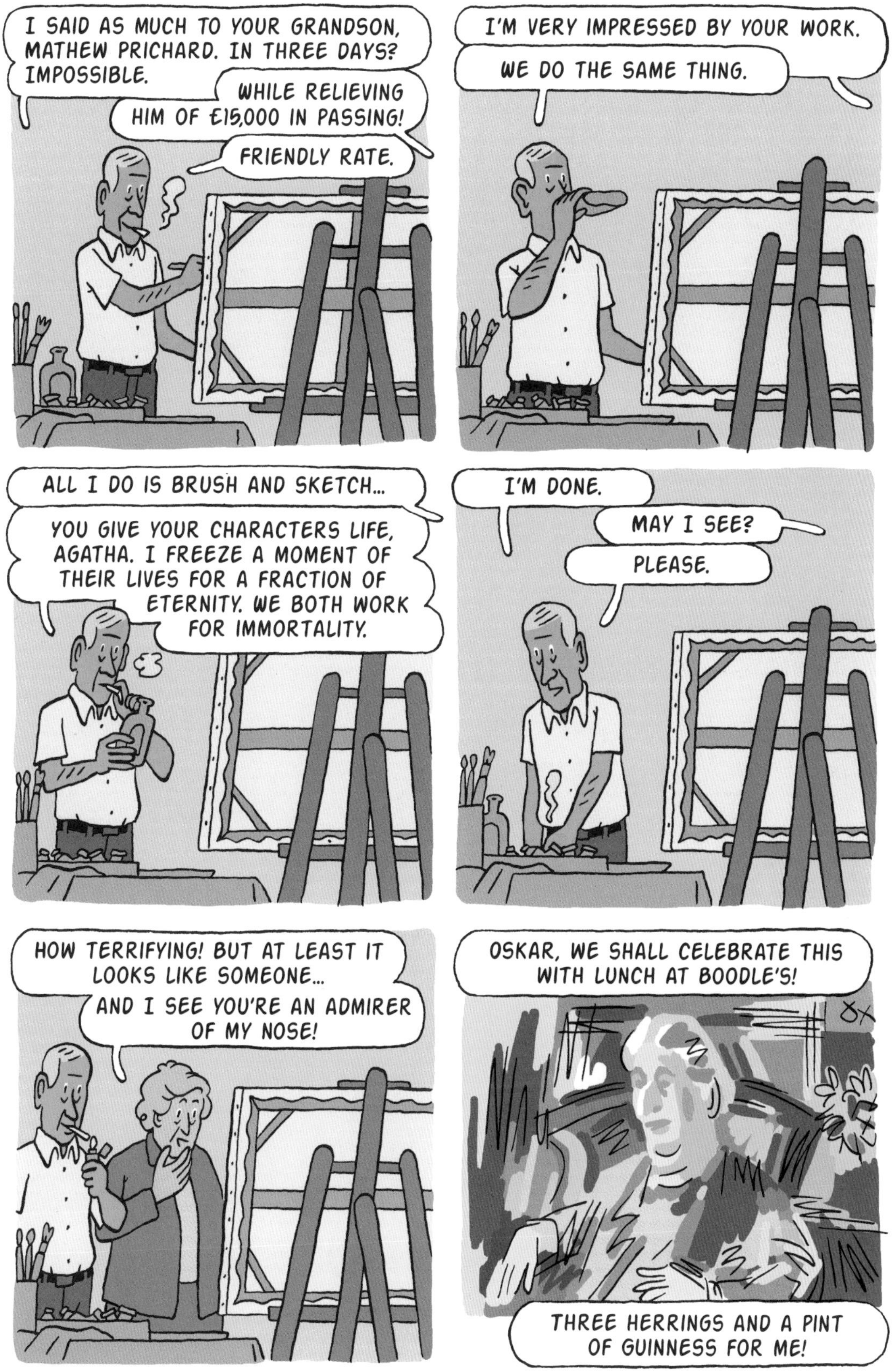
I SAID AS MUCH TO YOUR GRANDSON, MATHEW PRICHARD. IN THREE DAYS? IMPOSSIBLE.
WHILE RELIEVING HIM OF £15,000 IN PASSING!
FRIENDLY RATE.
I'M VERY IMPRESSED BY YOUR WORK.
WE DO THE SAME THING.
ALL I DO IS BRUSH AND SKETCH...
YOU GIVE YOUR CHARACTERS LIFE, AGATHA. I FREEZE A MOMENT OF THEIR LIVES FOR A FRACTION OF ETERNITY. WE BOTH WORK FOR IMMORTALITY.
I'M DONE.
MAY I SEE?
PLEASE.
HOW TERRIFYING! BUT AT LEAST IT LOOKS LIKE SOMEONE...
AND I SEE YOU'RE AN ADMIRER OF MY NOSE!
OSKAR, WE SHALL CELEBRATE THIS WITH LUNCH AT BOODLE'S!
THREE HERRINGS AND A PINT OF GUINNESS FOR ME!

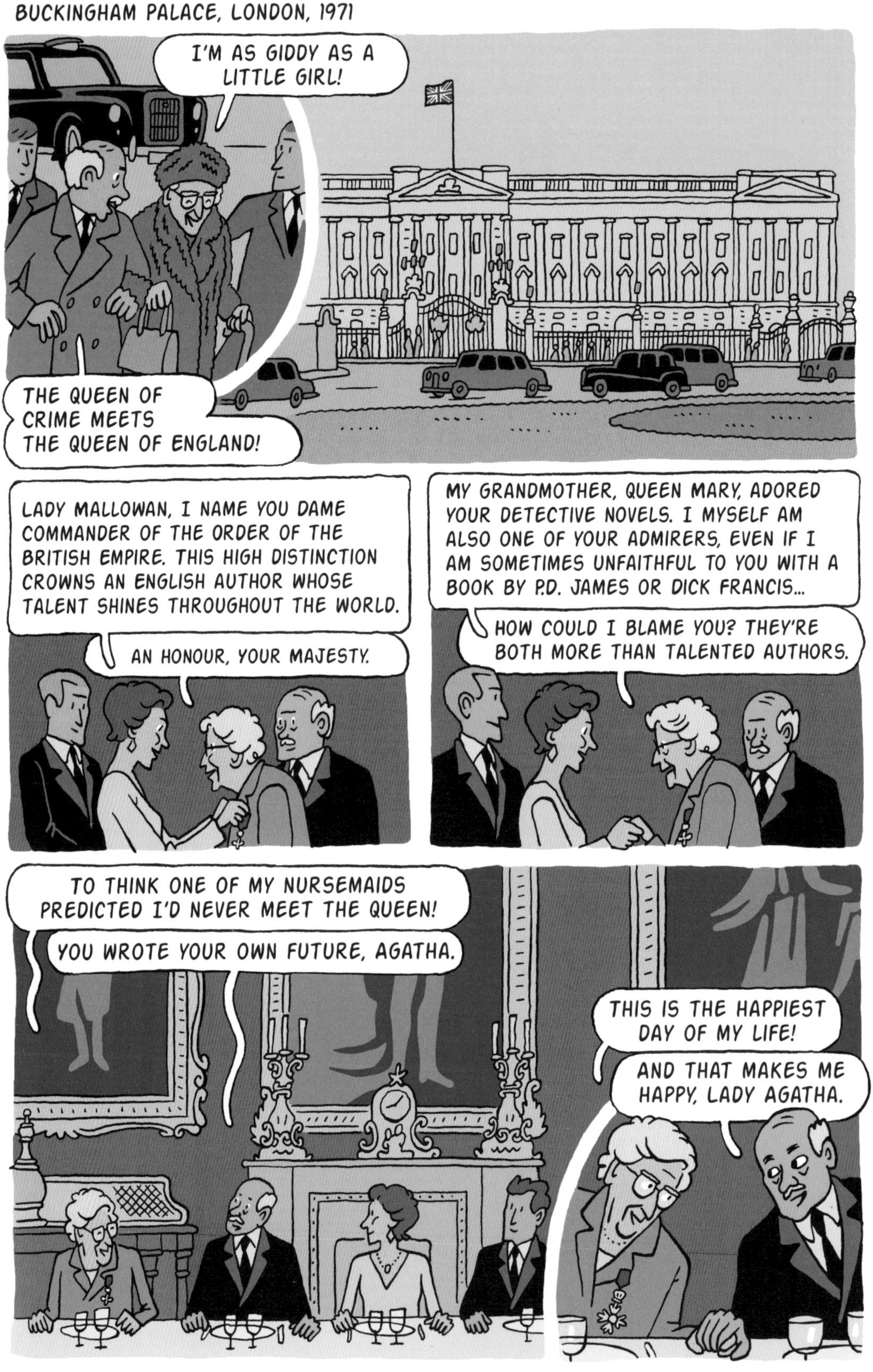
BUCKINGHAM PALACE, LONDON, 1971
I'M AS GIDDY AS A LITTLE GIRL!
THE QUEEN OF CRIME MEETS THE QUEEN OF ENGLAND!
LADY MALLOWAN, I NAME YOU DAME COMMANDER OF THE ORDER OF THE BRITISH EMPIRE. THIS HIGH DISTINCTION CROWNS AN ENGLISH AUTHOR WHOSE TALENT SHINES THROUGHOUT THE WORLD.
AN HONOUR, YOUR MAJESTY.
MY GRANDMOTHER, QUEEN MARY, ADORED YOUR DETECTIVE NOVELS. I MYSELF AM ALSO ONE OF YOUR ADMIRERS, EVEN IF I AM SOMETIMES UNFAITHFUL TO YOU WITH A BOOK BY P.D. JAMES OR DICK FRANCIS...
HOW COULD I BLAME YOU? THEY'RE BOTH MORE THAN TALENTED AUTHORS.
TO THINK ONE OF MY NURSEMAIDS PREDICTED I'D NEVER MEET THE QUEEN!
YOU WROTE YOUR OWN FUTURE, AGATHA.
THIS IS THE HAPPIEST DAY OF MY LIFE!
AND THAT MAKES ME HAPPY, LADY AGATHA.

WINTERBROOKE, FEBRUARY 1971

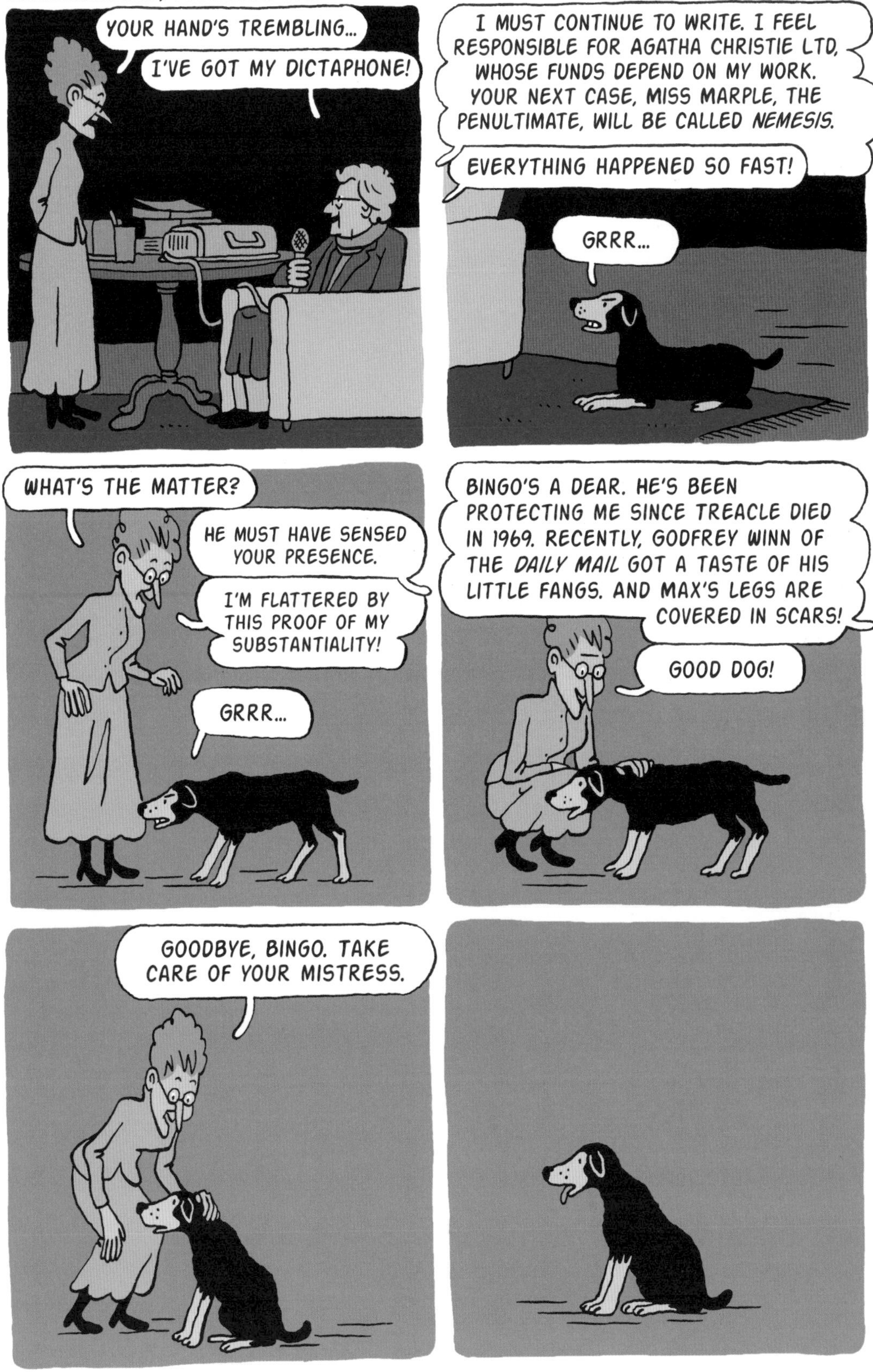
YOUR HAND'S TREMBLING...
I'VE GOT MY DICTAPHONE!
I MUST CONTINUE TO WRITE. I FEEL RESPONSIBLE FOR AGATHA CHRISTIE LTD, WHOSE FUNDS DEPEND ON MY WORK. YOUR NEXT CASE, MISS MARPLE, THE PENULTIMATE, WILL BE CALLED *NEMESIS*.
EVERYTHING HAPPENED SO FAST!
GRRR...
WHAT'S THE MATTER?
HE MUST HAVE SENSED YOUR PRESENCE.
I'M FLATTERED BY THIS PROOF OF MY SUBSTANTIALITY!
GRRR...
BINGO'S A DEAR. HE'S BEEN PROTECTING ME SINCE TREACLE DIED IN 1969. RECENTLY, GODFREY WINN OF THE *DAILY MAIL* GOT A TASTE OF HIS LITTLE FANGS. AND MAX'S LEGS ARE COVERED IN SCARS!
GOOD DOG!
GOODBYE, BINGO. TAKE CARE OF YOUR MISTRESS.

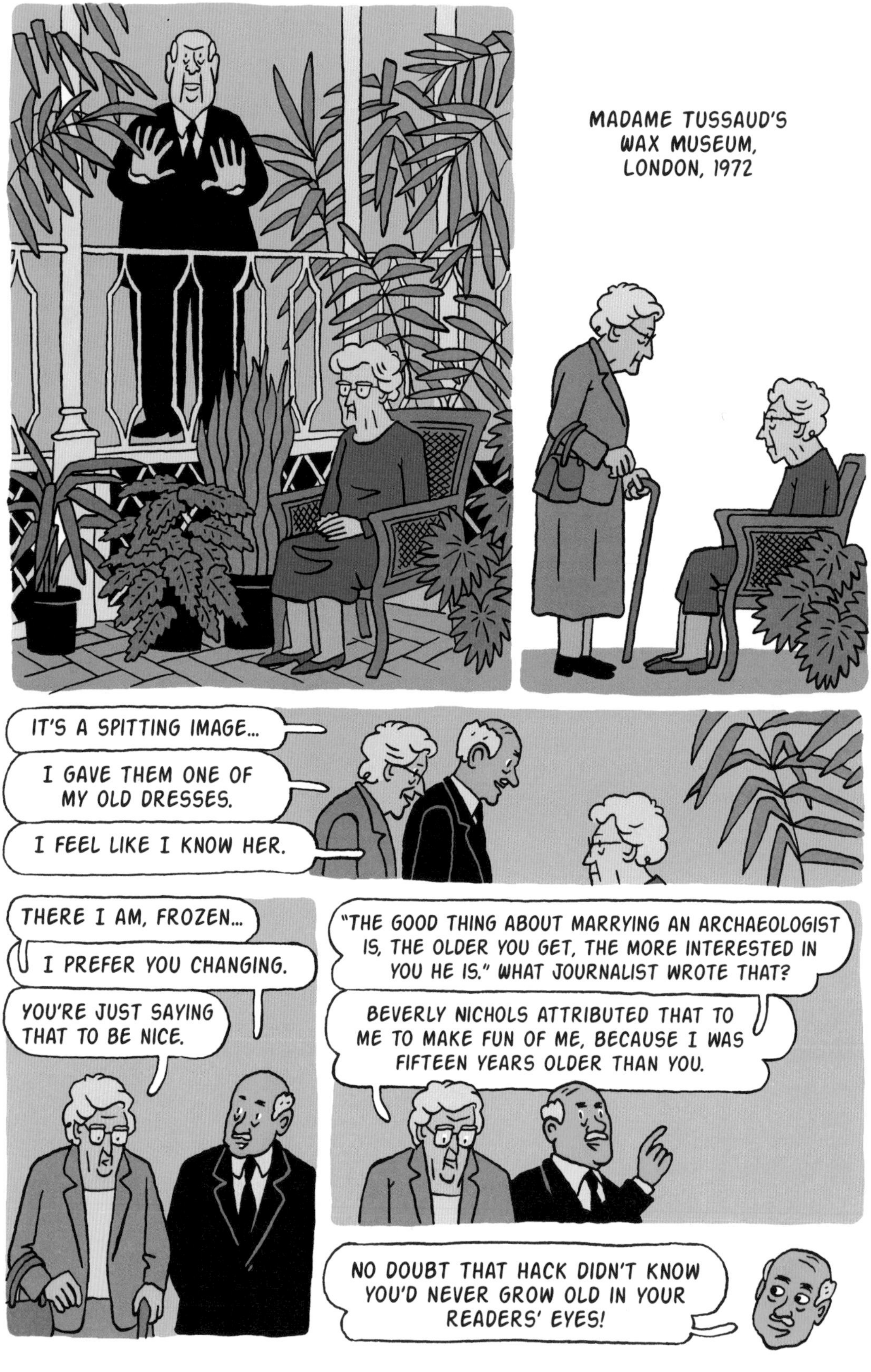
MADAME TUSSAUD'S WAX MUSEUM, LONDON, 1972
IT'S A SPITTING IMAGE...
I GAVE THEM ONE OF MY OLD DRESSES.
I FEEL LIKE I KNOW HER.
THERE I AM, FROZEN...
I PREFER YOU CHANGING.
YOU'RE JUST SAYING THAT TO BE NICE.
"THE GOOD THING ABOUT MARRYING AN ARCHAEOLOGIST IS, THE OLDER YOU GET, THE MORE INTERESTED IN YOU HE IS." WHAT JOURNALIST WROTE THAT?
BEVERLY NICHOLS ATTRIBUTED THAT TO ME TO MAKE FUN OF ME, BECAUSE I WAS FIFTEEN YEARS OLDER THAN YOU.
NO DOUBT THAT HACK DIDN'T KNOW YOU'D NEVER GROW OLD IN YOUR READERS' EYES!

WINTERBROOKE, 1973

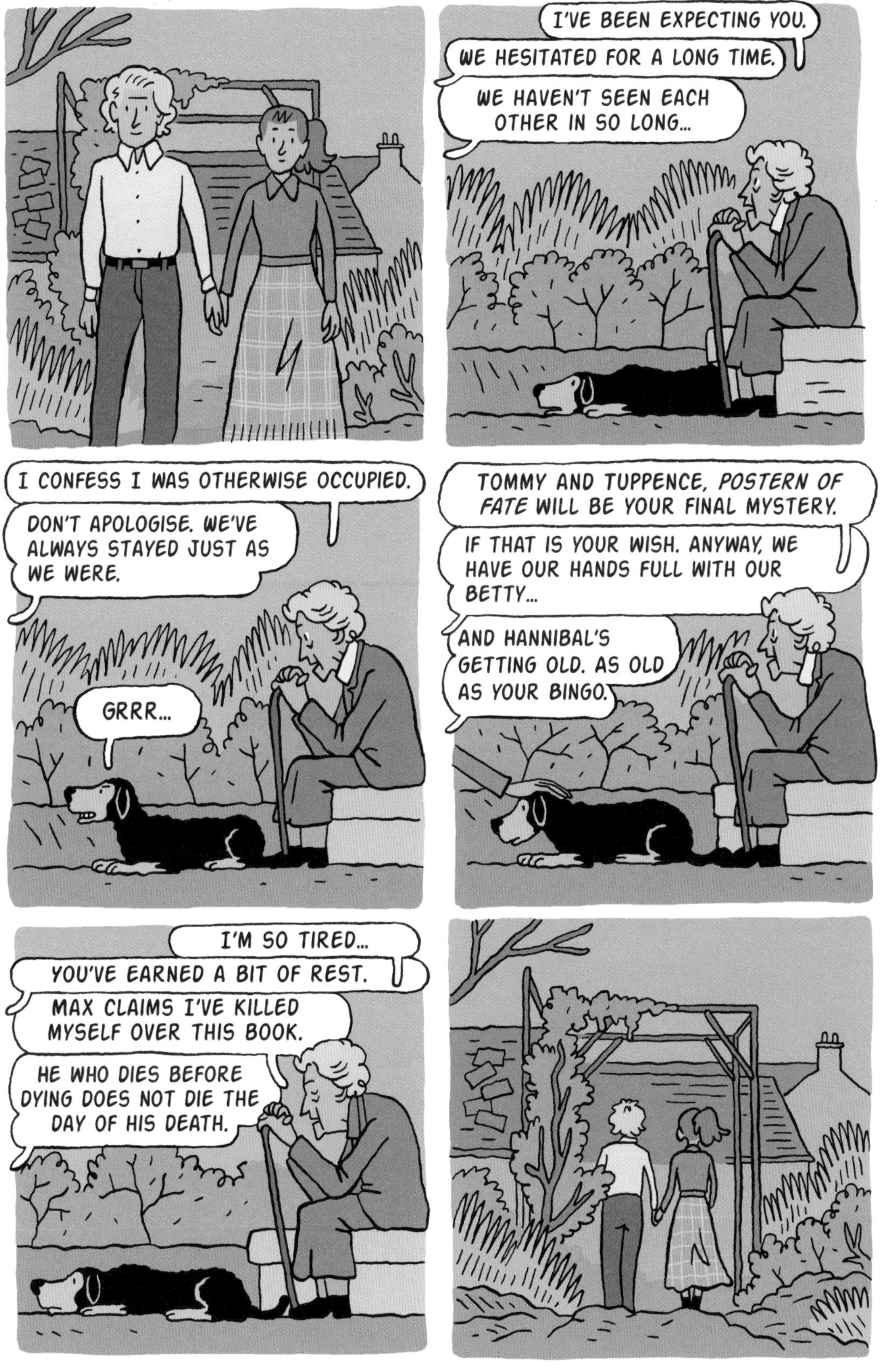

I'VE BEEN EXPECTING YOU.
WE HESITATED FOR A LONG TIME.
WE HAVEN'T SEEN EACH OTHER IN SO LONG...
I CONFESS I WAS OTHERWISE OCCUPIED.
DON'T APOLOGISE. WE'VE ALWAYS STAYED JUST AS WE WERE.
GRRR...
TOMMY AND TUPPENCE, *POSTERN OF FATE* WILL BE YOUR FINAL MYSTERY.
IF THAT IS YOUR WISH. ANYWAY, WE HAVE OUR HANDS FULL WITH OUR BETTY...
AND HANNIBAL'S GETTING OLD. AS OLD AS YOUR BINGO.
I'M SO TIRED...
YOU'VE EARNED A BIT OF REST.
MAX CLAIMS I'VE KILLED MYSELF OVER THIS BOOK.
HE WHO DIES BEFORE DYING DOES NOT DIE THE DAY OF HIS DEATH.

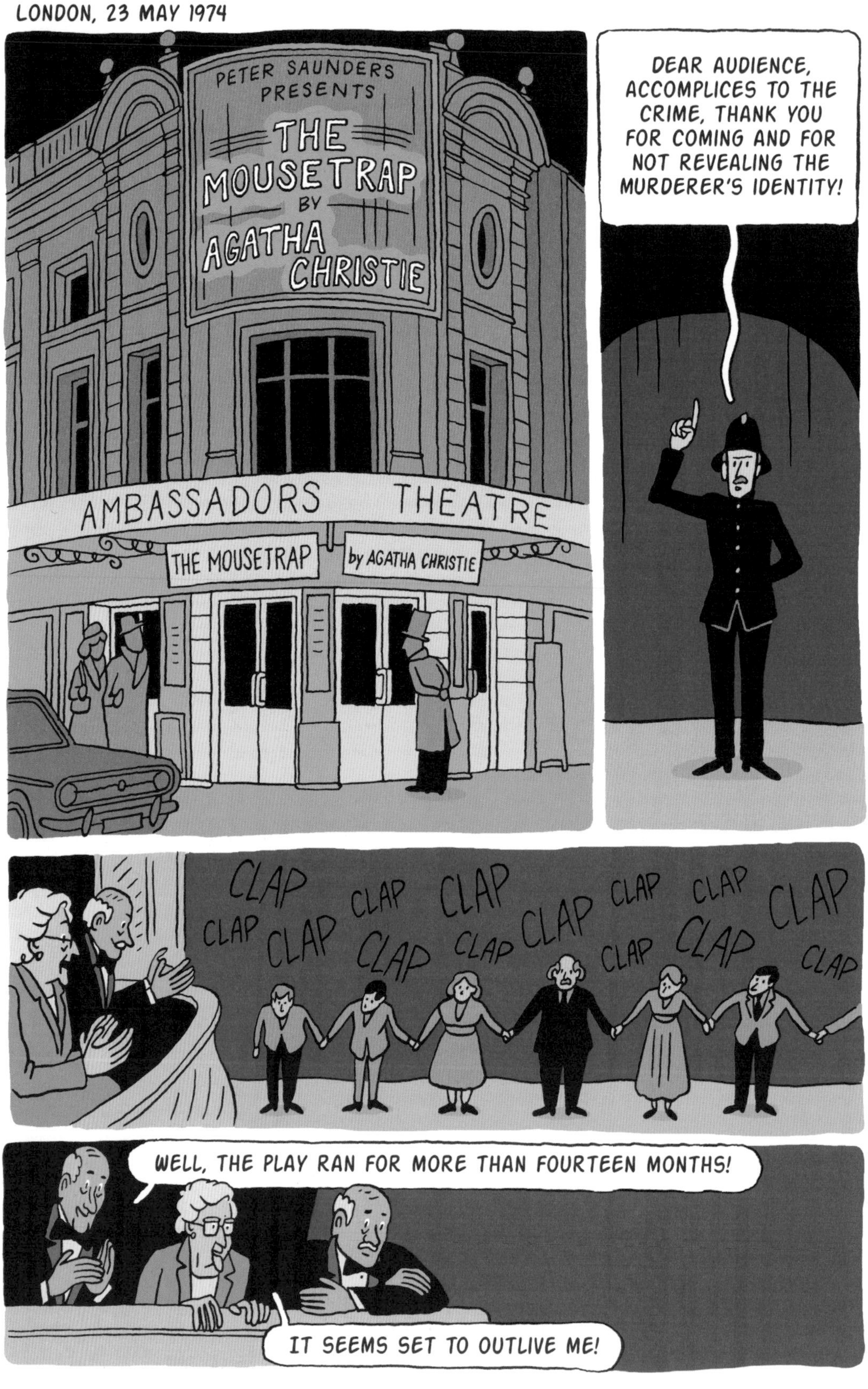
LONDON, 23 MAY 1974
PETER SAUNDERS PRESENTS
THE MOUSETRAP BY AGATHA CHRISTIE
AMBASSADORS THEATRE
THE MOUSETRAP
by AGATHA CHRISTIE
DEAR AUDIENCE, ACCOMPLICES TO THE CRIME, THANK YOU FOR COMING AND FOR NOT REVEALING THE MURDERER'S IDENTITY!
CLAP CLAP CLAP CLAP CLAP CLAP CLAP CLAP CLAP CLAP CLAP CLAP CLAP CLAP
WELL, THE PLAY RAN FOR MORE THAN FOURTEEN MONTHS!
IT SEEMS SET TO OUTLIVE ME!

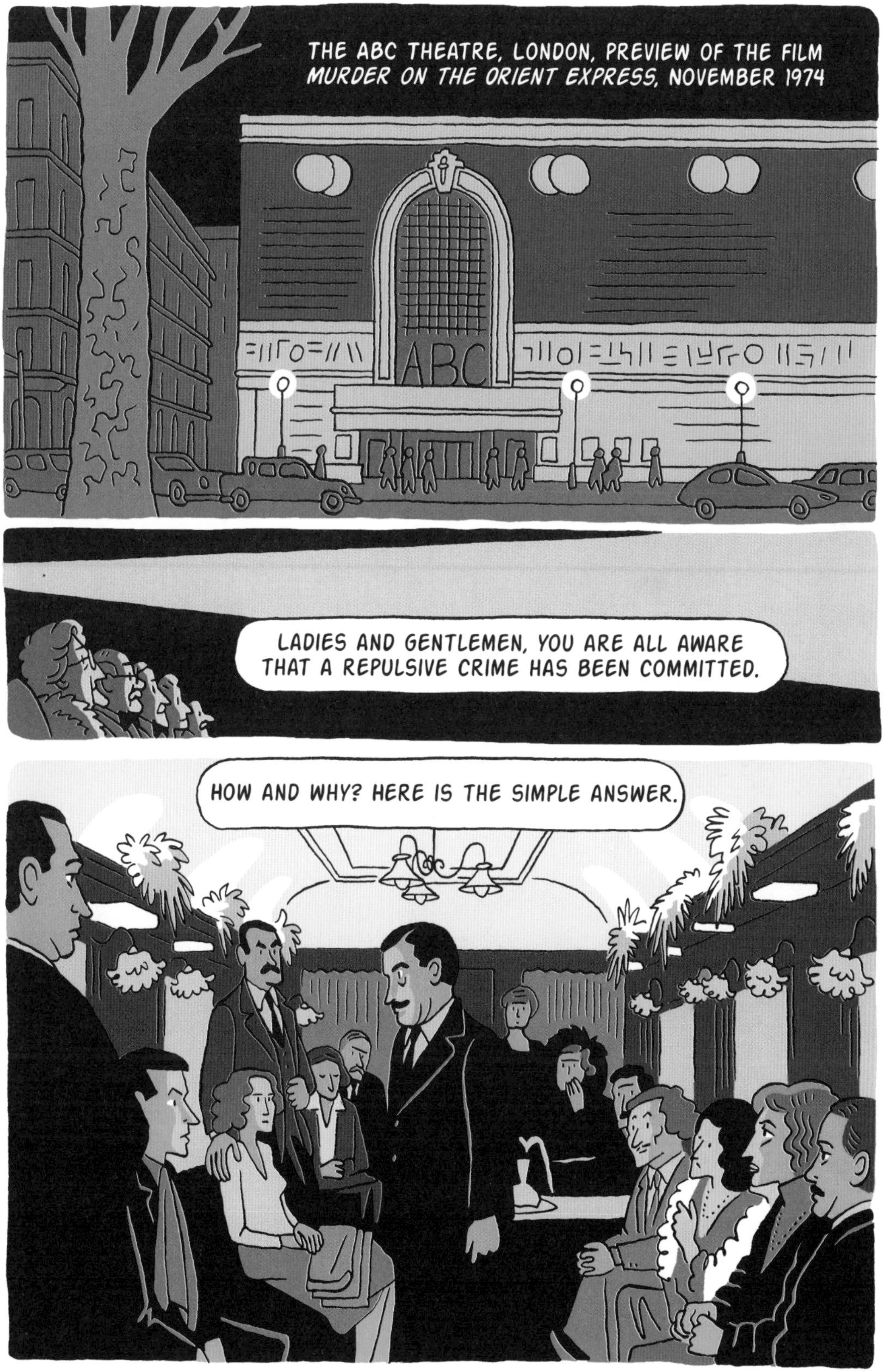
THE ABC THEATRE, LONDON, PREVIEW OF THE FILM *MURDER ON THE ORIENT EXPRESS*, NOVEMBER 1974
ABC
LADIES AND GENTLEMEN, YOU ARE ALL AWARE THAT A REPULSIVE CRIME HAS BEEN COMMITTED.
HOW AND WHY? HERE IS THE SIMPLE ANSWER.

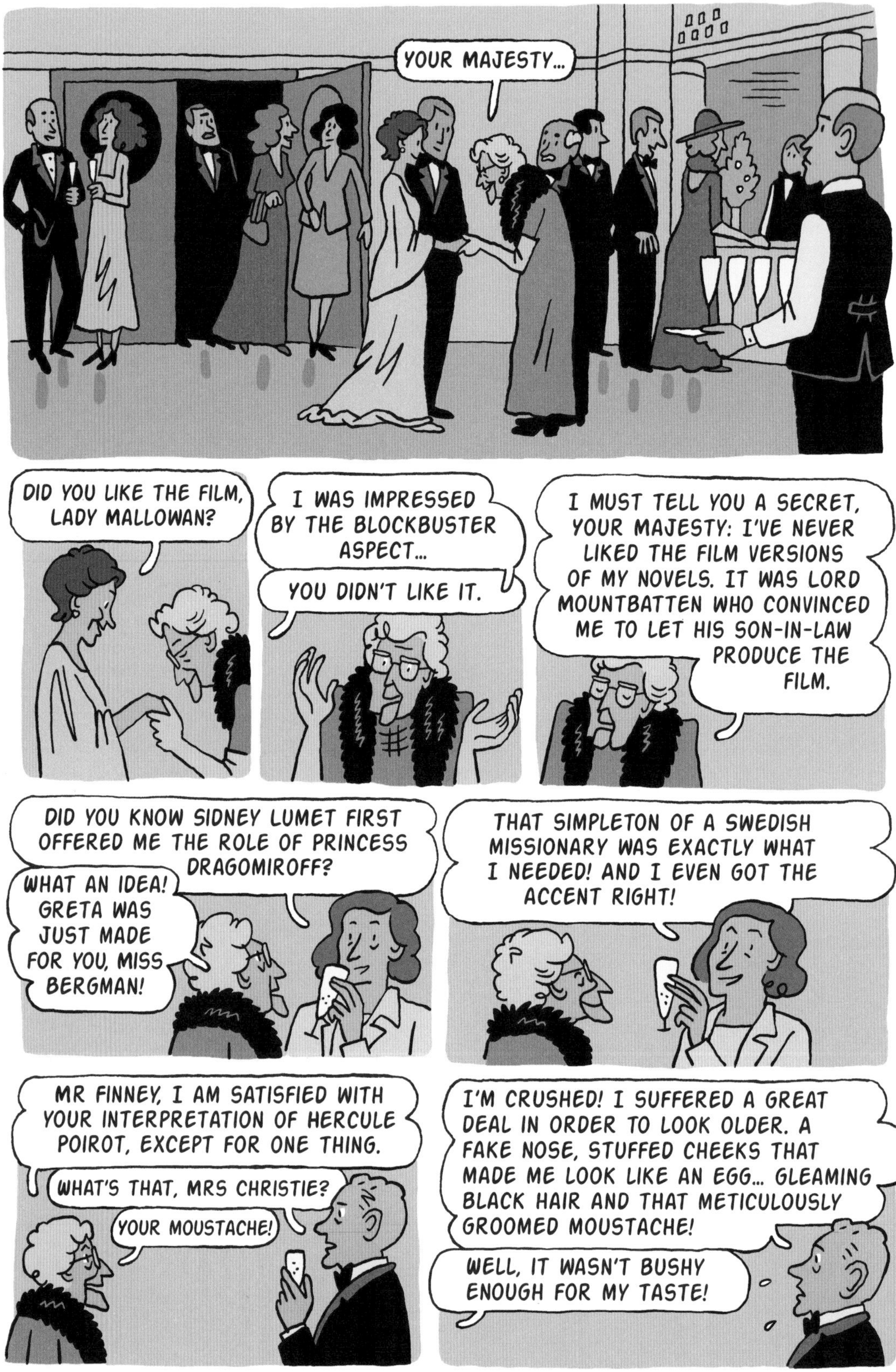
YOUR MAJESTY...
DID YOU LIKE THE FILM, LADY MALLOWAN?
I WAS IMPRESSED BY THE BLOCKBUSTER ASPECT...
YOU DIDN'T LIKE IT.
I MUST TELL YOU A SECRET, YOUR MAJESTY: I'VE NEVER LIKED THE FILM VERSIONS OF MY NOVELS. IT WAS LORD MOUNTBATTEN WHO CONVINCED ME TO LET HIS SON-IN-LAW PRODUCE THE FILM.
DID YOU KNOW SIDNEY LUMET FIRST OFFERED ME THE ROLE OF PRINCESS DRAGOMIROFF?
WHAT AN IDEA! GRETA WAS JUST MADE FOR YOU, MISS BERGMAN!
THAT SIMPLETON OF A SWEDISH MISSIONARY WAS EXACTLY WHAT I NEEDED! AND I EVEN GOT THE ACCENT RIGHT!
MR FINNEY, I AM SATISFIED WITH YOUR INTERPRETATION OF HERCULE POIROT, EXCEPT FOR ONE THING.
WHAT'S THAT, MRS CHRISTIE?
YOUR MOUSTACHE!
I'M CRUSHED! I SUFFERED A GREAT DEAL IN ORDER TO LOOK OLDER. A FAKE NOSE, STUFFED CHEEKS THAT MADE ME LOOK LIKE AN EGG... GLEAMING BLACK HAIR AND THAT METICULOUSLY GROOMED MOUSTACHE!
WELL, IT WASN'T BUSHY ENOUGH FOR MY TASTE!

YOU KILLED ME! I'M OUTRAGED!

I'VE KEPT THIS BOOK IN A SAFE FOR THIRTY-FIVE YEARS. IT WAS TO APPEAR ONLY AFTER MY DEATH, BUT WILLIAM COLLINS, MY EDITOR, INSISTED. CLEARLY, THE MOVIES HAVE GIVEN THE BOOK SALES A PUSH.

YOU'RE BREAKING MY HEART.

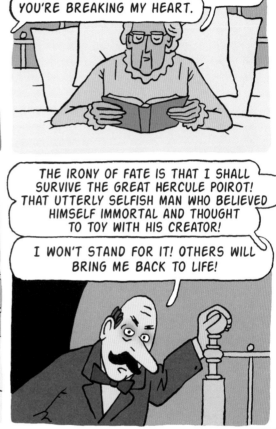

AND MISS MARPLE?

I'M GRANTING HER WHAT I REFUSED YOU: ONE LAST CASE.

I HATE YOU!

THE IRONY OF FATE IS THAT I SHALL SURVIVE THE GREAT HERCULE POIROT! THAT UTTERLY SELFISH MAN WHO BELIEVED HIMSELF IMMORTAL AND THOUGHT TO TOY WITH HIS CREATOR!

I WON'T STAND FOR IT! OTHERS WILL BRING ME BACK TO LIFE!

CURTAIN!

Hercule Poirot Is Dead; Famed Belgian Detective

By THOMAS LASK

Hercule Poirot, a Belgian detective who became internationally famous, has died in England. His age was unknown.

Mr. Poirot achieved fame as a private investigator after he retired as a member of the Belgian police force in 1904. His career, as chronicled in the novels of Dame Agatha Christie, was one of the most illustrious in fiction.

At the end of his life, he was arthritic and had a bad heart. He was in a wheelchair often, and was carried from his bedroom to the public lounge at Styles Court, ~~~ in Essex,

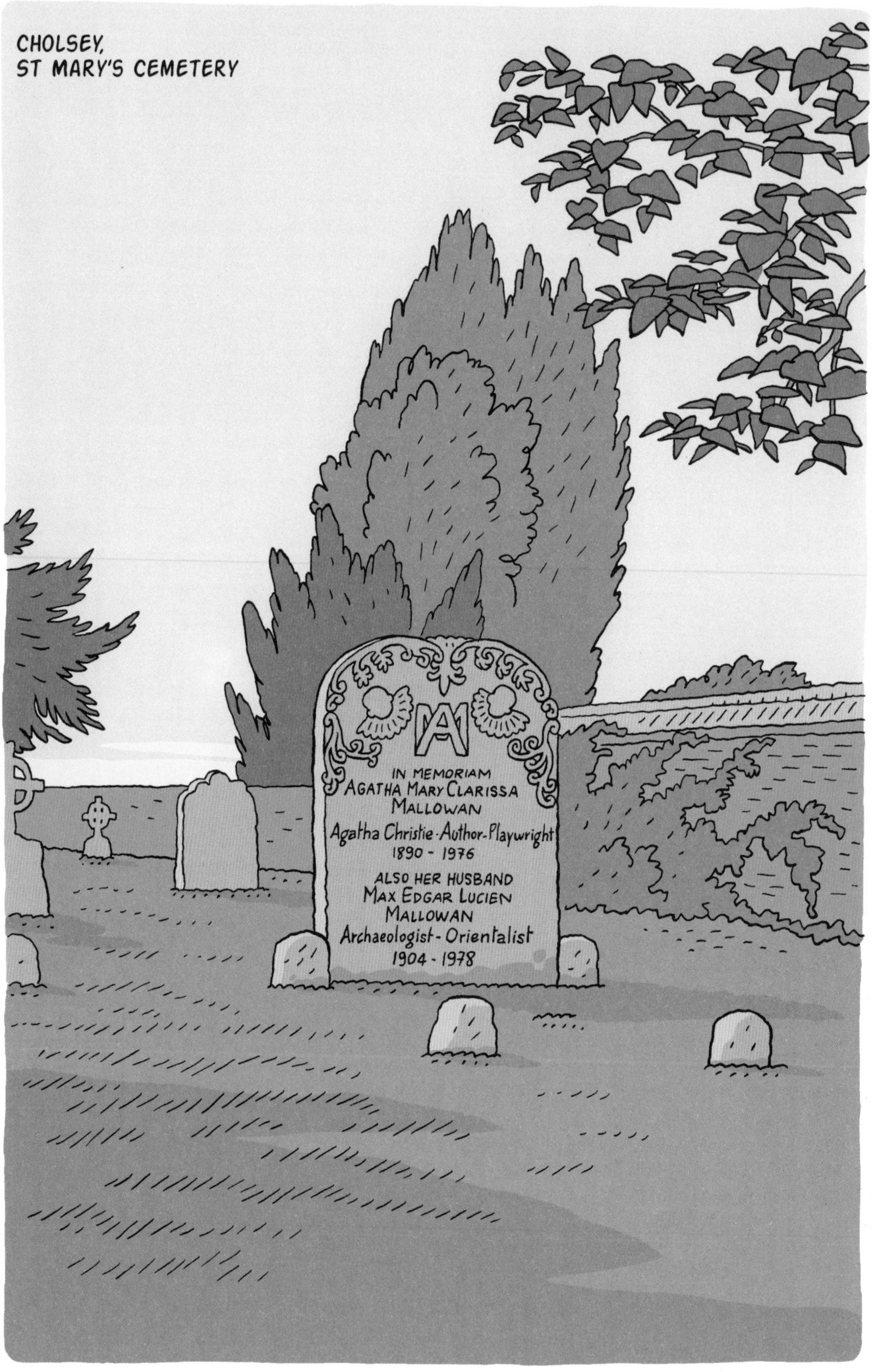
CHOLSEY,
ST MARY'S CEMETERY
IN MEMORIAM
AGATHA MARY CLARISSA
MALLOWAN
Agatha Christie - Author - Playwright
1890 - 1976
ALSO HER HUSBAND
MAX EDGAR LUCIEN
MALLOWAN
Archaeologist - Orientalist
1904 - 1978

APPENDICES

Timeline

15 SEPTEMBER 1890
Agatha Mary Clarissa Miller is born in Torquay, Devon. Her father, Frederick Alvah Miller, is American, a stockbroker by profession. Her mother, Clarisse Margaret Boehmer, is English, the daughter of an army captain. The couple will have three children: Margaret "Madge" Frary (1879-1950), Louis "Monty" Montant (1880-1929) and Agatha.

1900
Agatha's brother Monty enlists in the Boer War in South Africa.

26 NOVEMBER 1901
Her father dies of pneumonia. This is the beginning of the family's financial hardships.

1902
For the first time, Agatha is enrolled in a school in Torquay, Miss Guyer's Girls School.

SEPTEMBER 1902
Madge marries James Watt.

1906
Agatha is sent to Paris to complete her schooling. She is educated in three pensions: Mademoiselle Cabernet's, Les Marroniers in Auteuil, and then Miss Dryden's, a finishing school. There she discovers the "Paris-Brest," delighting in its praline-flavoured butter cream...

1908
Agatha writes her first novel, entitled *The House of Beauty*, in two days – thirty pages written on her sister's typewriter, under the pen name Mac Miller, Esq.

WINTER 1910-1911
Agatha spends three months with her mother in Cairo, Egypt.

10 MAY 1911
Agatha climbs aboard a plane and takes her first flight.

EARLY 1912
Agatha meets Reggie Lucy, an artillery officer. He declares his love, but gives Agatha time to consider the possibility of marriage.

12 OCTOBER 1912
Agatha meets Archibald Christie at a ball thrown by Lord and Lady Clifford in Chudleigh, near Torquay.

24 DECEMBER 1914
In Bristol, Agatha is married to Lieutenant Archibald Christie of the Royal Field Artillery. They spend their honeymoon at The Grand Hotel in Torquay. Then Archie leaves for war, and Agatha becomes a volunteer at the Red Cross Hospital in Torquay, where she puts in 3,400 hours between October 1914 and December 1916.

1916
Spurred by an earlier bet with her sister Madge, Agatha resolves to write her first detective novel. Over the course of two weeks at the Moorland Hotel in Haytor, she writes the first half of what will become *The Mysterious Affair at Styles*.

30 APRIL 1917
She is certified as a dispenser, or pharmaceutical assistant, by The Worshipful Society of Apothecaries of London.

5 AUGUST 1919
Her only daughter is born in Ashfield. Rosalind is named after the heroine of Shakespeare's play *As You Like It*.

SEPTEMBER 1919
Agatha, Archie and Rosalind move to an apartment at 5 Northwick Terrace, St John's Wood, London.

OCTOBER 1920
In America, John Lane publishes Agatha's first novel (written in 1916), *The Mysterious Affair at Styles* – the first appearance of Hercule Poirot.

21 JANUARY 1921
The Bodley Head publishes *The Mysterious Affair at Styles* in Britain.

1922
Agatha travels around the world with Archie on a ten-month tour of the dominions of the British Empire.

JANUARY-MARCH 1922
Agatha visits South Africa and learns to surf at Muizenberg Beach.

JANUARY 1922

British publication of *The Secret Adversary*, the first appearance of Tommy and Tuppence.

AUGUST 1922

Agatha surfs at the beach in Waikiki, Hawaii, on a board named Fred. Today, she is considered the first female English surfer!

APRIL 1926

Death of her mother from bronchitis.

JUNE 1926

Williams Collins, Sons publishes *The Murder of Roger Ackroyd* in Britain.

3 DECEMBER 1926

Around 9.45 PM, Agatha, distressed by her mother's death and her husband's infidelity, vanishes. She turns up again 11 days later in Yorkshire.

7 DECEMBER 1926

The Daily News offers a reward of £100 for any information concerning Agatha's disappearance.

14 DECEMBER 1926

Agatha is discovered safe and sound at the Swan Hydropathic Hotel, an establishment in the spa resort of Harrogate. She had checked in under the name of Mrs Teresa Neele – the surname of her husband's mistress. Agatha Christie claims to have experienced temporary amnesia. She will never shed any further light on her fantastical disappearance.

29 OCTOBER 1928

Her divorce from Archie is finalised.

16 NOVEMBER 1928

Archie is remarried to Nancy Neele.

1928

For the first time, Agatha travels aboard the Orient Express. She visits the archaeological site at Ur in Iraq, and there she meets archaeologist Max Edgar Lucien Mallowan.

1929

With the earnings from her books, Agatha buys a house at 22 Cresswell Place in Chelsea. She writes her first play, entitled *Black Coffee*.

20 SEPTEMBER 1929

Her brother Monty dies of a cerebral haemorrhage in Marseille.

APRIL 1930

The first of six novels written under the pen name Mary Westmacott is published, *Giant's Bread*. Mary Westmacott's true identity will remain a secret until 1949, when it is revealed by the *Sunday Times*. The pen name is inspired by Agatha's maternal grandmother, Mary Ann West.

11 SEPTEMBER 1930

Agatha marries Max Mallowan in Edinburgh at either St Cuthberts (according to the marriage licence) or St Columba (according to her autobiography). Max is fourteen years her junior. The two begin travelling to archaeological digs. Agatha writes one to two novels a year.

1931

Agatha and Max travel to Egypt, where they visit Tutankhamun's tomb in the Valley of the Kings and meet Howard Carter, its discoverer, during their stay at the Winter Palace in Luxor.

DECEMBER 1931

On the way back from Niniveh, Agatha is stuck on the Orient Express for 24 hours due to inclement weather. This incident inspires the plot and characters of one of her most famous novels.

JUNE 1932

British publication of *The Thirteen Problems*, a collection of 13 short stories that debuts the famous Miss Jane Marple.

JANUARY 1933

Agatha takes part in the dig at Tell Arpachiyah in Iraq, excavated by Max Mallowan. That same year, she takes a cruise along the Nile with her husband and Rosalind. During this trip, she stays at the Cataract Hotel (rechristened the Old Cataract years later) in Aswan, where she will write a few chapters of *Death on the Nile*.

JUNE 1933

Publication of *Death on the Nile* in the form of a short story in *Nash's Pall Mall Magazine*. Mr Parker Pyne, and not Hercule Poirot, is the detective!

1 JANUARY 1934

British publication of *Murder on the Orient Express*.

DECEMBER 1934
The Mallowans buy Winterbrook House in Wallingford.

1 NOVEMBER 1937
British publication of *Death on the Nile*.

OCTOBER 1938
Agatha buys Greenway Estate, a vast Georgian home on the River Dart in Devon, for £6,000.

6 NOVEMBER 1939
Publication of *Ten Little Indians*. It will sell more than 100 million copies worldwide.

JUNE 1940
Rosalind marries Hubert de Burgh Prichard, a British infantry officer.

21 SEPTEMBER 1943
Agatha's only grandchild, Mathew Prichard, is born in a Cheshire clinic.

AUGUST 1944
Hubert de Burgh Prichard dies in combat in France.

OCTOBER 1948
Rosalind is remarried to Anthony Hicks.

2 APRIL 1950
In the ruins of the ancient city of Nimrod in northern Iraq, Agatha begins her autobiography. During this dig, she cleans fragments of ivory with beauty products!

1950
Death of Agatha's sister, Margaret Frary Miller.

6 OCTOBER 1952
The hit play *The Mousetrap* premieres at the Royal Theatre in Nottingham. It goes on to break the record for the longest theatrical run.

MAY 1956
Agatha travels the US, stopping in Los Angeles and New York, where the 645th and final performance of *Witness for the Prosecution* takes place on 30 June.

13 SEPTEMBER 1956
The Mousetrap celebrates its 1,998th performance.

1957
Agatha succeeds Dorothy L. Sayers as the President of the Detection Club, an association of British mystery writers founded in 1930.

13 APRIL 1958
The Mousetrap is declared "the longest continuously running play in the whole history of the English theatre".

SUMMER 1958
Death of Nancy Neele, Archibald Christie's second wife.

1959
The Index Translationum, an international bibliography of translations published by UNESCO, states that Agatha Christie has been translated in 103 countries and has sold 400 million books.

20 DECEMBER 1962
Death of Archibald Christie.

11 OCTOBER 1965
Agatha finishes her autobiography at her house in Wallingford.

AUTUMN 1966
Agatha leaves for the US with her husband, who is giving a series of lectures in major cities.

1968
Max Mallowan is knighted.

1971
Agatha is appointed Dame Commander of the Order of the British Empire by Queen Elizabeth II, thus becoming Dame Agatha Christie.

MARCH 1972
A wax statue of Agatha is put on display at Madame Tussaud's.

6 AUGUST 1975
Announcement of the death of Hercule Poirot. *The New York Times* publishes his obituary.

SEPTEMBER 1975
British publication of *Curtain*, Hercule Poirot's final investigation written by Agatha Christie.

12 JANUARY 1976
Death of Dame Agatha Christie at her home in Wallingford. She is buried in the churchyard of St Mary's, Cholsey.

NOVEMBER 1977
British publication of *Agatha Christie: An Autobiography.*

Bibliography

NOVELS AND STORY COLLECTIONS FEATURING HERCULE POIROT

The Mysterious Affair at Styles: A Detective Story, John Lane, October 1920

Murder on the Links, John Lane, 1923

Poirot Investigates, The Bodley Head, March 1924

The Murder of Roger Ackroyd, Collins, June 1926

The Big Four, Collins, January 1927

The Mystery of the Blue Train, Collins, March 1928

Peril at End House, Collins Crime Club, March 1932

Lord Edgware Dies, Collins Crime Club, September 1933

Murder on the Orient Express, Collins Crime Club, January 1934

Three Act Tragedy, Collins Crime Club, January 1935

Death in the Clouds, Collins Crime Club, July 1935

The A.B.C. Murders, Collins Crime Club, January 1936

Cards on the Table, Collins Crime Club, November 1936

Death on the Nile, Collins Crime Club, November 1937

Dumb Witness, Collins Crime Club, July 1937

Murder in the Mews, Collins Crime Club, March 1937, collection of four stories:
1/ "Dead Man's Mirror"
2/ "Triangle at Rhodes"
3/ "The Incredible Theft"
4/ "Murder in the Mews"

Appointment with Death, Collins Crime Club, May 1938

Hercule Poirot's Christmas, Collins Crime Club, December 1938

Sad Cypress, Collins Crime Club, March 1940

One, Two, Buckle My Shoe, Collins Crime Club, November 1940

Evil Under The Sun, Collins Crime Club, June 1941

Five Little Pigs, Collins Crime Club, January 1943

The Hollow, Collins Crime Club, November 1946

The Labours of Hercules, Collins Crime Club, September 1947, collection of twelve stories each named for one of the mythic labours.

Taken at the Flood, Collins Crime Club, November 1948

Mrs McGinty's Dead, Collins Crime Club, March 1952

After the Funeral, Collins Crime Club, May 1953

Hickory Dickory Dock, Collins Crime Club, October 1955

Dead Man's Folly, Collins Crime Club, November 1956

Cat Among the Pigeons, Collins Crime Club, November 1959

The Adventure of the Christmas Pudding and a Selection of Entrées, Collins Crime Club, October 1960, collection of six stories, of which five feature Hercule Poirot:
1/ "The Adventure of the Christmas Pudding"
2/ "The Mystery of the Spanish Chest"
3/ "The Under Dog"
4/ "Four and Twenty Blackbirds"
5/ "The Dream"

The Clocks, Collins Crime Club, November 1963

Third Girl, Collins Crime Club, November 1966

Halloween Party, Collins Crime Club, November 1969

Elephants Can Remember, Collins Crime Club, November 1972

Poirot's Early Cases, Collins Crime Club, September 1974, collection of eighteen stories:
1/ "The Affair at the Victory Ball"
2/ "The Adventure of the Clapham Cook"
3/ "The Cornish Mystery"
4/ "The Adventure of Johnnie Waverly"
5/ "The Double Clue"
6/ "The King of Clubs"
7/ "The Lemesurier Inheritance"
8/ "The Lost Mine"
9/ "The Plymouth Express"
10/ "The Chocolate Box"
11/ "The Submarine Plans"

12/ "The Third Floor Flat"
13/ "Double Sin"
14/ "The Market Basing Mystery"
15/ "Wasp's Nest"
16/ "The Veiled Lady"
17/ "Problem at Sea"
18/ "How Does your Garden Grow?"

Curtain: Poirot's Last Case, Collins Crime Club, September 1975

Problem at Pollensa Bay and Other Stories, HarperCollins, November 1991, collection of two stories featuring Hercule Poirot: "Yellow Iris" and "The Second Gong"

While the Light Lasts and Other Stories, HarperCollins, August 1997, collection of two stories featuring Hercule Poirot: "Christmas Adventure" and "The Mystery of the Baghdad Chest"

Black Coffee, novelisation by Charles Osborne of a play by Agatha Christie produced in 1930, HarperCollins, November 1998

Superintendent Battle mentions Hercule Poirot in *Towards Zero*. Tommy and Tuppence mention him in "Partners in Crime".

NOVELS AND STORY COLLECTIONS FEATURING MISS MARPLE

The Murder at the Vicarage, Collins Crime Club, October 1930

The Thirteen Problems, Collins Crime Club, June 1932, collection of thirteen stories:
1/ "The Tuesday Night Club"
2/ "The Idol House of Astarte"
3/ "Ingots of Gold"
4/ "The Blood-Stained Pavement"
5/ "Motive vs Opportunity"
6/ "The Thumb Mark of St Peter"
7/ "The Blue Geranium"
8/ "The Companion"
9/ "The Four Suspects"
10/ "A Christmas Tragedy"
11/ "The Herb of Death"
12/ "The Affair at the Bungalow"
13/ "Death by Drowning"

The Body in the Library, Collins Crime Club, May 1942

The Moving Finger, Collins Crime Club, June 1943

A Murder is Announced, Collins Crime Club, June 1950

They Do It with Mirrors, Collins Crime Club, November 1952

A Pocket Full of Rye, Collins Crime Club, November 1953

4.50 from Paddington, Collins Crime Club, November 1957

The Mirror Crack'd from Side to Side, Collins Crime Club, November 1962

A Caribbean Mystery, Collins Crime Club, November 1964

At Bertram's Hotel, Collins Crime Club, November 1965

Nemesis, Collins Crime Club, November 1971

Sleeping Murder: Miss Marple's Last Case, Collins Crime Club, October 1976

NOVELS AND STORY COLLECTIONS FEATURING TOMMY AND TUPPENCE

The Secret Adversary, John Lane, January 1922

Partners in Crime, Collins Crime Club, September 1929, collection of eighteen stories:
1/ "Partners in Crime"
2/ "A Fairy in the Flat"
3/ "A Pot of Tea"
4/ "The Affair of the Pink Pearl"
5/ "The Adventure of the Sinister Stranger"
6/ "Finessing the King"
7/ "The Gentleman Dressed in Newspaper"
8/ "The Case of the Missing Lady"
9/ "Blindman's Buff"
10/ "The Man in the Mist"
11/ "The Crackler"
12/ "The Sunningdale Mystery"
13/ "The House of Lurking Death"
14/ "The Unbreakable Alibi"
15/ "The Clergyman's Daughter"
16/ "The Red House"
17/ "The Ambassador's Boots"
18/ "The Man Who Was No 16"

N or M?, Collins Crime Club, November 1941

By the Pricking of My Thumbs, Collins Crime Club, November 1968

Postern of Fate, Collins Crime Club, October 1973

NOVELS WITHOUT RECURRING PROTAGONISTS

The Man in the Brown Suit, The Bodley Head, August 1924

The Secret of Chimneys, The Bodley Head, June 1925

The Seven Dials Mystery, Collins Crime Club, January 1929

The Sittaford Mystery, Collins Crime Club, September 1931

Why Didn't They Ask Evans?, Collins Crime Club, September 1934

Murder is Easy, Collins Crime Club, June 1939

Ten Little Niggers, Collins Crime Club, November 1939

Towards Zero, Collins Crime Club, July 1944

Death Comes as the End, Collins Crime Club, March 1945

Sparkling Cyanide, Collins Crime Club, December 1945

Crooked House, Collins Crime Club, May 1949

They Came to Baghdad, Collins Crime Club, March 1951

Many Steps to Death, Collins Crime Club, November 1954

Ordeal by Innocence, Collins Crime Club, November 1958

The Pale Horse, Collins Crime Club, November 1961

Endless Night, Collins Crime Club, October 1967

Passenger to Frankfurt, Collins Crime Club, September 1970

PUBLISHED UNDER THE PSEUDONYM MARY WESTMACOTT

Giant's Bread, Collins Crime Club, April 1930

Unfinished Portrait, Collins Crime Club, March 1934

Absent in the Spring, Collins Crime Club, August 1944

The Rose and the Yew Tree, William Heinemann Ltd, November 1948

A Daughter's A Daughter, William Heinemann Ltd, November 1952

The Burden, William Heinemann Ltd, November 1956

The Floating Admiral, Hodder & Stoughton, December 1931, co-written with Dorothy L. Sayers

POETRY

The Road of Dreams, Geoffrey Bles, January 1925

Star Over Bethlehem, Collins Crime Club, November 1965

Poems, Collins Crime Club, October 1973

AUTOBIOGRAPHY

Come, Tell Me How You Live, Collins Crime Club, November 1946

An Autobiography, Collins Crime Club, November 1977